GOD'S WORKBOOK:
Shifting into Light

*How to Transform Your Life
& Global Events with
Angelic Help*

GOD'S WORKBOOK:
Shifting into Light

How to Transform Your Life & Global Events with Angelic Help

Tiffany Snow
Fr. Billy Clark

Spirit Journey Books
San Diego, California

GOD'S WORKBOOK: SHIFTING INTO LIGHT
How to Transform Your Life & Global Events
With Angelic Help
Copyright © 2007 Tiffany Snow, Fr. Billy Clark

Printed in the United States of America
First Edition

Published by
Spirit Journey Books
P.O. Box 61
San Marcos, CA 92079

Toll-Free (800) 535-5474
The Divine Wellness Institute

For more information please visit:

www.TiffanySnow.com
www.TheFourthHealing.com

Edited by:
Fr. Billy Clark, Tiffany Snow
Cover Design by:
Tiffany Snow, Cat Stevenson

Library of Congress Catalog Number:
International Standard Book Number:
ISBN 978-0-9729623-2-2

1. Spirituality. 2. Religion 3. Inspirational

DEDICATION

Thank you God of unconditional Love,
for you have taught me that
Love is beyond fear.
And though the dark is getting darker,
the light is getting lighter,
and Love wins!

Thank you Heavenly Father,
for letting me hear your voice so well,
and the Holy Stigmata that you have
shared with me to brighten all of us.
For indeed it has been a transformation
not only of body, but of mind and spirit.

You have taken the foolish things of the world
and made them wise.
You have taken the things that are not,
and made them so they are.
This you have done with me.

Thank you for letting all of your earthly children
participate in this time of global shift.
For you desire all to be the mystic,
to hear your voice and sing your song,
and witness the Love firsthand,
and the Angelic transformation
of our beautiful earth home.
My heart is yours.

- Blessed Tiffany

TIFFANY SNOW (BLESSED TIFFANY) carries the Holy Stigmata upon her body, and is an evidence-based miracle healer and award-winning author, medical intuitive and public speaker. She has been called a modern-day mystic, along the spiritual paths of Teresa of Avila or Padre Pio. Tiffany simply calls herself, "A Worker for The Big Guy." Her near-death experience by lightning-strike eight years ago first awakened her gifts, and experiencing the Stigmata consistently since July of 2005 has led to empirical revelations beyond any religion of mere habit, past muddy metaphysics and into Divine Love.

Blessed Tiffany - she is called this because of the physical healing miracles and blessings that come by her hand - is also able to help people remember their purpose and to see the potential each one has to accomplish the missions, dreams and desires placed in their heart. She helps them to heal and make connection to God, to one another and to themselves, developing a mind of tranquility and gratitude in the empowerment of unconditional and pure love.

The detailed information and profound spiritual insights received during Blessed Tiffany's Stigmata is an ongoing revelation and continues to help greatly in this time of world shift. With our free will interaction and this God-given information, we can each become a junction point between heaven and earth, where the miracles manifest everyday, thus helping the earth and our families live a life of Divine guidance, Angelic protection, vibrant health, full abundance and peace. This is an opportunity to replace fear, depression, anger and darkness and transform it into unconditional love and hope, amazing joy and Divine light throughout your neighborhood and the entire world.

Blessed Tiffany continues to share through Miracle Healing Day conferences in different cities, and live teleclasses and downloadable recordings on a wide variety of subjects through her website. She is an award-winning author. Classes on The Divine Decrees are taught continually. You are invited to sign up for her newsletter to keep current of events and information, as new revelations for each of us continues to unfold. www.TiffanySnow.com (800) 535-5474

FATHER BILLY CLARK is a priest in the Old Holy Catholic Church, and has been a consistent witness of Blessed Tiffany's Stigmata since its beginning. Father Billy has a B.A. in psychology from Villanova University, and works with Blessed Tiffany at the conventions and coordinates every aspect of this work, having a calling and spirit easily moved by God. Father Billy specializes in prayers of deliverance and breakage of generational bondage and spiritual counseling. Stating emphatically "God is not about religion, " he is the primary caretaker and teacher of the information given through Stigmata, including worldwide classes on The Divine Decrees, such as "Becoming the Mystic – The Power to Transform All Things." His genuine warmth and kindness of heart continues to move thousands to clearly recognize God's voice of love for themselves, and to discern what is of love and what is not. Father Billy and Blessed Tiffany are happily married and live in Southern California. www.TheFourthHealing.com (800) 535-5474

"For years Father Billy & I have been working together, and from the beginning I have been impressed by his kindness, depth of spirituality, wisdom and sense of humor. He is a true warrior-priest; he protects and teaches the deeper things of our own spirit and God's Spirit. He has been a consistent witness of my Stigmata and his has been the flawless pen that has written down the guidance and prophetic information Father has brought through those times. He was personally commissioned by God to expand The Divine Decrees throughout the world. Father Billy helps each person to recognize and remove all blocks to attaining their God-given true potential."
Blessed Tiffany

"I have been working with the power of prayer in healing, counseling and deliverance for many years. Each and every moment we can actively choose to be fully protected and guided directly by God, Our Father - right here, and right now. There is power and protection given through The Divine Decrees, and true freedom in hearing Father's voice in your own life, guiding you everyday. I am here to help you with that communication and to help you remember how powerful you are as a child of God and the Love written upon your heart. And to remind you – Love Wins!" Father Billy Clark

CONTENTS

****

****

CALLED AND COMMISSIONED
A Minister's Manual for Specific Blessings

****

THE TWELVE BOOKS OF ACTS OF THE LOVE OF GOD
The Divine Decrees All Together   281

CHAPTER 1

You Are Living at This Time for a Reason
You Were Created to Change the World

Would you like the power to change the world? How about an unlimited ability to help the environment, and to globally influence positive change in politics and religion? Have you thought about what you would do, or how to go about doing it? Did you come up with realistic answers and strategies? Do you have the resources behind you to facilitate such an endeavor? You have these desires placed in your heart because *you were created to change the world,* and this book will share with you everything you need to know to access the tools and power needed to accomplish it. And it will show you that much of this can be fully accomplished without leaving your neighborhood, your home, or even your couch.

All can see the problems facing the world. We look around and see that things are not the way they are supposed to be in any country, whether they are considered affluent or not. We need to look no further than the news, or our own families, neighborhoods, communities and governments to see the escalation of darkness. And it touches and pains our heart, to the point that we don't want to look anymore. Why do these things happen? We know that people should be kind to one another. We know that people should be more loving. We also know we would like to help those having struggles, but how? Closer to home, we seek to protect the ones we love, to make sure they know they are loved, to provide for them and see them happy and healthy. But even then, we worry, since the escalation of darkness hits so close to home.

We see the need for change. The desire to help is there, but what can we do? The problems are numerous and obvious while the solutions seem to escape us. Many feel helpless, hopeless and ignored, many feel slighted, marginalized and underprivileged. Many have turned to numbing the pain they feel or trying to ignore it, loath even to watch the news or read the paper because it hurts to see it. My dear loved ones, there is much you can do!

The information shared in this book is for all that are moved by the events of the world, those that feel the compassion to do something, those who feel called to action. We share the inspired tools that have waited until now to be shared with the world, to ease the suffering of all mankind in this period of time, including for each one of us and our families. And you are living at this time to participate in this change.

You Are Made in the Image of God

You were made in the likeness of God. What does this mean? We know that it goes way beyond the physical body. God doesn't have flesh, hands and legs. So what does it really mean to be made "in the image of God?" Simply put, we have the same spirit. We are each a spark off the Divine Flame, spirit created from Spirit. *"Then God said, 'Let us make man in our image...so God created man in his own image, in the image of God he created him; male and female he created them...and God blessed them..."* (Genesis 1:26-28)

We Were Created to Be Powerful

During the experience of sharing the Holy Stigmata, I learn many wonderful things, and after witnessing and then experiencing the redemption of mankind, entire books are displayed and opened to me. During this time, conversation with God and his Angels is allowed and much information is given. Besides receiving the information presented, I often get to ask questions. And I always learn so much more than what I originally ask for. During one of these times, my question was, "What is the role of the Guardian Angel?" The answer revealed how closely the Guardian Angel works with us, but also included something else. We humans were *created to be co-creators* with Love for manifesting positive change in our environment.

Being a co-creator is not just about having babies. It includes the ability to *manifest things with our intention.* This is how powerful we were created to be – and still are! God never takes away his gifts, we still have them. But because of bad choices by our original parents and other things along the way, we have now lost our purity of focus and have an imperfect connection.

2

Our heads can also become foggy because of outside manipulations by negative intention and thought. But through it all, this wonderful gift is still there. There are three pieces to it. (1). Our Negative Intentions (2). Our Own Good Intentions (3). Unlimited Divine Power with Our Own Good Intentions.

Here's how it works with your negative intentions: let's say you are driving down the road, and you see an oncoming car. If, for just an instant, the thought flickers through your mind that the other car would swerve into your lane and hit you, in that instant, *that is exactly what would happen!* But the role of the Guardian Angel is this – the Angel uses his power to immediately prevent it from occurring. Yes, it may happen by another way, but it will not occur by that *random negative flicker of thought* that just went through your mind. This is how powerful we were made, and the safety feature that has been added so our random thoughts don't create undue havoc. At this time, a person has to go further than just thinking about it to do bad things. With just this amount of information, do you see that if we have a tendency toward negative thoughts, how our Guardian Angel may spend much time just guarding us from ourselves!

Now, what happens to our own good and positive intentions? They are allowed to fly free! But, they are buoyed and supported by our own energy. That is why the more excited we are about something, the more likely it is to come to fruition. But it is also why it may not go as far as we would like it to, and why we may also feel exhausted and drained by it, because it is fully supported and fed by our own power. This is as far as many programs and ideas have gone with this, but *it is no secret* that this does not go far enough.

Now, there is a third piece. This is where we choose by free will to go beyond our own bubble of energy and connect to Unlimited Energy. Here is where our positive good intentions are combined with limitless power. Now instead of feeling drained by our intentions, we actually become a positive and necessary instrument in the mix, and also receive of the flow going through us. So instead of feeling exhausted by pouring out, we now feel exhilarated and powerful, because we are a channel of the flow pouring in and through. This is where everything happens, where everything transforms.

This is where great healing miracles occur, where polluted lakes are purified, all wars cease, and severe storms become gentle breezes. This is where we interact and connect with God and his Holy Angels, and all things are made new. All things!

Remembering Who You Are

Has this thought ever crossed your mind – "if I was God, I would change things." Well, guess who wants you to do just that. All the good things you want, he wants too. The Big Guy wants you to remember who you are, how powerful you are and in what you are here for. He has given you his Spirit, and has equipped you with tools to participate in co-creating a new world. The world is not just escalating in fear and darkness, but in love and light too. We are now living in the great shift foretold that has been foretold for thousands of years in all cultures. It is a shift between light and darkness, and light wins! *You are of that light!*

CHAPTER 2

First Comes Our Personal Shift
Love or Fear? There are Only Two Choices

Is your life happy, are you living it to the fullest? Do you have emotional peace and calm? Do you wake up each morning anticipating the joy of the adventure of the day ahead? Do you feel secure about your future and the future of your loved ones? Can you actually feel Presence upon your life and the warmth of personal guidance? Do you have a sense of purpose? Are you attaining your biggest dreams? If you do not have these things, what is holding you back? Much more than you may consciously realize.

There are only two choices in life. Love or the opposite of love; and the opposite of love is not hate, but fear. Love always moves us forward, fear stagnates and freezes us. This is a simple yardstick to help us distinguish any place of stagnation in our lives and to make new choices. When we see what has been the true motivating factor behind our decisions, it gives us the power to change things and make it better. And something else takes place. When we consistently choose love over fear, an incredible transformation occurs around us, because light and darkness can't be in the same place together. They simply cannot exist jointly as one, they are of two different natures. So a great shifting occurs in our lives, for the better.

With every choice that we make for love, we move ahead on our journey and become brighter. And if darkness tries to move toward light, *it either has to transform into light to be near us,* or move away even to exist. Nothing harmful is able to stay near us. Nothing. Think of it this way, when we bring a lit candle into a darkened room, look what happens to the room - the entire area transforms, and the area closest to the flame is the brightest. Now, do we have to be afraid that the darkness will overwhelm and put out the candle? No, it doesn't matter how dark the room is, the darkness can never put out the candle. But, the candle can put itself out. In human terms, this happens when we buy into the ideas of unworthiness, separation and doubt, the ugliness that the darkness tries to convince us that we are.

5

But we are not of the darkness, we were created of light, and when we remember this our flame will never go out. It does not matter what darkness tries to imply or manipulate us into thinking. We were created of light and love. And when we remember our true nature it doesn't even matter if we are accepted or rejected by others, because we remember who we are in the eyes of God. We are loved.

Shifting into a Vibrant and Joyful Life

When we always choose love, it creates a great shift around us in our jobs, relationships, even in our personal health. As we have seen, everything has to be positive and loving to be near us, or it has to transform or move away. And since our physical health cannot move away from us, every time we make a choice motivated by love we make a choice for good health. Perhaps you have heard of spiritually adept people throughout the world who have exceptionally vibrant and healthy lives well into old age. This is why.

When we choose love, we actively choose our God-given birthright to how our lives are *supposed* to be. It is our true and full potential to embrace loving and long-term relationships, financial abundance, and effervescent physical health. With the expanded clarity that comes from advancing in love, we can also more easily identify further opportunities of light around us. This helps us make better decisions by recognizing the Divine interventions of love placed before us, choosing these, and then fully following through with them.

Now in regard to everything else, we must realize that the shifting that occurs around us can be initially difficult to witness. Yet, it is for our soul's greater and highest good, and all those connected with us. When we discern this, it helps us trust and accept the changes taking place. Love is always the better way. That is why trust and bravery is essential to advance forward in love, for fear limits our ability to allow or follow through with changes. Many times people stay in situations that are not good for them simply because it is familiar. Trusting in love helps us actively step outside of our comfort zone onto new, higher ground. That new ground is where the new world awaits, with new opportunities; and like any explorer traveling to new lands, faith is needed to leave the old things behind.

"Faith is being sure of what we hope for, and certain of what we do not see." *(Hebrews 11:1)* In that new world that we find ourselves in, we also find that we are a new person as well, a joyous and more connected and loving one. And we never find ourselves alone. Our relationships, jobs and everything else around us will be brighter and healthier for us too, for we actively discern the healthier opportunities placed before us. And as we continue to expand in light, we become more aware of living a joyous life fully guided by love, and the larger positive ripple effect our interactions have with others. We become aware of our spiritual need. We become aware of prayer. And we become aware that much of what we might have been taught doesn't ring true with the essence of our spirit anymore. What then?

Do Not Give Your Power Away – Discerning What is Right for You

This is your life, yet others desire to influence you on what you should or should not do. And the opinion of what you should do will differ from person to person; depending on what that person believes and wants you to believe as well. What will you do? Will you still choose love over fear? Or will you be fearful of others? Will you put your own flame out by giving your power away to others? Will you fall prey to doubt and turn aside from what your heart tells you, even to your own misfortune? Or can you step forward no matter what others may say, and make your own choices, and stick to it whether it's a popular one or not. Really, how do you know what is right for you?

People, books, radio, TV – they can tell you anything and everything, and wish to make all your decisions for you; what to buy, what to wear, what to eat, how to connect with your mate, how to think. Will you live as a specter or a ghost in your own life, or will you actively think, speak and feel for yourself? When you remember who you are, a bright spark off the Divine Flame, a beloved child embraced by Love, your spirit will yearn to move ahead and the confidence in the gifts you were given will grow. Those gifts include your free will. And, that means you can hold up all the information and choices presented to you from any source and will be able to discern for yourself if it is of Love or not, if it is of God, if it is of Spirit. And the things that are of Love will resonant within you, and you will feel it.

7

And this will happen because you know it in your spirit, not because someone else told you so. This is how it is supposed to be. God wants each of us to be able to hear him clearly without distraction. He wants each of us to be the mystic, one who directly has experience with the Divine, and to live a purposeful life guided unswervingly by love. Being a truly enlightened person is not something you do, but something you choose to become, and are continually becoming. Love is beyond limits, unconditionally. In that place of unconditional love, you are beyond limits too.

Who Do You See God as Being?

No matter what your religion, faith, culture or background, if you see God as a personification of Love, you will be able to hold all things up to that, and you will know if it is of God or not; and correspondingly, if it is for you or not. God was here before religion, and he will be here after it. An excellent spiritual connection is what Love desires for us, and the tradition or path a person takes to receive it varies on what the person can recognize at the time.

God is neither male nor female, but has maternal and nurturing qualities as a woman does, and the protective and supportive qualities that a man does. Most people refer to God as male, and as a father figure, and this is what Christ did as well. One question I asked of Love is what his name is. I was told that even if it was given me just as a series of numbers, by the time I got done saying it, it would be wrong! This is because God, just like love, continues to expand. So no matter if you call God: Heavenly Father, Almighty Lord, Divine Love, The Big Guy, Alpha & Omega, etc, it is not going to encompass all that he is, but because of the bubble of free will, the important thing is just to call him! God knows what his full and true name is, and all that it stands for. And much of what he stands for has been openly shared with mankind since the beginning of time. He stands for Love.

This may seem a difficult answer for many. Many have been taught that God is similar to a strict high school principal, or a prison warden. Many are taught we have to earn love, to be perfect and never make mistakes or there will be real fiery consequences.

8

These are all manipulations and scare tactics that have been handed down by men, traditions of fear to control mankind, and do not reflect the real nature or characteristics of God. Much truth about God's love can be found in the Bible, but much twisting of the beauty of it continues to occur by those seeking to influence and control by fear for their own gain.

For example, let's take the basic teaching about hellfire, and we will look at it through analytical eyes first. If you knew Greek, Hebrew and ancient history you would understand there are three words translated as "hell" in the scriptures. "Haides" and "sheohl" simply translate as "pit" or "grave." "Gehenna" is translated "Valley of Hinnom," which was a garbage dump kept perpetually burning outside the walls of Jerusalem, and was especially noticed when the wind changed and blew noxious odor and smoke over the city. It truly was a place "where the maggot does not die and the fire does not go out." (Mark 9:48) Christ and his apostles used this dump to illustrate a point about being *kind* to one another.

At that time, if you died and no one loved you enough to claim the body, either because you were a criminal or a hateful person, the city authorities threw your body out to be burned with the trash. No one alive was ever thrown in. Of course, this demise was not wished on anyone, especially since any respectful funeral or memorial arrangements didn't happen. This illustrated the point very well for the people of that time, so it was used for those particular people at that particular time to help them understand love better. Simply put, it was an encouragement to be loving toward one another, so when you die you will be mourned and properly buried instead of thrown out with the trash.

The Bible abounds with literal and symbolic language, and if something is read and interpreted as God not being loving or kind, just reasoning it through with common sense and holding it up to your essence of love will give you the right answer. Now let's look again at the concept of God placing bad people in a fiery hell to burn forever. If God is love, does it make sense that if a person is bad for all his life, let's say 70 years, that the right thing to do is torture him for all eternity? Do we as loving parents take the hand of an unruly child and place it on a hot stove burner to teach him a lesson? No!

9

Also, if there is a fiery hell where people are sent for demons to burn and torture, doesn't that mean that God and the devil are in league together, and that God created the devil to work for him? If that is true, there is no difference at all between good and evil, and light and dark, and nothing really matters at all.

But, none of that makes sense, does it? It doesn't make sense to God either. In fact, in Biblical days there was a pagan ritual of sacrificing children to false gods by burning them to death in fire, and God shows his repugnance for that by saying: *"The people of Judah have done evil in my eyes...they have built the high places of Topheth...to burn their sons and daughters in the fire – something I did not command, nor did it come up into my heart." (Jeremiah 7:30, 31)* It is not in the heart of a loving God to do such a thing, it is unreasonable. And this is why we don't have to be trained scholars or considered wise in the ways of the world and figure out all the arguments and translations of ancient words to know the heart of God. The truth of his love is written in our hearts. He is a God of Love. May the arguments about God being anything but love be laid to rest. *"I praise you Father, Lord of heaven and earth, because you have hidden these things from the wise and learned, and revealed them to little children." (Matthew 11:25)*

Physical Signs and Wonders are Increasing throughout the World

Just as parables and illustrations have always been part of teaching about love, God has always used physical signs and wonders to show that he not only exists, but that he cares for us and wants to participate in our lives. Miracle healing, true prophecy, Holy Stigmata, words of knowledge, intuitive gifts, visions, dreams – all and more are opportunities for us to see and know that we are not alone, never have been, and never will be.

Whether it is something we witness, or something we have participated in, the bottom line is the outcome. The "proof is in the pudding," as they say. In other words, God will verify what is of him and what is not, and he will back it up in more than one way. Why does he do this? Because he knows it is difficult for us because he is invisible, as is the spiritual world around us of Angels and loved ones.

10

The wind is also invisible, but we can see the leaves move on the trees so we know the wind is there, because we see and experience the physical results with our analytical brain. Our 10% of the brain acts as a bridge or barrier to receiving spiritual information. So the more experience we have had with spiritual events, the more we readily receive and understand it, and can better utilize it. *"Taste and See that God is Good…" (Psalm 34:8)*

This is why gifts always come together, and why we each have more than one of them, and why you will be able to verify what is true and what is not with all things around you. The same applies to what we are sharing with you in this book. We invite you to experience the leaves moving on the trees in your own life. The information here has come through the sharing of Holy Stigmata through Blessed Tiffany, who God has also given the gift of miracle healing. But even with this, if you have not seen the spontaneous opening of her wounds of Christ, or experienced a healing at her hands, how would you know if it is true or not? You don't. But you can test it out. Hold all the things we are sharing with you up to Love and see if your essence rings true with it. Also use the validation of personal evidence, empirical experience, by seeing if the information makes positive changes and differences in your life that you can experience, see and feel for yourself.

It is because of the strength of empirical, first-hand experiences why more people will be gifted with more miracles. This is part of the speeding up of things in the world, for as the darkness gets darker, all light, including yours, is encouraged to get brighter and brighter. But why is there darkness to begin with? If God is a God of love, and so powerful, why does it continue? If Love made all things, where did darkness come from? Truly, why is there evil in the world, and what is being done about it?

CHAPTER 3

Love Beyond Limits, Unconditionally
Why the Dark is Getting Darker & the Light Brighter

Why is there darkness in the world, and what is being done about it? Why is there an escalation of it right now? If God is love and all powerful, why doesn't he simply rid the earth of any problems? Why has it gone on for so long? Will it ever stop? Yes, these are all good questions. *And all the answers are here for you.* This is a sacred time in history - the time that darkness disappears forever! What does this mean, and how does it happen?

The Bubble of Free Will

Love created mankind with free will. It is like a strong bubble around us where we can choose to do our own thing, and also where we experience the ripple effect of our choices. This is why we can have an addiction such as smoking, and though it's not good for us, the cigarettes do not fly out of our hands. Love would not do that since it would be a manipulation of free will. In fact, God loves us even in the midst of our imperfections. So would he love us more if we didn't have addictions? No. But he is happy for us when we make the better choices not to, because of the harmful cause-and-effect they have on our bodies and lives. God created free will, and this is how much he respects the gift he gave us; he will not interfere to change things unless we ask him to.

The love of God will not cross the line and break into our free will. He does not coerce or manipulate. But when we ask for help, as through the intention and connection of prayer, we are making a free will choice to go beyond our own energy and our limited wisdom to receive more than we have on our own. This is where we can also receive physical, emotional and spiritual healing, protection, guidance, and much, much more. *But we have to ask for it,* we have to actually make the choice to go beyond our bubble to where that transformation occurs. But damage can happen to this bubble, and although God will not manipulate it, other things can. How does this happen?

13

To understand this, think of this strong bubble of free will also as a suit of full-body armor. We go into battle everyday. Perhaps we sustain some damage. Any place of dents or scratches is noticed and pinpointed by the enemy, who then focuses all attacks there until a gapping hole appears where the damage had been. Now we are unprotected where these holes are, and we can be badly injured there, which might take us out of battle or even worse, which is what the enemy was hoping for in the first place.

These holes can occur to our free will by two ways. Holes can be punched through from the outside through damage from physical abuse, emotional abuse and sexual abuse. From the inside we can also damage ourselves through unforgiveness of ourselves or others, by addictions, by doing things we know we shouldn't do but doing them anyway (willful sin), and places where we may be weakened through grief, high anxiety, fear, hatred, anger and other negative emotions. As we have seen, when we have a weakness in the armor we are attacked there; it is like putting blood in the water for sharks. And these sharks of darkness attack the same three things they have for thousands of years – physical health, family/relationships, and finances. This darkness wants us to feel isolated, alone, separate from God, from our true selves, and from one another. To make us feel we are not loved or lovable. To make us forget who we are.

It is like a negative voice sitting upon your shoulder constantly speaking into your ear: "You will never be happy. You will always be alone. You will never have good health. You will never have what you need. No one really cares about you. Etc, etc." *This voice is not from you.* That is why when we hear these things, it causes such a strong trauma inside our heart, because we know that is not the way it should be. We know in our spirit that we can be joyful and happy, vibrant and healthy, to have abundance in all things, to have long-term loving relationships, because that is how it is supposed to be. It is our God-given gift of how we were created to live! *This negative voice that you hear is not God.* If it is not you and it is not Source, who is it? This darkness is the voice of unHoly Angels who have come through the holes in your free will to manipulate you.

14

These unHoly Angels know that their darkness cannot put out your flame. But the flame can put itself out, by buying into their tauntings of unworthiness and doubt. So they try to make their voice seem like your own, to make you forget the light you are and the power you have and the Love you were created in and for. Is there anything we can do to heal the holes they have created? Yes, you now have the Deliverance prayer to heal the holes. This is only one of the wonderful tools you will find in this book, along with many other inspired and Divine words to heal, protect and transform. But your awareness was necessary first. And your continuing awareness of shifting into light will help you transform many places of injury in your life and the lives around you. But why, you may ask, would anyone do this? Who are the unHoly Angels? And what about the other Angels, where are they in all this?

Angels Have Free Will Too

The very first things that God made were the Angels, and they were given free will as well as mankind. Love does not want mindless robots operating around him; he wants those around him who choose to be there only because they want to be there. All Angels, Spirit Beings and humans were created with free will. In the design of things, mankind is made *"a little lower than the Angels."* *(Hebrews 2:7)* Angels are not just a religious thing, though pictures of Angels are shown in many religions. God is not a religious thing either, although God is worshipped in many religions. All that we are sharing goes beyond any borders or limits placed by mankind's current interpretation.

All Angels were created Holy and perfect. But some of these Angels chose to separate from God and become unplugged, unwilling and unable to hear God anymore or expand in love. Now there were two camps of Angels, and the brotherhood was divided between Holy Angels and unHoly Angels. Why does this matter to mankind?

When mankind was first placed upon the earth, we were beautiful new sparks, and our Father had placed all kinds of kindling wood around these flames, there were many opportunities to help us expand and brighten.

15

We were created of and for the earth, as caretakers of this earth garden, and the plants and animals upon it. We were created in the image of God to co-create, manifest and design many beautiful and extraordinary things. And that was just the beginning, the expansion of mankind would start here, and God would guide us perfectly into more and more of his universe of love. We would continue to polish all the multiple facets of love, in timelessness and full physical health. We were created without imperfections, and would continue to live through timelessness, without any degeneration, disease or death. We could perfectly see, learn from and converse with God and his Holy Angels at any time. So what happened?

Why there is Darkness on the Earth

Whenever anything is new, it is at its most vulnerable. It was at this time that an Angelic son of God *misused* free will and chose to rebel, and thus made himself an unHoly Angel. He unplugged himself from God and the responsibilities he was created for, and from the brotherhood of other Holy Angels. He manipulated the situation upon earth to his own benefit, and like a bully picking on the new kids in the neighborhood, enticed mankind's first parents into making bad decisions. But his motives went further than that – in his desire to create separation, confusion and destruction of all good things that Love had created, he even brought up questions about God himself, and that Love was not the best way to do things. And with God being the amazing personification of love, this brought up the issue of God's right to rule, not just mankind, but the entire cosmos as well.

The Original Issues – Is Love the Best Way?

Three questions were raised: (1). Mankind can rule himself successfully without God. (Genesis 3:1-5) (2). Mankind only comes to God for what he can get out of God. (Job 2:1-10) (3). If threatened to his very life, man will always turn from his integrity and curse God. (Job 2:1-10)

With this development, why didn't God just ignore the questions raised, quash the Angelic rebellion, and end the lives of our original parents and start over again?

Because these questions were brought up in front of all the Angels and Spirit Beings, and the consequences of the misuse of free will needed to be clearly seen. This was misuse because it also included manipulation of truth and the withholding of facts. In his patience and confidence, Love allowed the question to stand, and since the question was raised on earth and included mankind, it needed to be settled on earth with mankind. So God basically said, *'I know love is the best way, and I've got faith that even these very new children will recognize that.'* Is God's way, love, the best way? After all, it seemed to be working well in the rest of the cosmos. But now the question was raised, and it needed an answer that would stand as a basis for all eternity.

Why was this a misuse of free will? The misuse of free will is similar to this: we trust our kids to be nice to one another and not hurt themselves, others or personal property. The misuse of free will is when they usurp the free will of others causing damage to themselves, others and their surroundings. As another example, the proper use of free will is to be able to choose from 31 flavors of ice cream, not to pull out a gun and kill the ice cream man. There is a big difference. The unHoly Angels misused their free will when they started manipulating the free will of others.

So now a question was raised that needed answers. Similar to a court case, time had to go by for the evidence to present itself. This question would take thousands of years and many generations of mankind "doing his own thing" to answer. Now, the evidence speaks for itself. We are peering into a celestial courtroom, where the attorney is compiling the mound of evidence. The final conclusion will stand forever, will not be brought up as a challenge ever again, and will never be changed throughout all time, in any part of the galaxies.

What Has the Evidence Shown?

Question (1). *Mankind can rule himself successfully without God.* How have our governments been doing? Through all the many methods, ways and thousands of years, you would think mankind would almost have it perfect by now. Is that the case? No, it has only gotten worse.

There is no government on earth that has been successful for all the people under it. Even on an individual basis, most see it is difficult to figure things out on their own, and do not have the fully happy, abundant, healthy lives they desire. Case closed.

Question (2). *Mankind only comes to God for what he can get out of God.* People seek God whether they receive miracles or not, and whether they receive gifts or not. They seek him even if they have not had accurate information about who God truly is, they still seek him. No matter what time or culture, the desire to look for higher direction has been there, and so has the desire to worship. Worship is about giving, about praising, about talking to him, singing, and lifting up the heart. This is who we are at our core, we need to do this, it is part of our joy, and can be seen throughout time in all civilizations. Case closed.

Question (3). *If threatened to his very life, man will always turn from his integrity and curse God.* Man has been tested to the death over and over again, and many have been successful to trust love instead of succumb to fear. Whether it was being thrown into the lion's den in ancient times, or a gas chamber or gun held to the head today, millions have chosen to lose the body rather than their integrity to God. Case closed.

Another example about this, a simple yet profound truth is what happens when we are about to get into an accident, often the thought "Help me God!" will go through our heads. This is testimony as well that when threatened, often mankind turns *to* God and *not away* from God. This is in direct contrast to our original parents, which shows that the original pair where not *created* with faulty judgment, but chose it on their own. In addition, mankind not only seeks out God but also looks to do Love's will, even when there is great hostility upon him if he does so. Even when standing in the face of great adversity, mankind often demonstrates their choice of love, the choice of God.

Look at the love that mankind is stimulated to when a disaster hits. Many think it is a natural inclination for people to only think of themselves. But what do you see instead?

18

A great outpouring of energy, love and support occurs, whether it is a complete stranger or not, people give whatever they can, with many even risking their own lives to help another. This is the goodness of humanity in full force, that place of recognizing "love thy neighbor as thyself." And no one forced them to do it, for it is written on their hearts, by the spirit of Love.

Case Closed - Love Wins!

Why do we say "case closed?" Because just like there is an end to a court case when the evidence is compiled and the verdict reached, *so it is now!* We are living in the blink of time between the conclusion being reached and it being pronounced. It is as if the foreman of the jury has been handed the folded piece of paper, he is unfolding it, and about to pronounce it to all. Knowing that all three issues are closed is one of the many blessings of information that has come through Holy Stigmata. We knew two of the original issues had been settled for a while, but the last one *just finished in 2006.* What does this mean? It means exactly what we are seeing around us – things are speeding up. A great shift, a great transition is now upon us, to take us back to the original plan for mankind and the earth. God's first plan has never changed; we just had a little bump in the road, and the Divine plan for the earth and mankind will come to be. *"...my word that goes out from my mouth; it will not return to be empty, but will achieve the purpose for which I sent it." (Is. 55:11)*

Is it easier to understand now why there is darkness upon the earth? Can you see now that it is not just about humankind, but there is something bigger happening here, something much greater? Those Angels that have chosen to be true to Love, 2/3 of all of the Angels created are helping God's Will to come to fruition. Those Angels that have chosen to separate from Love, 1/3 of all the Angels created are looking to oppose God and God's Will, and have made themselves unHoly Angels. These are seeking to cause as much destruction and damage as they can to God and what he loves, which includes earth and mankind.

The unHoly Angels know the case is closed and that they lost.

Like a criminal bent on murder and ruin, they are destroying everything they can as quickly as possible before they are placed where they can do no harm. So especially at this time they seek any holes in the bubble of free will to puppet as many people as possible. They manipulate them to make bad choices, and exploit them like pawns in a chess game to hurt one another and the environment. And as long as people are not informed about their power to use their free will to heal their armor and call in God and the Holy Angels, the unHoly Angels are getting away with it. Or so they think - because in the bigger picture, they are not. This is because even if not a single human remembers who he is and participates with God in transforming the world, the change will still happen, and the Holy Angels will do the cleansing through God's free will alone.

This time of our human participation with the Holy Angels is another example of God's love, in that he is still allowing the unHoly Angels - who were once in his Presence and once Holy too - to learn and see how love benefits all. Even now it is not too late for any of them who have rebelled to turn from their ways and come back home. Then they would be welcomed again into the Angelic brotherhood, and be plugged back into the connection of God's love.

Our Participation with the Holy Angels

Light and darkness cannot exist in the same place together, and the unHoly Angels cannot interact with their Holy brothers of Light any longer. And since we have seen this question had to be solved in our world, the darkness is now limited to the jurisdiction of where the case was presented, the earth.

"And there was war in heaven. Michael and his angels fought against the dragon, and the dragon and his angels fought back. But he was not strong enough, and they lost their place in heaven. The great dragon was hurled down - that ancient serpent called the devil, or Satan, who leads the whole world astray. He was hurled to the earth, and his angels with him...Therefore rejoice, you heavens and you who reside in them! But woe to the earth and the sea, because the devil has gone down to you! He is filled with fury, because he knows his time is short." (Revelation 12:7-9, 12)

20

The unHoly Angels know that the time is short, and the marketing and advertising program of brainwashing people against the belief that a personal God *exists,* let alone loves and cares about us, is fully underway. This lie is one of the reasons that Love allows supernatural events (such as miracle healing), and signs and wonders to occur - it is a supreme Holy marketing program of Love's own making, and also acts as a direct lifeline to his children. It also underlines that we have the powerful free will ability to end any manipulation against us, our family, and even the world we live in. It also underlines why we can send forgiveness and love back to any people or situations where people have harmed us, because we know *it wasn't really them.* This knowledge alone can bring great comfort and peace to us, knowing that people behave the way they do from unconscious brainwashing and influence of negative forces, by manipulation. It is not in mankind's true nature to harm another.

For example, during a time of sharing during the Holy Stigmata, Blessed Tiffany witnessed that when Christ was looking down from the cross, he saw one of those who had tortured him. The man was sneering, and had a wretched, evil look upon his face. Then Christ spoke the words, *"Forgive them Father, for they know not what they do." (Luke 23:34)* Immediately, a dark shadow moved out of the person; and a *face of childlike innocence* replaced the one of evil. This really drives home the point. This is why we can forgive even the worst terrorist or murderer, and all those who have ever harmed us or threatened to harm us. Because *it is not them,* they are being manipulated like a puppet. It is not the true nature of the spirit of mankind to do such things; he is not capable of it on his own unless darkness enters in.

What Happens to the Darkness?

How deep is God's love? Remember that he asks us to love and forgive any who have harmed us. Would God ask us to do anything that he himself is not willing to do? No! This is why God wants even the unHoly Angels to come back to him, to turn from their dark ways and join again the brotherhood with his other Holy sons.

21

In that same blink of time that we are living in, the unHoly Angels are asked to put an end to the manipulation they create upon mankind and the earth, and the manipulation that they create for one another as well. Since they cut themselves off from love, a gang-mentality reigns among them, so they war against and manipulate one another too. But God longs to have all of creation in unity under Love and in peace. And that includes *all* the Angels, even those who have once caused trouble.

The parable in Luke 15:11-31 of the lost prodigal son demonstrates profound love and mercy. It tells of a younger brother who leaves his father's house, squanders his inheritance, and finally comes back repentant and half-starved. Upon seeing his young son coming down the road to him, the father prepares a feast, and welcomes the lost son with jewelry and takes care of all his needs. In this illustration, the older brother who stayed all the years at home to help his father, becomes upset at all the kindness bestowed upon his younger brother, and doesn't understand how his father could forgive so easily and welcome back such a wayward soul. This is what the father answered his older son: *"'My son,' the father said, 'you are always with me, and everything I have is yours. But we had to celebrate and be glad, because this brother of yours was dead and is alive again; he was lost and is found.'"*

Though the lost son made bad choices, we can see the excitement of the father when this son returns. Now can you imagine the joy when a fallen unHoly Angel returns to God? God is the one who is fit to judge, no other. God is the one who will correct and guide. We are all Love's creation, man and Angel alike, and Love is in charge, and rules out of all the facets of love, including compassion, mercy and forgiveness.

What if the unHoly Angels Don't Change?

All along the way, the unHoly Angels have known and seen the consequences for bad behavior. They have been warned to not cross certain lines. And all along there have been unHoly Angels who just don't care about any lines, and don't really think any consequences will come from their behavior. Because of this attitude of audacity, many have been removed from the scene all throughout time, since even though they were warned, they just didn't care.

You can see that Love has always truly been in charge.If God had *not* set parameters and restrictions upon what the unHoly Angels could do to mankind and the earth, we would all be dead today and the earth already destroyed. That fear is also a manipulation the unHoly Angels still place in the minds of mankind; that life is uncertain, and that at any instant all of us could be destroyed in a nuclear holocaust, everything going up in a mushroom cloud of smoke, the earth will flood from melting ice caps, the poles will shift, ozone layer depletion, chemical warfare, global infertility, genocide, worldwide plague, etc. But there is no need to worry, again, God is in charge. So where there would be a demonic "death wound" only a bruising occurs. The original purpose of joy for mankind and the earth will still happen.

It is because of Divine intervention that we still survive. The unHoly Angels who have crossed the line, and do not heed the warnings, have their Holy brothers to contend with. God sends his True Sons to take these fallen ones out of commission. God sends the Holy Angels by his own request, *and he sends them in request to human prayer as well.* The unHoly Angels do not go willingly, and the Angels that Love calls to do this work have the rank and responsibility of Warrior Angels. The unHoly Angels are placed in a confinement where they can do no harm to themselves or others; it is like a large sheet of glass that they can see out of, but cannot move. They have no further interaction with other unHoly Angels, the line of communication is completely broken; and they have no power to manipulate anyone or anything, or to be manipulated by each other. From this immobile position, they can clearly continue to see the outworking of God's love upon mankind and the earth. They are not tortured. A God of love would not do that. And even in this state, we are still in the period of time that all they have to do is say the word, and God will welcome them back.

But when all is said and done, there is a time when all decisions are final, and since Love wins the war, there is no place for anything not of Love. Energy cannot be destroyed, only changed. So there comes a moment when the energy that the unHoly Angels were given in wave form is now turned into particle, and they will then simply become a part of the ground the earth is made of.

More About Angels – Who Are They?

Angels are some of the most beloved creatures the universe has ever known. Both the Greek words *ag'ge-los* and Hebrew *mal-akh'* actually mean "messenger" or "spirit messenger" and occur in the scriptures nearly 400 times. Angels were individually created by the will of the Most High; they are not people who were once alive. They were created before mankind ever came on the scene, and have their own responsibilities. Angels travel at tremendous speed, past anything we could compare to on earth. They are superhuman in power, and have more intelligence than we do.

All Angels have individual and group duties, responsibilities and rank. Their appearance is iridescent, like shimmering light, and in the core of their spirit are different multifaceted colors sparkling and flickering, like rotating gemstones. These correspond to the responsibilities each was created for, and the gifts they have. Some specialize in healing, others in protection, communication, environment, death (the "homing" Angels, taking us home) and much more. How many Angels are there? There are thousands of references to them in the scriptures. This is what the prophet Daniel saw around God: *"thousands upon thousands attended him, ten thousand times ten thousand stood before him." (Daniel 7:10)* And those are just the Angels to attend to and praise God! In the garden of Gethsemane, Christ could have cried out to his Father for 12 legions of Angels to protect him, if he had wanted to. Just one "legion" corresponded to the largest unit of the Roman army, consisting of 3,000 - 6,000 soldiers. One Angel is known to have killed 185,000 people all by himself. (2 Kings 19:35, Isaiah 37:36). They are very, very powerful.

Angels each have their own name and personalities too. Only two Angel names are given in the Bible, Michael and Gabriel; since Angels are dispatched by God, in *his name*, and not their own. There are several references about people in the scriptures asking Angels for their names, or wanting to worship them; but they were told by the Angels, *"Be careful! Do not do it! I am a fellow servant with you and with your brothers who hold to the testimony of Jesus. Worship God!" (Rev. 19:10)*

24

If you are not sure if you are in the presence of a Holy Angel or an unHoly one, asking this one question will solve it: *"Do you love Jesus now?"* Any unHoly Angels will either disappear, try not to answer the question, or say unflattering and dark things. They know the power of the name. You will see why that is important in the next chapter, no matter what religion you are. *"If you make the Most High your dwelling - then no harm will befall you…for he will command his angels concerning you to guard you in all your ways." (Psalm 91)*

Angels are sexless; they don't marry or procreate. But, they are generally referred to in the scriptures as males, although in most paintings they are represented as females. Their wings are not actually feathers. They are likened more precisely to radiant beams of shimmering light. They have control over this light to be in any shape they desire, including wings. They can be very huge – I've seen one almost 40 feet tall, standing head and shoulders over a house that had just been spiritually cleansed. They can also be very, very tiny, and may be where the idea of fairies came from in some cultures. There is no limit on the variety of spiritual beings that God has made. Most of the time Angels are invisible, but sometimes they are a mist, bright light, or look like shimmering heat waves or high vibrating energy. At rare times (only) Holy Angels are even allowed to manifest in human form. Remember what Einstein said? "Matter is just slowed down energy."

Most of the time you will not see anything with your eyes - you will just have a knowing sense that you are not alone, and sometimes it can get very cold. It is a profound experience to be in the company of Holy Angels. And they desire to not only be in your company, but to help you remember what you are called to do, to assist it to come into fruition, to guide you, and protect you. But without your free will participation, nothing can happen. Holy Angels cannot go further than what you or God allow. This is why we are encouraged not to ask the Angels to only *watch* over us, since this is a place of inactivity that they do anyway, but to help, guide and defend us. Then they can do much. And God allows much. He even sends out his Angels to help humans rearrange and change the world.

CHAPTER 4

Participating with Angels – Words Create Worlds
Aligning with Divine Will through the 50 Decrees

Can you see that no matter how dark and intimidating the world may seem, love is even now winning the war? It is a time of shifting, brightening, and a rearranging of the world back into love. There are many misconceptions about this time, which are based on needless fear. But as we have seen, just by using common sense many of these misconceptions can be identified and thrown away. For example, some people fear that the earth itself will be destroyed, but that is not the case. The earth is a beautiful gem in God's eyes and will last forever.(Psalm 37:10,11) For another example of common sense, if you owned an apartment building and one of the tenants was causing a disruption for all the others, would you destroy the apartment building, or just oust the bad tenant? All of it can be reasoned out by going back to this, "If God is a God of love, would he…?" People may want to argue many points, but if that is the yardstick they measure Love by, much clarity can be found. This also cuts out much misinformation and fear that the unHoly Angels have presented to intimidate us, to keep us from recognizing the time we are living in and what is really going on. Now, let's learn how to help with this shift, because *starting today,* you can change the world!

Changing How Man Treats One Another

For all those whose hearts are touched with compassion by the struggles seen in this world, this is what is offered to you – you can work freely and in unlimited amounts by being a touchstone of free will between heaven and earth. What a story of transformation and adventure we will be able to tell into timelessness, and share with whomever we meet along the way. Indeed, mankind is known throughout the cosmos as *the only creation that doesn't believe it was created.* This doesn't have to be the case for you! Now, this change will happen whether mankind interacts in it or not, but how wonderful that we are asked to participate! The original issues needed to come to closure before humankind could get back to what we were created to do and be.

Now we are on the verge of this new world, and with alignment and connection with The Big Guy we are asked to start the re-creation of it *now!* But how do we do that? How does this really work? How do we connect to God and the Angels? And if this is through our free will, are the words important – what do we really say to cover it all?

Yes, because of free will, the right words are very important, and we talk through prayer. We don't pray to the Angels, but to the one who sends them, since Love knows which ones are the correct ones with the corresponding responsibilities and gifts to send to get the work done. Many of us know prayer manifests change – but what if you were given written prayers *specifically worded by God* to help you perfectly manifest guidance, protection and healing for you and your family now, in the past, and the future? What if these prayers already carried God's approval and power to protect the earth, cleanse the governments and religions, calm the storms, feed the hungry, transform the environment, and were created specifically to expand our brightness in this time we are living in? What if there were words to flawlessly align our will with the perfect Will of Love? Wouldn't you want to be part of that? That is what we are able to share with you now - perfect words for perfect alignment, for our perfect shift into Love.

Because we are spirits of God born as humans here on earth, we are each a touch-stone between heaven and earth. Among other things, it means that we can bridge the gap. For example, when we specifically ask for help (pray) for governmental officials to recognize better choices and to be aware of the effects of their actions before they even take them, in the past present and future, *God can do much.* He sends a Holy Angel with the right gifts and responsibilities to create another opportunity for that person to recognize what to do, and it creates a better different ripple effect. Because we each have free will, Love will still not go against someone else's free will, but will give them greater opportunity to recognize right choices. It is as if God places in front of each of us a field, and plants beautiful rose bushes here and there, hoping we will recognize the rose bushes. When we pray, a Holy Angel is sent and another rose bush is planted; another prayer, another rose bush; until the entire field may be filled with roses.

28

It is still up to the person involved to recognize that there are rose bushes in the field, and to make better choices, but there are now numerous opportunities abounding in front of him to do so.

Changing Severe Weather

Now how does our free will affect things that aren't human, things that don't have free will themselves, such as storms and severe weather conditions? We see the problems all around us; tornados, hurricanes, flooding, mud slides; so much loss of life and destruction. Millions homeless and sick, many lost from their loved ones. Is there anything that we can do to change the weather? The unHoly Angels utilize many ways to stimulate fear and destruction, and manipulating the environment is one of them. When we ask for a Holy Angel to help with those things, instantly one is sent, and because there is *no conscious free will* in the storm, there is immediate and powerful change! *"He got up and rebuked the wind and the raging waters; the storm subsided, and all was calm."(Luke 8:24)* Christ said that those who came after him would do even greater things, (John 14:12), and calming storms is another sign and wonder that we can participate in on a worldwide scale, bringing calm and peace in the midst of panic and fear.

The Wording is Important

"Lock the door." "Lock the door now." "Lock the door now on the front side of the house." "Lock the door on the front of the house but be sure to leave the side door open for Suzy." Do you see the difference in the meaning of the words as additional information is given? Words are important, because for free will not to be compromised, access has to be given, an alignment of will. For mankind to have the most participation, guidance and protection in this time of shift as possible, and for the most access and freedom for the Holy Angels to do their job, the wording is *essential*. To help with this, God gave us perfect wording to align mankind's free will with his Will. They are called The Divine Decrees. These are 50 prayers written by God to allow our participation with the Angels for perfect and immediate change.

29

The Power of Love through You

We are given these Divine Decrees at this crucial time so that suffering may be eased and many of our brothers and sisters may be granted further opportunity to hear the voice of Love, recognize Love and choose the way of Love. These Decrees are what God has blessed the children of man with to assist them in this crucial time of shifting into the timelessness of Love. God knows how many are suffering, and has shown numerous times that it is through the spoken word that the power of transformation takes place. Through these words, Love has now given his human children additional ways to become stronger and interact with the Holy Angels to assist you in choosing Love over fear, and to help manifest changes to transform the world.

During Holy Stigmata, we were shown an image of how prayers were brought to God; they were like wafts of incense that the Angels gathered and brought to God. Prayers are gathered according to their purpose, such as prayers for health, prayers for forgiveness, prayers for love, and prayers for peace and so on. Prayers differed according to the brightness of the ones praying them; some were smoky-colored prayers, ("God I don't know if you are there or not but…") and some were very, very bright ("God! I know you hear me!"). So the brightness comes from the connection of the one who is praying and the strength of their faith and trust. The brighter a person is, the brighter their prayer is – so those that know Love hears prayers actually make their own prayers brighter. And the brighter a prayer is the more attention it attracts. We see this demonstrated here by what an Angel said: *"Do not be afraid Daniel, for since the first day you set your mind to gain understanding and humble yourself before God, your words were heard and I have come in response to them." (Daniel 10:12)*

Daniel was a man of faith and had set his mind to gain understanding. He had humbled himself and his words were heard, and a Holy Angel was sent in response. This is how the Divine connection of Love is meant to be for all of us. We ask, and help is given. So now you see how prayers work, and how the brightness can vary greatly because of us.

But a Divine Decree is very different. *A Divine Decree is like a laser beam that shoots brightly and directly to God!* With an immediate impact, the Decrees enable us to be covered in every conceivable aspect by guidance, protection and the transformation of love. There is no difference in brightness; they are each one brilliant and immediately heard.

Prayer and The Divine Decrees

The Divine Decrees are to be used with your prayers. Do not stop praying! Again, the Decrees are given to be used *in addition* to our own prayers to God.

Your prayer is your love song to God. The time of connection to Love is a personal time of union and sharing in trust our deepest thoughts, feelings, needs and gratitude. Similar to a high-speed internet download, much happens in prayer, and it is never just a one-way conversation. When you connect, you are receiving. You may or may not be conscious of it, but peace, answers and guidance is placed in your spirit. In prayer, you are making a conscious free will decision to go beyond the bounds of your self and align with unlimited energy. You are also thinking of what needs to happen for yourself or for another. You run through your mind asking for healing, for love, for forgiveness, for a softening, for an awakening and for all sorts of things. We do this through our own ideas of what we think needs to happen for another or for ourselves, through our own imperfect wisdom. The Divine Decrees *are God's love song to his children.* With the Decrees, it is what God, in perfect wisdom and love has given to us for perfect alignment, to take care of all our needs and desires, and all that we may not even know enough to ask about.

A Recipe for Perfect Love!

Another example of the difference between prayer and The Divine Decrees is this: prayer is like a family recipe for a wonderful apple pie. We may have the recipe in our head, or even by word of mouth it may have been passed down from generation to generation: a pinch of this, a handful of that. Each time the pie comes out it may taste very good, just not the same way each time.

That is like our prayers. The Divine Decrees are like having the perfect ingredients and the perfect measurements, the perfect setting for the oven and the perfect pie, *every single time!* That is an easy way to think of the difference. Both are good and appreciated, but the perfect pie is even more precious!

Laser Beam Prayers

Given by God, The Divine Decrees are already blessed. They have an immediate reaction of advancing and brightening the person who says them, and shoot right to God like a precise and focused beam of perfect light. Love has given us incredible protection; the Holy Angels to assist us and our families, our loved ones, and even all those we have ever met and those we have yet to meet. It is an opportunity given to all those that are moved by compassion to heal the world, for they ease the suffering and bring more peace, hope, trust, discernment, faith and hope into this special time. Divine Love created us to co-create with him, and part of that glorious gift is now to re-create the earth we live in.

When you take a look at the Decrees you will begin to understand the many things that are covered for you. This is beyond religion, this is all about love. Anyone from any religious path can say these Divine Decrees, there are no restrictions unless you place them there yourself. Those who recognize Love and the way of Love will be able to see the Love within. These Decrees help us to be the bright reflection of the love of God, for ourselves, our loved ones, our community, nation and world. And we are doing this work in full conscious awareness, so our spirit expands into brightness, connection and joy. We invite Love in as the solution rather than doing it on our own power. We connect with God and his Holy Angels so there is no limit of energy flow or exhaustion on our side. These Decrees are tools for the alignment of free will to help transform darkness into light. Love knows how difficult it is now and the further challenges that lie ahead of us. And he knows that less will suffer now in this world through this gift of love, The Divine Decrees.

The Desire is already placed in Your Heart

Can you see the Decrees for what they truly are? Can you see that through these you may accomplish all the things that *he has already placed within your heart to do?* All the ways to help others, bring about peace, love, joy, hope and faith? Can you see that it is recognition of who you are, and his Spirit within you that makes the difference? God doesn't just give us the desire without any tools to make it happen. Many people think that being a mystic is about being passive. It is just the opposite - it is about being an activist, and fulfilling our God-given role to consistently and bravely look fear fully in its face, and transform it.

Here is a wonderful way to describe what we have been given. A plane is flying and the Captain comes over the PA and says: *"...just to let you know, we will be experiencing some turbulence. There is no need to be afraid; we will be through it shortly. If there is a need for it, the oxygen masks will deploy from above you and we suggest you place them on yourself first, then on the one sitting next to you, should they require assistance. Have no fear; we have the finest of equipment available to you. We will be landing safely and we appreciate your trust in us. Have a good day."*

The Divine Decrees are the oxygen masks that will help us through the tough times. By saying them, we take care of ourselves, those we love and those we are inspired to help. These are powerful and can affect change way beyond our ability to comprehend their impact. For it is *"not by power, nor by might, but by My Spirit, says the Lord Almighty"* (Zechariah 4:6)

What is Holy Stigmata & How Did The Divine Decrees Come to Us?

These Divine Decrees were given to us through the sharing of the Holy Stigmata experienced by Blessed Tiffany, which first began in July 2005. Holy Stigmata is a spontaneous manifestation of bloody wounds on a person's hands, feet, forehead or back - similar to the wounds of the crucified Jesus. History tells us that many have received these marks of the Passion of Christ with corresponding and intense sufferings. These are called visible Stigmata.

Others only have the sufferings, without any outward marks, and these phenomena are called invisible Stigmata. Stigmata at its simplest form is God's way of saying, "I understand fully what the human condition is, I too have felt life at its bones and sinews." Currently there are 102 bearers of the Holy Stigmata in the world, in all different cultures and religions, this is because the redemption of mankind from dark into Light by Christ is not about religion, just as God is not about religion. This number will continue to grow, as another sign and wonder in this period of time. All Stigmata-bearers have additional gifts as well, to validate who the Giver of the gift is.

God is light, and darkness and light cannot be in the same place. So before Jesus, none were bright enough for God to feel human life through. What Love experienced through Jesus at the moment of our karmic redemption from darkness back into light, included pain, suffering and death. He broke the bonds of sin upon us. So sometimes when God visits, he will use this to show he understands the fullness of humanity.

Holy Stigmata is true communion - except this time, Love consumes us as the bread and wine. The experience is Graced by a high state of peace and tranquility mixed within the suffering. This is because God wants us to feel joy and love above all, in this reality of Divine connection with him, in bridging heaven and earth, the visible and the invisible, man and God, replacing sin and death with forgiveness and life. One of the reasons there is pain with Stigmata is because the flesh is imperfect, so there is a dying off of it, and a re-creation of it at the same time, as perfect Love visits the person. So Stigmata is like death and resurrection while still in the body. This shifts the person's veil as well, and expands greatly the spirit of the person who has chosen to be vulnerable to Love. Blessed Tiffany first sees Christ as third-person, from a distance. Then she becomes superimposed with him, and sees and feels what he saw and felt at the time of breaking the bonds of darkness.

At the height of the pain, she is pulled out, and experiences many visions, including reading of great books and ability to ask questions of God and the Holy Angels of what she sees and hears. At times she is visited during Stigmata by Mother Mary, who appears beautifully and tenderly as Mother of All the Nations.

She encourages her and reminds her to stay upon the earth to finish the work. Through all of this, she is either semi-conscious or fully out of body. If she is semi-conscious, she will whisper the words given to her which are immediately written down. If she is out of body, she will give the information when she returns. It is truly a time of great learning, and in Blessed Tiffany's case, hundreds of pages of information have already been compiled, which will continue to be published, for it is for the children of mankind that the words are given.

As the months went by and Blessed Tiffany continued to go through this Sharing (which is what Stigmata is called on the other side) for about 3 – 5 days every month, she brightened to a point where spiritually, emotionally and physically she was ready to receive them. This included being able to consciously and clearly hear and see while in the company of several Holy Angels over a span of three weeks while writing the words in her own hand. After this, The Divine Decrees were to be given to a priest that God had chosen that he may share the blessings everywhere. Can you see the balance and equality of the way Love brought forth the words? Through the Christ-wounded hands given to a spiritual woman, mother and healer who originally never believed in such things, to the ordained hands of a religious priest, encompassing male and female, spiritual and religious, ordained and common? The Decrees are truly a gift to be shared to all, no matter what background or belief system.

Father Billy Clark was the priest called to be the protector of The Divine Decrees, which are in their entirety called The Twelve Books of The Acts of the Love of God. It was only after he was ordained as a priest in December 2006 that they were to be shared with him by Blessed Tiffany, who had completed them in November. It is our honor to be part of the opportunity during this time of shift to teach and assist others in hearing the voice of Love and aligning with such powerful transformation. It is not about us – Love has always made his own choices regardless of outward appearance, cultural or social standings or worldly qualifications. All we had to do was say "yes!" That is the same choice all of us have, to either say "yes" or "no" when offered an opportunity. We are all in this together; and none of us are any greater or lesser than anyone else.

We are all his kids and welcomed up on his lap, all are loved, and all have gifts. The Divine Decrees are a very special opportunity to change the world. What do you say? Will you say "yes?!"

What Happens When I Say The Divine Decrees?

The easiest way to understand what is occurring when you say The Divine Decrees is to look at them through the illustration of a plant and super powered fertilizer. Every plant must go through its own growth, one plant cannot grow for another. When a plant is mature and ready for more than just the basic nutrients, fertilizer or plant food can be applied. Depending on the quality of the new food the plant can grow and develop quickly. The plant must be able to absorb the new food at a balanced rate. When we feed a plant we do not put the fertilizer on it every day. We must water it and tend to it every day, but even that must be done in balance with the growth of the plant. If we were to fertilize the plant daily simply because we wanted it to grow rapidly and produce quickly, we would risk harming the plant. This is how we can look at The Divine Decrees.

The Divine Decrees expand dramatically our spiritual growth when we align our will with the Will of God. And they come with instructions at the bottom of each one which gives the span of time in which to repeat them. For example, The Protection Act states that it is recommended that it be repeated in 5 days. If you were to say it on the first day of the month, you would again say it on the 6th, 11th, 16th, 21st, 26th and 31st (when applicable) of the month.

See it as your door having a lock. If your door is locked, it doesn't matter when the thief comes to enter, you are prepared. If your door is unlocked, the thief may or may not come at that time, but any damage could be avoided if you are prepared. To ensure that your door stays locked, simply say The Divine Decrees in the suggested times.

It is not necessary to say all The Divine Decrees everyday. This is overdoing it and it can cause harm. The reason it can cause harm is because of the continual push for spiritual expansion without regard or respect for the physical body.

It is not a bad thing to seek spiritual growth; this is part of why you are given the information, to encourage you in your path to Love. This is about balance, and God doesn't want us harmed in the process of seeking Love. God has given the times needed for everyone to be powerfully and abundantly covered through the times given, just stick to that.

What Happens If I Push for Expansion Too Hard, Too Fast?

Signs that you are pushing too hard for the spiritual growth without care for the body: bloody nose, inability to concentrate, constant lightheadedness, headaches that do not go away with water, food, sugar or the deliverance prayer, being too loose in the body and having trouble staying grounded in the physical body, or fatigue. All these signs point to the fact that you are pushing your body too fast for it to recuperate. The Decrees are powerful and are to be treated with respect. Read them at the times suggested. Please remember - *it is not necessary to say all The Divine Decrees everyday* and it could even cause harm to the physical body as the spiritual progresses faster than the body can assimilate the information. You are seeking to align your will with God's Will. This is a wonderful gift and blessing of enlightenment. Be gentle on yourself in the process and have respect for God's gift for you.

Balance is necessary. Pushing yourself too fast is not helpful for accomplishing your purpose here on earth. Many of these get in the way and can cause more problems as your body attempts to rectify the damage done, which is a distraction that gets in the way of the work that Love has for you. It is essential you continue to do the things needed to balance the body especially when seeking spiritual enlightenment. Make sure the body gets what it needs for food, water, sleep, play and exercise so that you have the ability to do the greater work spiritually. God is looking for shining stars that can provide the light for a long period of time - he does not ask us to be shooting stars that give their light for but a moment. There is a lot of work to do and you are needed. Take care of yourself so that you can be utilized for the greater work. It is suggested that your body have all the requirements of food, water and sleep before putting exercise in the mix. In this way, you keep from burning out your system.

We have been shown that when we are out of balance, we cannot be given greater responsibility. Greater responsibility requires greater ability to not only do the work *but to recover.* Take bilocation for example. Bilocation is where the body appears at 2 places at the same time. God has used many people for this throughout time. Blessed Tiffany is one that Love has used for this as well. Bilocation is not easy on the body; it takes a lot of water and energy to be able to be called for this purpose. If you are well rested, well fed, have enough water and are in balance, Love can use you to do fantastic work. If you are not, it would be a detriment to your body, so you would not be called to do this. This is why it is essential that we balance, so we can be used by God for greater supernatural work of all kinds!

Do The Divine Decrees Keep Me from All Harm?

The Divine Decrees prevent many things from happening to you than you will be able to see or recognize. These you will clearly see in the bigger picture at a different time. But it is not about never having anything bad ever happen again. What it is about is *transformation.*

Here is why: the unHoly Angels seek to cause you harm, even to destroy you, to hurt you, to keep you from doing the work of Love and to harm Love by hurting what Love has created. While the unHoly Angels still attack to try to convince you to lower or extinguish the candle, the full intentions of harm will not be allowed to manifest. Take for an example if they wish to create a deadly car accident to harm you. You are bright and you say your Decrees without leaving any opening or gap within the times suggested. You even know enough to do the Deliverance Prayer for yourself whenever anything comes against your health, finances or relationships. You have your bases covered. So while the unHoly Angels seek to create a horrible car accident to kill you, instead you may have only slight bumper damage with no real damage to your health. You have just participated in transforming your life. Will you have eyes of faith to know there was a bigger picture going on? Or will you give up on the Decrees because you were not saved from having a bent fender?

The Divine Decrees are in place for your protection and are given at this crucial time to *drastically cut down* on the suffering for all of mankind. They are not for *ending* the suffering of all of mankind! That will come soon as well, but the shifting into light must come first, and the darkness knows this and chooses to attack more furiously. This is why we have The Divine Decrees now, so that when attacked and the enemy seeks our destruction and death, for the most part it is only a glancing blow. For many people, this will translate to the attacks only giving a bruise where the unHoly Angels sought to break a bone. We can still get hurt, yes, and some will still die, but it will not be to the extent that was originally schemed. The Divine Decrees are a powerful and loving gift.

Recognizing Love beyond Restriction!

God is in control. Love Wins! The Divine Decrees are specifically given to help us through this tough time, for we are told, *"For then there will be great distress, unequaled from the beginning of the world until now - and never to be equaled again. If those days had not been cut short, no one would survive, but for the sake of the elect those days will be shortened"* (Matthew 24:21)

This is God's great love for us, that we may be uplifted and have hope for what is to come and the faith needed to make it through whatever comes our way. There is no need to alter the wording in any way. The Divine Decrees were given and worded this specific way for us. We do not need to question the wisdom behind the words nor the one who bestowed them upon humanity.

Even if you only say The Divine Decrees once, you have brightened. Many Holy Angels are put into work as soon as the Decree is stated. So much happens that we cannot see and the ripple effect is fantastic. Remember, these Decrees were given to ease the suffering of the sons of mankind, and the earth. Many besides yourself and your family will be helped by these, more than you can imagine. Let's begin!

CHAPTER 5

BOOK ONE – The Unification Act
Unity of the Soul with God, Self and One Another

(1). I Decree as a Spirit of God, born as a child of man, full alignment, communication and unity of this soul's Holy Prayers and Holy Intentions with God, the Word of God, the Holy Spirit, the Holy Ones, Guides assigned, All Holy Angels assigned (and my husband/wife and those under my care). By free will I agree to receive and connect with Love to strengthen Love, choose the way of Love, encourage Love and expand Love wherever it may be found, whenever it may be found, in whatever amount it may be found, throughout all creation that has been formed, is being formed and will be formed.

(2). I Decree full authority and free will interaction to All Holy Angels assigned to utilize the indent of this soul through all interactions past, present and future to continue the experience and expansion of the Love of God.

(3). I Decree this as binding on earth as it is in heaven by the alignment of the will of God and man, bridging all past, present or future events until the One King of the Kingdom of God assumes full authority by the order of the Unification Act as ordained by the Blood of the Covenant as witnessed and given through the Holy Spirit by the Love of God, Amen.

(Visualization: Falling snow, blanketing everything. Color: White. Duration: 5 days. Repeat the Unification Act again in 5 days).

Understanding the Unification Act:

(1)…I Decree as a Spirit of God, born as a child of man… The first Decree states who we are: a Spirit of God, born as a child of man. This is how all the Acts will begin, recognizing that we are "of God" and where we are now as a "child of man."

41

The best way to explain this is to give you the background of spirit, soul and body. The definitions that have been shared with us through the sharing of Holy Stigmata are as follows; a spirit is who we truly are; a Spirit of God, a creation *"made in the image of God." (Genesis 1:27)* Our spirit could have been made and placed elsewhere, but we were born here as a child of man. The spirit can exist separate from the body. This spirit is what lives on even after the death of the body. It is the spirit that is eternal, not the body. The body is the temple that houses the spirit of God. *"Do you not know that your body is a temple of the Holy Spirit, who is in you, whom you have received from God?"(1Corinthians 6:19)*

The soul is the combination of the body and the spirit. The body is a gift of Love that enables us to accomplish our commission that we set out to do in life. We are here to learn and apply the various facets of love, which helps us know more about God, ourselves and one another; and to be an instrument of Love's transformation in the world. This is what is summed up in the golden rule; loving God and our neighbor as ourselves. (Matthew 22:37) We are offered the choice to be an opportunity of love that God can share with our extended family here on earth, and the environment, and to work hand in hand with the Holy Angels to create positive change. We learn that the alignment of our will and Divine will creates helpful change for ourselves, our immediate family, and all the things our heart is passionate about. We learn there are no limits when we go beyond our own strength, and flow with unlimited and unconditional Love.

Through all The Divine Decrees we will be stating who we are as "a Spirit of God, born as a child of man." This is how we start all the Decrees: declaring who know and recognize who our soul is, before delivering the message and our connection with it. It is an acknowledgement of self.

…full alignment, communication and unity of this soul's Holy Prayers and Holy Intentions…The message in this first Decree within the Salvation Act is about full alignment, communication and unity. Let's break this down to understand it more fully. First, we are asking for this from a soul level (the combination of our spirit and our body).

42

This is a personal declaration, a personal statement and testimony that no one else can make on our behalf as well. This alignment is an expression of our free will, "this soul." As such, *we cannot say this for another* since this could violate their free will. We can, however, state these aloud *with* another and they can say an "Amen" at the end to demonstrate their free will agreement. This is how the Decrees can be said in groups, with a joint audible agreement at the end. Also when the Decrees are read aloud in this way if someone is unable to speak for whatever reason, God himself hears their internal agreement or reservation to what was said.

In this first Decree what we are seeking is full alignment, communication and unity of our Holy prayers and Holy intentions. This is a huge statement! By choosing to align our energy, our spirit, our passion and compassion, we become the true power and potential we were originally created to be. When we align our Holy prayers and Holy intentions we unite as one force for good, together in harmony with God and one another. How beautiful to align with Love in one will – truly this is a place of power beyond one soul acting alone, even with the best of intentions! With this alignment of will, nothing is limited or weak, nothing is left separate or isolated, nothing is unsustainable, nothing is impossible – and you will see and feel the ripple effect of your participation within your own life and that of your family.

...with God... Let's take a look at who we are uniting with, first and foremost: God - our Creator, the God of Divine Love, Creator of all that is, the one who is the true personification of unconditional Love, the One we came from, long to be with, and learn more about. We are sparks from his Divine Flame, we are of him, through Love and for Love. God has a personal Presence and core, and many people who have come back from near-death experiences (NDEs) tell about the bright white light they witnessed, and the overpowering Love and acceptance they felt while in that Presence. Blessed Tiffany had this experience as well; by a lightning-strike she was killed and brought to the God of unconditional Love. It is a powerful and detailed story which many people know about, so it will not be retold here, though you may read it on her website or in previous books.

Though God has a personal core and Presence, he is also connected and aware of all things, but he is not the things he created. For example, you are here because of your mother and father coming together, and your DNA and flesh are of them. You wouldn't exist without them - but, you are not them. You are *of* them, but you are *not the same* as them. This is also the difference between seeing God as "your higher self" or worshipping the creation or nature instead of the Creator.

...the Word of God... Next, the Word of God, who was known on earth as Christ Jesus. Christ is the *"Word of God."(Rev. 19:13)* This is not to be confused with the many references to the word of God coming to people with a message. Jesus was the first creation, the first-born son, the first thing that God made. Through him the word of God has been and continues to be accomplished and fulfilled, including the inspiration of sacred texts and creation of the earth and cosmos, and the karmic redemption of mankind from dark into light. *"In the beginning was the Word, and the Word was with God, and the Word was God. He was with God in the beginning. Through him all things were made..." (John 1:1)*

...the Holy Spirit... The Holy Spirit is the power of Love going out, fulfilling God's Will and returning to him. It is like God's hands and feet. Nothing sent out by God comes back to him without being accomplished. The Holy Spirit brings Love to many; he heals, teaches and clarifies messages, creates, and does all the things God wishes to be done. It is an extension of Divine Will and the ability and energy to do all things.

...the Holy Ones... These are humans *living and dead* who are, and have been, devoted to him and continue to seek to do his will. They have completed polishing the basics of the facets of love. You are praying for the brotherhood of saints and to strengthen your connection with all workers of light. These let nothing stop them from expanding the love of God throughout the earth and the cosmos.

...Guides assigned...A guide is a Spirit of God that was born as a child of man, lived as a human and died, and is now in spirit form to help guide another human.

44

This is a Holy One who has completed the minimum facets of love required. These no longer have to come back into a body to learn the basics of love. As such, they were given the choice to go off world or to come back as a human, or as a spiritual guide for a human. Guides are assigned by God to help those of us here in these bodies accomplish our commission, what we agreed to with Love for this life. Since Guides are out of body, they have perfect hearing and connection to Father, his Holy Angels and all other Spirit Beings and other Guides. And with their additional understanding of how it was to be in a body and human, they can help us understand things easier and put things in a way that we can easily identify with and understand. Unlike our personal Guardian Angel who stay with us through our entire life experience Guides are assigned and reassigned by Love as needed, depending on what we need and are working on at the time, and level of growth. Guides are often assigned that have similarities to our own personality and have accomplished skills in what we need and are working on at the moment.

...All Holy Angels assigned... These were created before all other creation. Just a simple recap here: all Angels were made perfectly and given free will as well as mankind. All of them were created for different responsibilities, and have different gifts. They all have the ability to choose the way of Love or to separate from Love.

The Holy Angels are those who continue to choose Love. Our personal Guardian Angel is always a Holy Angel. The unHoly Angels are those who were part of the created brotherhood of God, but chose to disconnect and misuse free will to harm the will of others. The Holy Angels are still allowed to manifest human form as directed on occasion, and desire no glory for themselves, but do all things for the Glory of him who sent them. They have the freedom to move through the expanses of heaven and earth as needed. The unHoly Angels are now limited to the earth and can go no higher into the expanse than the moon. They are not allowed to manifest human form, though they puppet people through any holes in their shields of free will. The unHoly Angels have no additional information of prophecy, spiritual growth or knowledge since the moment they unplugged from God. They still have the gifts of God that they were originally created with, which they now use to harm the things that God loves, which includes mankind and the earth.

Father still desires for the unHoly Angels to turn from their destructive ways, come home, and be part of the brotherhood again. Especially now that the time left is diminished before his original will and purpose for the earth and mankind is fulfilled, and the transformation of all things not of Love is here.

...(and my husband/wife and those under my care)... For those who are married, one spouse can stand in for the other, since they have already asked before God for an alignment of wills between themselves. *And those under our care* means children who are under the legal age for the area they live in, and also those we are taking care of who are unable to take care of themselves. This can also include the elderly and those who have other challenges to health or emotional well-being.

...By free will I agree to receive and connect with Love to strengthen Love, choose the way of Love, encourage Love and expand Love wherever it may be found, whenever it may be found, in whatever amount it may be found, throughout all creation that has been formed, is being formed and will be formed... This shows our free will choice to align as one force, one team - unified by, for and under the love of God. This is the unity we seek! Now we see what the full purpose is and are giving our agreement with receiving and connecting with it. It is all about Love. *"For whoever does not love does not know God, for God is love." (1 John 4:8)* This love is throughout time and creation - past, present and future. It is about recognizing who Love is, and we are, and each other is, in the whole of Love. This also shows that Love continues to expand, and that creation continues to be formed even now as we speak! We will never get tired or bored, or know all there is about Love, since there is no stagnation in love, but it compels onward all it touches. Our journey now becomes a blessed path, and this alignment brings us into a life that is Divinely guided in all things.

(2)...I Decree full authority and free will interaction to All Holy Angels assigned to utilize the indent of this soul through all interactions past, present and future to continue the experience and expansion of the Love of God... This is the power of our free will expressed, to invite in the Holy Angels.

46

Granting full authority and free will interaction to All Holy Angels assigned demonstrates that it is about God's plan and we recognize our place and ability in it. This Decree lets Love assign the Holy Angels and utilize the indent of who you are throughout every interaction that you have had, are having and will have; to experience and expand Love in past, present and future situations. What is even more amazing is that it could be several Holy Angels assigned, several thousand or even several million! Can you imagine the number of people you have met in your life, the interactions you have had, the experiences you've shared? Can you see the power of just agreeing that God can use the Holy Angels in all these occurrences to facilitate even more transformation and share even more Love? This applies even to change and transform struggles and difficulties that have already been experienced. It is amazing!

(3)… I Decree this as binding on earth as it is in heaven by the alignment of the will of God and man, bridging all past, present or future events... Right away we can see that with our declaration, our statement of our alignment of our will with the Will of God, it is an agreement that is binding. *"I tell you the truth, whatever you bind on earth will be bound in Heaven." (Matthew 18:18)*

This has a level of depth to it inherent in the statement that demonstrates the fullness of this work. In this Decree we are unifying our will with the Will of God and declaring that alignment for all to hear. This includes any Holy or unHoly Angels around us, our Guides, etc, and our recognition that there are no limits with Love even in relationship to space or time to manifest change. This is a powerful seal that will end every Act within the Twelve Books of the Acts of the Love of God.

…until the One King of the Kingdom of God assumes full authority…The King of the Kingdom of God is Christ. You will see this name shown in different ways through the endings of the different Acts but these are all titles referring to Jesus, the name God's son was known by on earth.

...by the order of the Unification Act as ordained by the Blood of the Covenant... This is the reference to the authority of each designated Act, and the seal and qualification given to indicate the power within. You could think of it as a presidential seal on the bottom of an important national declaration or law of a country, without which it would not be binding. Without the ordination of the Blood of the Covenant, the Decrees could not be offered, since the redemption of mankind was needed first, the freedom given us by breaking the generational bondage of our original parents, all the way back to the Garden of Eden.

...as witnessed and given through the Holy Spirit by the Love of God...by the active force of God, by his Will the idea and offering of Christ's redemption was made, and it was witnessed as accomplished and fulfilled by the Holy Spirit. If you looked at it similar to a legal document, the Holy Spirit is the second witness to its validation. This was also a precedent in Jewish law in Bible times, where Christ said: *"In your own Law it is written that the testimony of two men is valid." (John 8:17)*

...Amen... Every Act will end with "Amen." This demonstrates our agreement, participation and alignment, and gives the *go ahead* for it to occur through our free will. This is how much Love's children are respected, since the go ahead will not happen without our statement asking for it. Our "Amen" demonstrates our free will choice to share in its occurrence; it is our seal joining our alignment to God.

...(Visualization: Falling snow, blanketing everything. Color: White...

During Stigmata Blessed Tiffany was shown a perfect language that the Angels and all spirit creatures communicate with, which she has termed "Angelspeak." This language is created perfectly as it is spoken, and has the qualities of (1). Color, (2). Sound or Vibration, (3). Numbers, (4). Space, (5) Time, and (6) Dimension. It is a language that humans were also hard-wired with at our creation to use and understand, but we do not have the ability or clarity now to use it, because of the negative choices of our original parents and other manipulations along the way.

48

When we come back to the original perfection we were created to be, we will once again be able to communicate freely and accurately with everyone. Even now in our imperfection and lack of perfect understanding, we assign colors, sounds and letters/numbers to many things.

For example, if we think of the word "Elvis," we probably see a picture in our mind of what he looked like, or even hear one of his songs playing in our head. All the things that you correspond to your memory of "Elvis" is your indent to him. And the more experiences we have with a variety of sensory perceptions to something, the easier it is to remember and communicate. So if you went to one of his concerts, or toured through Graceland, you would have all of this as an indent as well, and your internal Angelspeak would encompass it all.

This is why today's business advertising and marketing use these things, to help us remember the brand or product, because we were created to express ourselves and learn that way. For another example, can you see why a college football team uses a theme song, town or state location, team colors, a mascot, and numbers? Do you see that the more senses we use with something, the closer we feel to it? We were made that way.

The visualizations, colors, and basic numbers are given from Father to help us indent to the theme of the different Acts and to remember and express them. The numbers assigned the various Decrees (1-50) are not Angelspeak numbers, but simply to help us coordinate them for referencing. If the actual Angelspeak numbers of the Decrees were given, each one would have a series of numbers several hundred digits long. Remember when Blessed Tiffany asked what God's true name was? She was told if it was only expressed in numbers, that by the time it was given and said out-loud, it would be wrong, since Love continues to grow and expand. But in the perfection ahead communication will happen through more than just the spoken word.
...*Duration: 5 days. Repeat the Unification Act again in 5 days)*...

The duration of the Decrees differ depending on the specific ones. Once we say something, there are changes that occur right away.

49

But just as we are asked to *continue* in prayer and not pray just one time, we are also asked to say and align ourselves with the Decrees more than one time. You can say them a day or so early if you need to, if you have something coming up that may distract your timing. This is better than being late or forgetting them.

Keep the Angels busy! They are very pleased to be working with you and doing Father's Will with you, and for you to be part of the transformation that is occurring. Whenever an Angel is sent to work through your alignment of will with Love, they rejoice. This is also why in our prayers we are encouraged not to ask the Angels to just *watch* over us, for witnessing our choices is what they do already, and is a place of inactivity for them. Instead, we are encouraged to ask the Angels to *help* us and *interact* with us. And this is what The Divine Decrees allow us to do, perfectly.

CHAPTER 6

BOOK TWO – The Arrival Act
Allowing the Soul to Act in Past, Present or Future Events

(4). I Decree as a Spirit of God, born as a child of man, full trust and opportunity to allow my soul or spirit to manifest and aid as needed in any past, present and future event of God's Love. By free will I accept full escort and call in All Holy Angels assigned to render harmless any unHoly indent while interacting in the body or in the spirit, granting safe passage to this soul and any Guides assigned as well. By free will I accept and ask for transformation of any gift or material made by man or substance of creation darkened by unHoly intentions or manipulations, and

(5). I Decree a cleansing of these through All Holy Angels assigned including a purification and bringing back the perfect creation within agreed parameters of interaction of the creations of the children of man to the fullness of potential made.

(6). I Decree full authority and free will interaction of All Holy Angels assigned to protect any and all methods of communication, interaction and information devices from manipulations and unHoly intentions, including any present methods and future methods and inventions.

(7). I Decree this as binding on earth as it is in heaven by the alignment of the will of God and man, bridging all past, present and future events until the King of All Dimensions in the Kingdom of God assumes full authority by order of the Arrival Act as ordained by the Blood of the Covenant as witnessed and given through the Holy Spirit by the Love of God, Amen.

(Visualization: The sun coming up over the horizon, going overhead and then the sun going down on the other side. Color: Yellow
Duration: 5 days. Repeat the entire Arrival Act again in 5 days).

Understanding the Arrival Act:

(4)…full trust and opportunity to allow my soul or spirit to manifest and aid as needed in any past, present and future event of God's Love. By free will I accept full escort and call in All Holy Angels assigned to render harmless any unHoly indent while interacting in the body or in the spirit, granting safe passage to this soul and any Guides assigned as well… The Arrival Act covers many things. It is being granted safe passage to a destination, being protected by the Holy Angels, which grants us a safe arrival without interference or manipulation. This covers actual physical transportation such as cars, trains, buses, boats, planes, bikes, walking and running. This covers every mode of transportation and ensures safe passage.

…By free will I accept and ask for transformation of any gift or material made by man or substance of creation darkened by unHoly intentions or manipulations… Another aspect that is covered is that of asking for a cleansing to occur, that any indent that is negative is released, purified and sanitized. This cleansing also protects us from any thing that is given to us by anyone with bad intentions, looking to cause us harm. This can be understood easily in the context of something that has arrived in your possession. In addition, this Act covers us even when we are doing work out of the body, such as dream work or bilocation or astral travel.

(5)…a cleansing of these through All Holy Angels assigned including a purification and bringing back the perfect creation within agreed parameters of interaction of the creations of the children of man to the fullness of potential made… With this cleansing is a re-creation of the original purpose in communication and the agreed parameters of what is allowed for interaction at this time. For example, although we know Angelspeak is the preferred and ordained method for interaction for all his creation, we are not stepping beyond our boundaries by asking for the fullness of this communication right now.

We are still limited at this time to the cloudiness and imperfections of having the dent from the mold of being one of Adam's children, and there is only so much that can be open to us as fullness of potential until our own transformation occurs in the Kingdom shortly to come.

(6)....to protect any and all methods of communication, interaction and information devices from manipulations and unHoly intentions, including any present methods and future methods and inventions... Next, any method of interaction whether through internet, phones, radio – all methods of communication is covered here in the Arrival Act. This protection ensures that the person not only has a safe arrival but the message to or from that person remains protected as well. Communication in a timely and accurate way is necessary for consistent interaction between one another. And, this covers all methods of communication that are currently being used and all the future ones to come.

Please take note of the difference between "unHoly intentions" and "manipulations." UnHoly *intentions* are what the unHoly Angels send against us. They want us to feel isolated, alone, separate and unable to communicate or be communicated with, for they know there is great power in unity. *Manipulations* come through *humans* that the unHoly Angels utilize against us by puppeting them through holes in their free will. Manipulations also come to us through *ghosts,* which are human spirits that have not yet gone to Father after death.

Free will is so respected, that even at the death of the body, we can decide to go with the Homing Angel back to Love, or not. Sometimes if people are taught traditions of fear, such as God expecting perfection, or the falsehood of hellfire, they may choose not to go, thinking they will be punished somehow. Or they may not believe they are dead, and think the Homing Angel and the transitioned friends and family with him are just a hallucination. This can happen in quick deaths such as accidents. Or sometimes the person may feel mistakenly that they have to protect someone here and can't let go yet. So even in death we can still refuse to go to Love. These are thereby open to attack and manipulation from fallen Angels in their unprotected state of choice, since they are vulnerable.

53

Since they have not gone to God yet, they are still holding all the misconceptions and weaknesses they had during their lives, such as unforgiveness of self or others, or feeling they have to earn love to be approved somehow, and that they could never earn enough so will never be approved.

The unHoly Angels are very smart, and recognize the weaknesses and seek to create more damage. Similar to how a street gang will offer a feeling of family and connection to manipulate and influence for destruction, the unHoly Angels manipulate the people who are now in a ghost state. Many ghosts fall into this brain-washing and are then called "manipulated ghosts." They may even forget they were once human, and the unHoly Angels give them a portion of their power to solidify the false idea that they are trying to perpetrate: that the ghosts never were human, but fallen Angels all the time. In this state of brain-washing, the manipulated ghosts are pawns sent against mankind by the unHoly Angels for all sorts of bad motives. The good news is this, this Decree and many others protect and defend us from them, and also there are prayers that can be said to help the ghosts remember who they are, and to be free and go home to Love. These prayers peel away the fake façade of what the unHoly Angels have led them to believe, and they see themselves again as humans and the freedom to make new choices. For those called into this line of Love's work, this prayer is included in the Called and Commissioned manual later in this book.

The concept of purgatory, being in a state of a "holding-pattern," is in reality only this ghost state. *God does not put anyone there,* but it is a choice of free will by the person. Not all ghosts are manipulated. But it is still better that they go home than to stay here. It is actually a better protection for the ones they love here and seek to protect, since their presence calls the unHoly Angels in over and over again to try to persuade them, and other manipulated ghosts. God periodically sends the Holy Angels and humans who have the gift of being able to see the other side to these to offer additional opportunities to go home to Father.

When we go to Love, we are allowed to come and go as we please after a short debriefing process of what we have learned in our lives, and a cleansing off of any baggage we may be holding onto. When we go to God, we are now a spirit, which is a much higher vibration than a ghost. Remember, Father is a God of Love, so will not hold us back from visiting our loved ones freely. And we have much more power as spirits of love to help our families than we do in a ghost situation.

(7)...until the King of All Dimensions in the Kingdom of God assumes full authority... Again, we seal this Arrival Act in a binding agreement, in recognition of Christ's higher authority and the given visualizations. He has the ability to move through all dimensions.

CHAPTER 7

BOOK THREE – The Transformation Act
The Full Alignment of the Will of God and Man

(8). I Decree as a Spirit of God, born as a child of man, full healing of this soul, spirit, body and mind by full alignment of the will of God and man by the receiving of wholeness and wellness in perfection, within the present parameters set by the original choices of man and agreed upon purpose and commission for this life. By free will I offer my faith and trust, in the power and Love of God as an indent for healing, for All Holy Angels assigned to offer aid of healing of the soul, spirit, body and mind to any and all of the children of man whenever they may call out to God for healing, knowing this will occur within the present parameters set by the original choices of man and agreed upon purpose and commission for these lives, and within the present parameters of the interaction of indents.

(9). I Decree full authority and free will interaction of All Holy Angels assigned to manifest additional opportunities and to aid these souls to recognize all choices of Love and healing and to choose without manipulations or unHoly intentions.

(10). I Decree this as binding on earth as it is in Heaven by the alignment of the will of God and man, bridging all past, present or future events until the King of Re-Creation of the Kingdom of God assumes full authority by order of the Transformation Act as ordained by the Blood of the Covenant as witnessed and given through the Holy Spirit by the Love of God, Amen.

(Visualization: Old becoming young, bodies deformed and bent standing straight and full, flowers going from bud to full bloom. Color: Orange Duration: 5 Days. Repeat the entire Transformation Act in 5 days).

Understanding the Transformation Act:

(8)...full healing of this soul, spirit, body and mind by full alignment of the will of God and man by the receiving of wholeness and wellness in perfection... The Transformation Act is another alignment of our will with Love, and God's Will for us to receive it! So right away we are asking to receive; and receiving wholeness and wellness in perfection. This is about our health, making the body and mind strong so it can be a vital house for our spirit, without distraction or restraint of ill health.

The unHoly Angels seek to damage health, relationships and finances. The unHoly Angels have focused on this since the beginning of time ("time" for mankind began after the fall of mankind in the Garden of Eden, before then, there was timelessness or eternal life; and will be again). In their perversion of what is natural and ordained for all mankind, the unHoly Angels seek to cause feelings of separation and confusion so we may doubt our connection to God and doubt his Love for us. Ill health is a distraction to what we want to do and how much we want to do it. So the Will of Love is for us to be healthy, that is the true potential we were created with, and asking to receive it is one of our God-given birthrights. We were made to be well!

...within the present parameters set by the original choices of man and agreed upon purpose and commission for this life... This is in reference to the acknowledgement of our imperfections because of the original choices of man, which acts almost as a generational bondage on our genetics. Also our agreed on purpose and commission for this life before we came into the body may have a physical effect on how much we are going to heal. For example, children born with Down's Syndrome have chosen to come in that way for a greater spiritual work while still lightly in the physical body. Also, in reference to one of the original issues, some healing is deferred or denied for a much larger reason. But nearly all cases of physical impairment is not natural or chosen, and can be wonderfully healed, no matter what the cause or age of the person.

This decree just reminds us of the awareness that we may have chosen purposes and commissions for this life, mind and body that at present we may not be aware of yet. And that our bodies are not in perfection yet.

…I offer my faith and trust, in the power and Love of God as an indent for healing, for All Holy Angels assigned to offer aid of healing of the soul, spirit, body and mind to any and all of the children of man whenever they may call out to God for healing…We often pray for good health or ask for improvement in health. We know instinctively that when we are well we can do more things. We are not the only ones who know this. The unHoly Angels seek to damage our health so we will not be strong enough to accomplish our purpose here on earth and our commission that we previously agreed to with God. If they can put us in a place of doubt and hopelessness it is easy to see how they can manipulate us even further. This may include us even doubting who we are which would dim the brightness of our Holy prayers and Holy intentions to God. Remember, it is not the darkness that puts out the candle, but the candle itself allowing the flame to grow low or even go out. It's light's natural reaction to the darkness to transform it into light.

…knowing this will occur within the present parameters set by the original choices of man and agreed upon purpose and commission for these lives and within the present parameters of the interaction of indents…This Transformation Act literally gives us the opportunity to help others and to be a dispenser of sending Holy Angels for all those who call out to God. Because of our stating this Act aloud, we can help others to heal anywhere in the world. This is not just about physical healing, but emotional and spiritual too. This has a ripple effect far beyond what we can see or even comprehend, yet it will not go against the free will and choices made by people in this life or before they came into it.

Stating this Decree creates a great difference in our personal body and spirit. Many of us who are sensitive to the emotions and energies of others may have had a difficult time being around very many people at a time because of the tugging of this on our own spirit.

Often a person will feel drained and seek to avoid crowds, or even avoid shopping when there are many people in the stores. When we state this Decree, now we have made an intention for all of these people to receive whatever is needed when their heart has cried out to Love. Now, we have become a touchstone of free will for them to receive, whether they know it or not, and whether we know they need it or not. This now creates a totally different reaction when we are around groups of people, since when the free will has been given, we are simply a touchstone for it, without needing any personal awareness of their spirit crying out to us to fix it. Instead, we become energized when around crowds instead of drained, since we have already aligned with God and his Angels for their healing. This decree alone changes the life of a sensitive person to move freely again whenever and wherever they wish, without feeling drained or exhausted.

(9)...to manifest additional opportunities and to aid these souls to recognize all choices of Love and healing and to choose without manipulations or unHoly intentions... This Decree also offers more Angelic opportunities to recognize love. Love offers all of us numerous opportunities to discern what is of him and what is not. Even then, he allows us to make our own choices, for right or for wrong. When we pray for more opportunities to occur for people to recognize love, more opportunities are given. It is as though God takes a field, and plants rose bushes here and there, and there again, to offer the person the opportunity to recognize there are rose bushes (right choices) in the field. When we pray more rose bushes are added. And the more often we pray, the more rose bushes are added, until the entire field may be full of Divine choices. Yet even then, because of free will it is still up to the person involved to recognize there are rose bushes planted there.

We all know the devastation that comes from using violence to quell violence. We have been told how to break this cycle - through forgiveness, through turning the other cheek. We know that love wins out and love wins the war! In this Transformation Act we are asking that others be provided with this precious opportunity to recognize love and be given a chance to choose without manipulation.

An illustration here proves handy: perhaps you and a friend are arguing over something, the argument escalates and emotions run high, one person ends up saying something hurtful and immediately wishes that he didn't. We all know this feeling. This is the place of manipulation, where we know what the right things is and how we feel pushed to do the opposite. In this example, the moment of manipulation is the lashing out rather than forgiving; yelling rather than listening; attacking and defending rather than responding kindly.

In asking for more opportunity to choose without the manipulation of the unHoly Angels, we are looking to diffuse the bomb before anyone gets hurt, recognizing that we need help and offering that same loving help to another. If we all recognized the aspects of Love around us, would we still choose fear or hatred? Could we see the truth of how love truly does conquer all? Can we recognize the power of Love to transform? This is how powerful this Transformation Act truly is, it gives us the ability to bring more love here for ourselves for healing, for others for healing, for others to recognize and see this love being beneficial for themselves and those around them and for us all to awaken to love and its many healing powers.

And, this is all done as to the agreed upon parameters, original choices and free will interaction of ourselves and all those involved. This honors both what we are asking for and how we are asking that it be done. Love delivered through love, harming none, violating the free will of no one, including ourselves before we came into this life.

(10)...until the King of Re-Creation of the Kingdom of God assumes full authority... Finally the Transformation Act is sealed as the other Acts before it, through Christ, the King of Re-Creation, who will soon assume full authority as God's designated King over his creation.

CHAPTER 8

BOOK FOUR - The Protection Act
Assigning Holy Angels to Defend, Protect & Render Harmless

(11). I Decree as a Spirit of God born as a child of man full protection of this soul, spirit, body and mind (and that of my husband/wife and those under my care) and all attending delegates by giving full authority and free will interaction to All Holy Angels assigned to render harmless any and all manipulations or unHoly intentions sent toward us.

(12). I Decree as welcome and valid all methods and signs approved by God and conducive to the further allowance of the veil, including full awareness of my spirit and any and all interactions of the human senses or God-given gifts to aid alignment with messages and power and action needed and made available through All Holy Angels assigned Guides assigned, and empowerment given to the faithful and aware children of man through all Divine Decrees and the Twelve Books of Acts of the Love of God.

(13). I Decree this soul's free will ability to call in All Holy Angels assigned and grant full authority and free will interaction to defend, battle, attack and render harmless as needed and to aid Guides assigned and all Holy Ones with containment of all manipulations and unHoly intentions sent.

(14). I Decree this soul's free will choice of asking for greater faith, trust and discernment of what my interaction is in every event and opportunity and utilizing this soul's abilities and God-given gifts when asked and in the parameters suggested and at the times recommended through all Divine Decrees and the Twelve Books of Acts of the Love of God.

(15). I Decree this as binding on earth as it is in heaven by the alignment of the will of God and man, bridging all past, present or future events until the Warrior Son of the Kingdom of God and his Holy Army assumes full authority by order of the Protection Act as ordained by the Blood of the Covenant as witnessed and given through the Holy Spirit by the Love of God, Amen.

(Visualization: Warrior Angels encircling and the sound of marching and shouting in unison. Color: Red
Duration: 5 days. Repeat the entire Protection Act in 5 days).

Understanding the Protection Act:

(11)... full protection of this soul, spirit, body and mind... This message is about protection, sharing how we can be kept safe. This greatly eases the suffering of all mankind, including our family and our own selves. This is a message of hope and love, trust and discernment.

...and all attending delegates... The Protection Act also uses the word "delegates" for the first time. This is different from those "under my care." A delegate is a pet, a domestic animal. So the Protection Act covers even our pets from manipulation by the unHoly Angels. How wonderful that our pets who bring us additional love and comfort are also afforded protection from those who seek to destroy love in whatever form it takes. *(See more on what delegates or animals are under "What is the True Nature of Animals" in the Called and Commissioned Manual).*

...by giving full authority and free will interaction to All Holy Angels assigned to render harmless any and all manipulations or unHoly intentions sent toward us... This Protection Act outlines for us what we need protection from, the unHoly Angels. We begin the Protection Act with asking for the Holy Angels to have free will to put an end to any harmful manipulations or unHoly intentions sent toward us. We are asking that the Holy Angels nullify any of the problems that the unHoly Angels have caused us. We are asking to be rinsed clean, to be cleansed from any evil sent toward us.

This does not take the place of a deliverance prayer but can go hand in hand with it, affording even greater protection.

Think about it this way: the unHoly Angels try to blot out the light wherever it is found. They seek our destruction, to create scenarios of fear and hatred, and to cause conflict and confusion. They seek to harm all the wonderful things created through love, and harm God in the process. *"But woe to the earth and the sea, because the devil has gone down to you! He is filled with fury, because he knows his time is short."* (Revelation 12:12)

It is no secret to the unHoly Angels that they have only a short amount of time now. We can see all around us the dark becoming darker and the light becoming lighter. God provides his children light even in the darkest of times so that they may have additional trust in his companionship and love. Father has always used signs and wonders throughout time in all parts of the world, and in all religions. Miracle healing is one of them, so is Holy Stigmata, and true prophecy, and many other things that God gives to help us to remember that we are never alone. Even the discoveries of sacred things once hidden, are uncovered and presented to the world at the right time for it, to encourage us.

Take for example, the stimulus to faith of the Dead Sea Scrolls, which were found in 1947, only a short time after World War II. God is good like that; Father has also revealed that as this transition occurs, many more supernatural signs and wonders will occur as well, to help us grow even further in faith. It could be discovery and verification of Noah's Ark, or even the Ark of the Covenant. And besides these things, the gifts in people will abound, including those enlightened ones (you) who will have specialized gifts such as: stopping severe storms, healing infertility, healing farm land from overuse and chemical abuse, etc. How wonderful is that!

Will you be one of his children that he can use as an instrument for these signs and wonders? Repeating these Decrees will help you to continually become brighter and become a more useful vessel in his hands of Love, and to grow in communication between you and him.

Nothing is beyond your reach when you go beyond yourself into All There Is, because nothing is beyond the hand of Love.

(12)...welcome and valid all methods and signs approved by God and conducive to the further allowance of the veil... Here we are asking for the further allowance of the veil. Simply put, the veil is what keeps us from remembering all the other lives we have lived, the facets of love we have polished, and the experiences we have had outside of this world. The veil necessary and is put in place to protect us and help us to focus on this current life, to fulfill our commission that we agreed to come here to complete now, without distraction.

The veil is only to be opened through God. There have been those that have tried to force open the veil or get a glimpse behind the veil through giving their power away to others (misinformed psychics or past life regressions) or by seeking to force it open themselves. This is dangerous and can cause tremendous harm, making it difficult to fulfill our commission here on earth, and for doing what we came here to do. When God lifts the veil, he does it as a confidence-builder and encouragement to help us fulfill what we are doing now. When it is opened haphazardly, all kinds of unfinished business and high emotional memories can occur, distracting us from what we are doing now and focusing on the past or trying to fix past wrongs.

It was probably hard while we were going through it, so why go through it again, opening it only at a human level instead of the higher awareness we saw for that life in the spiritual clarity of death? We already died in that life. We are already released from it, including any burden of things undone or mismanaged. Let Father open to you what is beneficial in the veil in his way and at the right time for it, and do not worry about the rest, because he doesn't. He only sees the love, and it is because you have been polishing the facets of love that you are reading these words now, and continuing to expand upon you awareness.

…including full awareness of my spirit and any and all interactions of the human senses or God-given gifts to aid alignment with messages and power and action needed and made available…First and foremost, we are never to give our power away to anyone. This power belongs to God. God is the one who is in charge! We are to have the confidence to go direct and not be afraid to ask the one who made us, who gave us these spirits and these bodies for help with them. No, they didn't come with a manual. But, they did come with a 24 hour servicing department with a toll-free number! And when we call, we get right in to the Boss!

Here is another awareness to have in mind for those who can see the other side. Just because a person may be able to see or hear spirits doesn't mean that they are tapping into a clean connection, and they may not even be aware of this. They may think they are communing with a Holy Angel, or a transitioned loved one or a Guide but they do not know for certain until they test them. We have been instructed to do this in scripture, testing the Spirits, *"Dear friends, do not believe every spirit but test the spirits to see if they are from God…" (1 John 4:1)* How do you do this?

The simple way to do this if you have the gift of seeing or hearing the other side is to ask the spirits: *"Do you love Jesus now?"* This is a perfect way to discern whose side they are on, for many unHoly Angels at one time loved Jesus as a brother. But once they chose to separate from God's love and Christ came down to break our Adamic generational bondage (as a ransom sacrifice for our sins), the unHoly Angels also rallied against Christ. If the spirit cannot answer "YES!" to the statement they "love Jesus *now*" they are unHoly Angels or manipulated ghosts sent by them and will seek to injure you to wrong actions and conclusions. This is a big reason why we are encouraged to go direct and ask God to lift the veil for us, to ask for a furtherance of the veil, for as we have seen, and for right discernment. The Big Guy does the lifting of the veil in the right way and according to perfect timing. When in doubt, go direct!

An illustration of this is as follows. Someone seeking answers goes to a psychic who does past life regression.

They are told that in one of their lives they were a monk and fulfilled all their spiritual work and didn't have to come back to earth at all, they learned what they needed to know about love and are here just to play and enjoy life. This may have a seed of truth, that they did have a wonderful spiritual life prior to this and they may have even polished enough facets of love that they did not have to come back. But the truth gets twisted and perverted to keep this person, this bright spot from being utilized by God through convincing them that they are only here to play.

Now if they are convinced that they are only here to play, what are the chances that they will seek to remember their true commission and what they chose to come back to do? This is how manipulation works, by putting poison in the sweet drink. Many have been manipulated this way and did not even know it. If we could smell the poison in the cup, would we drink it? No. But if the cup smelled sweet, with a little truth in it, would we now believe the rest of it and swallow the poison? Many have, for this is how manipulation works, mixing the good and the bad together. This Protection Act is about cleaning it up, removing the poison and putting up a shield to keep further manipulation from occurring.

...and empowerment given to the faithful and aware children of man through all Divine Decrees and the Twelve Books of Acts of the Love of God... Thus we are always asked to have discernment, for we are at serious risk for manipulation by the unHoly Angels, and this is a powerful reason why we were all given The Divine Decrees. As we continue to brighten, we each develop a keener sensitivity about what is clean and what is not. The Decrees in the Protection Act are about *you* personally receiving the gifts to understand God's messages better, and the empowerment to use them, and asking for the alignment with the Holy Angels to assist in this as well. This is a powerful realization. This discernment is why the empowerment is given "to the faithful and aware children of man."

(13)…ability to call in All Holy Angels assigned and grant full authority and free will interaction to defend, battle, attack and render harmless as needed and to aid Guides assigned and all Holy Ones with containment of all manipulations and unHoly intentions sent…This Decree speaks of the Holy Angels and what they are doing to assist us, battling, defending, attacking and rendering harmless the unHoly Angels and the manifestations sent toward us. There is also an important piece here that fills us in even more about God and his Love.

Here it is also good to note that the Holy Angels are the ones who defend, battle and render harmless, for they are the warriors, not Guides or Holy Ones. The Holy Angels aid Guides assigned and the Holy Ones with containment of all manipulations and unHoly intentions sent against us.

Now, why wouldn't God just *take away* the power of the unHoly Angels to create damage in the first place? This is because once God gives a gift, he never takes it away. As such, it is not about removing the gift(s) from the unHoly Angels but containing their misuse of power, that it not cause any harm to any of us or other creation. This too lets us know how much Love there is for all of us, that even when bad choices are made, God never takes away the gifts he has bestowed. Imagine how this works for all the gifts of the spirit that we ourselves have been blessed with, both past and present! We still have them all! This is another place of confidence that you can have with yourself. That if God is calling your heart and your heart is responding to that love and expanding toward gifts and life purpose, you can be confident that you have all the tools to fulfill what is asked of you. Remember you can have the confidence in yourself to do all things, since Love already does.

(14)…asking for greater faith, trust and discernment of what my interaction is in every event and opportunity and utilizing this soul's abilities and God-given gifts when asked and in the parameters suggested and at the times recommended through all Divine Decrees and the Twelve Books of Acts of the Love of God…This Decree speaks of asking for increased faith, trust and discernment of what we are to do.

69

We can trust in our Father as things get dark around us, we can trust in what has been shared with us that *"The Lord Himself goes before you and will be with you. He will never leave or forsake you. Do not be afraid, do not be discouraged."* *(Deuteronomy 31:8)* We are asking to have full discernment of what our interaction should be in every event and opportunity. Can you grasp the huge windfall of this declaration, what the ripple effect can be to know what our interactions should be at every moment, and to act on what we are called to do? This is a powerful statement!

(15)...until the Warrior Son of the Kingdom of God and his Holy Army assumes full authority... And we end this Protection Act with our seal, showing our faith in the beauty of trust, that the Warrior Son and his Holy Army will soon assume full authority. The side of Love, the side of God, always wins. Amen!

CHAPTER 9

BOOK FIVE – The Forgiveness Act
Erasing and Cleansing Harmful Intentions

(16). I Decree as a Spirit of God born as a child of man full forgiveness to all children of man who have harmed or intentioned to harm this soul (my husband/wife and those under my care). By free will I ask God for forgiveness and to erase and cleanse any indent of harm or intention to harm from this soul toward myself and all other children of man, attending delegates, the earth and all living creation in relationship to man, and any and all transgressions toward God, God's Word, The Holy Spirit, all Angels, Guides, the Holy Ones and all Spirit Beings, and I send Holy Prayers and Holy Intentions to all.

(17). I Decree full authority and free will interaction to All Holy Angels assigned to aid awareness of any and all opportunities where Love can be expanded by forgiveness in past or present events. By free will I agree with the continuing redemption of unHoly Angels as offered by the Love of God and stand as a representative of redeemed mankind accepted into unification and light once more and in this capacity and by the example of the Love of God, I grant forgiveness to all unHoly ones who have requested and gained forgiveness from God for their manipulations toward this soul (my husband/wife and those in my care).

(18). I Decree this as binding on earth as it is in heaven by the alignment of the will of God and man, bridging all past, present or future events until the Mighty Counselor of the Kingdom of God assumes full authority by order of the Forgiveness Act as ordained by the Blood of the Covenant as witnessed and given through the Holy Spirit by the Love of God, Amen.

(Visualization: One who is on their knees is tapped on the shoulder and asked to stand. Color: Brown
Duration: 10 days. The entire Forgiveness Act is to be repeated in 10 days).

Understanding the Forgiveness Act:

(16)…full forgiveness to all children of man who have harmed or intentioned to harm this soul (my husband/wife and those under my care). By free will I ask God for forgiveness and to erase and cleanse any indent of harm or intention to harm…All of these Twelve Books of the Act of the Love of God are beautiful and awesome. This book demonstrates God's Love and demonstrates how crucial forgiveness is, not only for us humans but also the huge role it plays for the unHoly Angels who have chosen to return to God as well.

In this Decree we start by asking for forgiveness for all humans who have harmed or intentioned to harm us, our spouse, or our delegates. We are also asking for forgiveness for ourselves, of wherever we have caused harm or even just intentioned harm. We are asking God to erase and cleanse any problem that has been caused as a result of our bad choices toward others, toward ourselves and even more so toward God, God's Word, The Holy Spirit, all Angels Guides, the Holy Ones, and all Spirit Beings. Jesus said, *"Love your enemies and pray for those who persecute you, that you may be sons of your Father in heaven. He causes his sun to rise on the evil and the good, and sends rain on the righteous and the unrighteous." (Matthew 6:18)*

…any and all transgressions toward God, God's Word, The Holy Spirit, all Angels Guides, the Holy Ones and all Spirit Beings, and I send Holy Prayers and Holy Intentions to all…Do you notice we are also asking forgiveness for any harm we have sent toward "all Angels?" This is *all* Angels, not just the Holy Angels but covers the unHoly Angels as well! By saying this we are underlining what is meant when we are asked to forgive and love our enemies, *"Love your enemies, do good to those who hate you." (Luke 6:27)* It is amazing and awe-inspiring show of faith. Those who have hurt so many of us, those who have sought our destruction and pain towards God, we are asked to forgive, just as our Lord forgives. This is how we know love, by the one who made us and taught us love! We teach through love, always through love. We learn, we live, we exist through the love of God.

The Forgiveness Act teaches us even more about this love and how powerful it can truly be. We ask for forgiveness for any of our transgressions toward those that have harmed in word or deed, and we send love back through Holy prayers and Holy intentions.

This is a good place to share what Blessed Tiffany was shown occurs in the battles between the Holy and unHoly Angels. When mankind asks for protection in the specialty prayers that we have been given to use, the Holy Angels are instantly sent into battle. What kind of battle is this? There is no killing, no torture; there is no manipulation or slander from the Holy Angels against the unHoly ones. Simply put, they are basically placed in a restraining device. Even in the thick of battle there is still opportunity for the unHoly Angels to turn back from their ways and return to God. When even the slightest flutter of desire to do this is shown, two Holy Angels immediately escort the unHoly one back to God. This flutter is the beginnings of the gems of color within them to shine and turn again, like the facets of love that continue to turn in the Holy Angels. When the unHoly had unplugged from love, they had become dark inside themselves, so no turning gems of light are seen. Blessed Tiffany was then shown the Angel is then started at a lower responsibility than originally given, but has opportunity to move from there into more responsibility later.

None are turned away, Father forgives and welcomes them all back, if they only desire it. During the battles, the unHoly Angels are silenced, since much filth comes from them against God and the Holy Angels and all God stands for, has purposed, and has created. There is no need for any creation to hear it. Then, the authority is given the Holy Angels to place the unHoly Angels in an encapsulation, a place similar to glass or plastic, where they are now cut off from the gang mentality of the other unHoly Angels, and where they are also powerless to do any harm, or to be harmed from other unHoly Angels. From this place of encapsulation, they are still able to witness the continual unfolding of the fruition of Love and his purposes, and the continuing testimonials and stories that come in from mankind to the original issues, even though the case is now closed and sealed forever, all testimonies are welcome and blessed, and will be shared openly for all timelessness.

The restraint of the unHoly Angels may be likened to a mentally unbalanced person being put in a straightjacket and in a padded room, where he may not harm himself or anyone else. This is quite different than how the unHoly Angels treat one another, where the ruthlessness and depravity is only escalated by the divisions between themselves and warring over various regions of the earth. In their system, anything goes, and it is an "eat or be eaten" attitude; and since death does not happen to them, the pain and suffering is continual. Any allegiances come and go as the different factions vie for power. It is in this place of constant destruction and turmoil created by their choices that *they are brought out of*. This restraint and encapsulation is God's way of love and further opportunity for these Angels to understand without manipulation.

(17)...to aid awareness of any and all opportunities where Love can be expanded by forgiveness in past or present events. By free will I agree with the continuing redemption of unHoly Angels as offered by the Love of God and stand as a representative of redeemed mankind accepted into unification and light once more and in this capacity and by the example of the Love of God... This is how loving God is! We can ask for expanded forgiveness and in his mercy, he allows it. This mercy continues on in asking for the expansion of love in all areas where forgiveness is needed, even in past events. Also included here is our agreement with God's plan that the unHoly Angels that have turned from their wicked ways and returned to Father and asked for his forgiveness are also forgiven. And we offer our own example of God's Grace as a representative of redeemed mankind, those who were ransomed by the perfect life and death of Jesus Christ.

...I grant forgiveness to all unHoly ones who have requested and gained forgiveness from God for their manipulations toward this soul (my husband/wife and those in my care)... In addition we state that we offer our forgiveness for all those who have harmed this soul, our spouse and those in our care. *"And when you stand praying, if you hold anything against anyone, forgive him so that the Father in Heaven may forgive your sins."(Mark 11:25)*

74

Forgiveness is very important. Unforgiveness leaves a big hole in our free will that can be manipulated and is considered a willful sin. It is a willful sin when we are told what to do, to forgive, and are given the examples of how to do it, and then choose to go the other way and not forgive. When we choose not to forgive, we are making the choice to do the opposite of what we know to be the right thing to do, we have "missed the mark," or sinned. We are to learn from the one who made us; we forgive as we have been forgiven. When we hold unforgiveness to ourselves or others, it is like holding a hex or curse of negative energy to sustain it. The unHoly Angels come running when there is unforgiveness, for they will prod that weakness to destroy you.

Additional Information: How Do We Forgive Others?

Many have said that they do not know how to forgive. We forgive in 3 ways, and we start by asking for energy beyond our own in prayer: forgive all those involved, forgive the situation and then forgive ourselves. Forgiving others allows for a healing for them as well as for ourselves. We transform the situation through love. Including forgiving ourselves helps to add love where it was missing. We are asked to forgive ourselves with gentleness, mercy and compassion just as if we were doing it for another person, with that same place of love in our hearts. In addition, forgiving the situation is extremely important. When we realize that people can be manipulated, that people who act out of fear, and those who lash out through anger have left themselves open to manipulation by the unHoly, we see why it is important to forgive the situation. Forgiving the situation brings an anointing of love, calming the circumstances and removing the high negative emotions. Remember that holding unforgiveness is like holding a curse over another and is kept active by emotional spider webs of energy that drain us to do so. When we forgive these webs are cut, and there is much freedom and lightness that comes with it. The Forgiveness Act covers these and raises the awareness of the importance of doing so.

Additional Information: How Do Ask for Forgiveness for Ourselves?

When we pray, asking to fully remember that we are loved, that we are the spark from the Flame, and are already redeemed through love, Grace and mercy. We can come before The Big Guy asking for forgiveness for any time we have done anything apart from Love's will for us, any time we have doubted rather than trusted, acted out of fear or anger rather than love, any time we have not remembered that we are his children and we are loved perfectly. With a humble and contrite heart, we ask to be forgiven for any choice, conscious or unconscious, where we have gone against his Will. We recall how God has already given us the perfect example of his son and that we, his imperfect children can still strive to be more like Christ in all ways. And we give thanks, again for his love, gentleness, compassion, instruction, correction and mercy.

It is important to remember that we are not the ones to judge, that is not our job. *"Who are you to judge someone else's servant? To his own master he stands or falls. And he will stand for the Lord is able to make him stand."* *(Romans 14:4)* Here we see clearly that whether it is a child of man or an unHoly Angel that has harmed another, it is not for us to judge for we are all servants to the one master, the one who created us all. It is not our place to judge, for we too are servants. Only God will judge. *"The Lord will judge his people."(Hebrews 10:13)* Remember, even Jesus did not rebuke the unHoly Angels, *"even the Archangel Michael when he was disputing with the devil about the body of Moses, did not dare to bring a slanderous accusation against him, but said "The Lord rebuke you!" (Jude 1:9)* Forgiveness is a healing for all those involved!

(18)…until the Mighty Counselor of the Kingdom of God assumes full authority…Christ is set as the Mighty Counselor of God's Kingdom in full authority. When one is counseled, there is comfort and deeper understanding of the issues and of themselves. What perfect comfort awaits us, where forgiveness flows as the rivers to the sea, until there is no need for forgiveness anymore, since all will be at that place of perfection as originally created by our God of Love and his Mighty Counselor.

CHAPTER 10

BOOK SIX – The Abundance Act
The Ability to Attain and Maintain Abundance in All Things

(19). I Decree as a Spirit of God born as a child of man full ability to attain and maintain abundance in all things beneficial to this soul (my husband/wife and those under my care) and

(20). I Decree full authority and free will interaction to All Holy Angels assigned to render harmless any and all manipulations or unHoly intentions toward health, finances or relationships and for expanded awareness of any and all points of damage or potential damage where conscious or unconscious choices need to be transformed and healed. I acknowledge this soul's birthright as a Spirit of God and my redemption as a child of man to live each day in full abundance and expansion of Love with God, one another and myself to the full potential of understanding and experiencing of Love this soul has been, is presently and will be accomplishing, including giving and receiving, and acceptance, gratitude and application of gifts and abilities.

(21). I Decree this soul's free will to share abundance with all children of man in whatever way it is most needed and is most efficient and beneficial and

(22). I Decree All Holy Angels assigned to aid in this recognition and completion through free will interaction and full authority and to render harmless any and all manipulations or unHoly intentions sent to impede this.

(23). I Decree this as binding on earth as it is in heaven by the alignment of the will of God and man, bridging all past, present or future events until the King of the Over-Flowing Cup of the Kingdom of God assumes full authority by order of the Abundance Act as ordained by the Blood of the Covenant as witnessed and given through the Holy Spirit by the Love of God, Amen.

(Visualization: Sounds of coins, the smell of fresh bread and a vision of golden fields of wheat that never end. Color: Green
Duration: 7 days. The entire Abundance Act is to be repeated in 7 days).

Understanding the Abundance Act:

(19)...full ability to attain and maintain abundance in all things beneficial... The Abundance Act helps us to attain the many good things in this world that we were all created to have, since abundance and prosperity is our natural birthright as a child of God. This goes beyond just necessary finances and covers all things beneficial to our soul, our spouse and those under our care, including love, health, shelter, peace, food and relationships. This abundance also includes our spiritual relationship with God, ourselves and one another.

Right from the start we see that it is not just about *attaining* abundance but it is also about *maintaining* it as well. This is what we are asking for, to enable us to accomplish our life's purpose, our commission here on earth, and to complete what we agreed to do in service to God and our brothers and sisters.

Here it is also good to mention that money is *not* the root of all evil. The *love of money* is. (1 Timothy 6:10) This scripture asks us what our focus it, and to have balance in all things. It is not about being rich is being bad; for a poor person can be more focused on attaining money than a person who has it. It depends on the choice of the person involved. In my experience, I have found many of the impoverished countries have a greater faith and yearning for spirituality than many in the more affluent nations do. Simply put, both have the opportunity to make bad choices by only focusing on money and attaining it at all costs; or not.

78

Money can be a very useful tool to do many things and to help many wonderful causes, yet if craved like an addiction, it can be destructive as well.

(20)...render harmless any and all manipulations or unHoly intentions toward health, finances or relationships and for expanded awareness of any and all points of damage or potential damage where conscious or unconscious choices need to be transformed and healed... In this Decree we are asking for a cleansing from any manipulation or unHoly intentions sent against health, finances and relationships. We follow this up by seeking to cleanse from any of our damaging choices, whether they were conscious or unconscious. For example, if you have caught yourself saying: *"this won't work, it never has, and it never will. I will always be (poor/single/sick/etc) no matter what I do,"* then you have fallen victim to the manipulations of unHoly Angels. You have bought into that dark voice planted on your shoulder and have made it your own. They want you to see these falsehoods as true for yourself, for you to give up and have no hope, and to make you feel worthless and separate from who you really are and from God and his purposes for you. But these falsehoods are NOT you! *We were created to have lives of abundance in all good things.*

This is why times of lack can create such high emotions, since in our heart we know this is not how it is supposed to be. But who are we blaming? Are we going to allow any frustration to be an opportunity for a weak spot in our free will shield of armor, where the unHoly Angels can then take advantage of a gapping hole in our defenses and our emotions be twisted and tweaked until we make damaging choices? God will save you out of your struggles, if you just let him love you. Call him in. Use any place of high emotion as a place of prayer and for calling in the Holy Angels to help you, and feel the calmness, peace and faith magnify.

God wants us to receive all that he has to offer. If we humans, even in our imperfection, desire all to have plentiful and healthy food and water, abundant finances and excellent living conditions, don't you think God in his perfection and all-powerful might desires it as well? Yes! Love wants his children to be happy and healthy, to enjoy abundance and use it and share it with others. God is a God of abundance.

He never plants just *one* wildflower on a hill! God never plants *one* tree in a forest, but surrounds it with more, an entire woodland. Not one grass, but thousands of grasses; not one fish in the ocean, but thousands! In the same way, God offers his children full abundance. How many times has Love set before you a table spread with all kinds of delicacies, yet you have eaten only the crumbs, or not even entered in to the bounty yourself, but escorted others toward it? Often we have neglected receiving for ourselves because of lack of self-confidence or unworthiness issues, or by pouring ourselves fully out until there is no strength left to eat anything for ourselves. Yet we are all worthy in God's eyes, and he asks us to find balance in giving and receiving.

Many opportunities for abundance Divinely placed before us we have not discerned, both because of manipulations from unHoly sources brainwashing us with ideas of unworthiness and lack, and also from our own lack of discernment of that is love and what is not. As we brighten, we see the opportunities plainly, and let go of any fear in pursuing them, for we recognize them as placed there by God and good for us.

….I acknowledge this soul's birthright as a Spirit of God and my redemption as a child of man to live each day in full abundance and expansion of Love with God, one another and myself to the full potential of understanding and experiencing of Love this soul has been, is presently and will be accomplishing, including giving and receiving, and acceptance, gratitude and application of gifts and abilities…Can you see why the unHoly Angels would focus on attacking our health? How about why they would target our relationships? Or our finances? When any of these three areas are attacked, it can distract us from our expansion into Love, for we feel uncomfortable and insecure. The unHoly Angels seek to cause disruption in our trusting God, trusting God in another person (family/relationships) and trusting God that we will be provided for (finances).

Too often we take a passive stance with these issues and give them over to God without any participation of our own. This is not what God wants us to do. God asks us to give him something to bless.

He wants us to choose the things that bring the most joy to our heart, and follow that, since joy will lead us to our recognizing our purpose. God always litters the path to our purpose with joy and abundance. This is also why we are asking in this Decree the full potential of understanding giving and receiving, and acceptance and gratitude and application of gifts and abilities. This is how we share everything with Dad, no matter how great or how small, for we are not just asking God to take care of it *for us,* but *with us* and *through us.* That is what we can see here in The Twelve Books of Acts of the Love of God, participation as a spirit of God born as a child of man. We are asking our Heavenly Father for help! These Divine Decrees are a way that he has given to us to cover us in every regard, to take care of his children, to let us know how much we are loved and to have faith, trust, hope and love, with abundance. God seeks to provide for us and ease our suffering. Let all *"who have ears to hear, let him hear,"* (Mark 4:9) God wants *you* to have abundance.

(21)…to share abundance with all children of man in whatever way it is most needed and is most efficient and beneficial…Next we have a crucial aspect to this work, sharing this abundance with all children of man. There is an important word here that helps us to understand the true unity of things; we are to share abundance with ALL children of man. This is without prejudice of race, sex, religion, culture, etc. We are all his kids, and by Divine right, all are our brothers and sisters. We are a family.

(22)…aid in this recognition and completion through free will interaction and full authority and to render harmless any and all manipulations or unHoly intentions sent to impede this... Here we are asking for protection from any manipulations or unHoly intentions sent to impede our abundance.

(23)…until the King of the Over-Flowing Cup of the Kingdom of God assumes full authority…This Abundance Act is sealed as the ones before it, binding on earth and in heaven. These Decrees within hold true until the King of the Over-Flowing Cup of the Kingdom of God assumes full authority. After that, there will be no need to ask, since abundance will be the norm. *"Mercy, peace and love be yours in abundance."* (Jude 1:2)

CHAPTER 11

BOOK SEVEN – The Purification Act
Powerful Transformation of the Air, Water and Land

(24). I Decree as a Spirit of God born as a child of man full cleansing of the air, water and land and all living creation in relationship to man and the earth through free will acceptance and interaction of All Holy Angels assigned to render harmless any and all manipulations or unHoly intentions including rendering harmless any and all harmful choices made by the conscious or unconscious mind of the children of man.

(25). I Decree full authority and free will interaction of All Holy Angels assigned to purify and sanctify any and all movements of elements beyond normal measures and to return all unHoly manipulations to the original parameters as first ordained by The Word of God, including peaceful and respectful interaction of man within the environment and man's transformation and balance of good and natural for all living creation in relationship to man and the earth in God's perfect plan of perpetual abundance as first ordained and commissioned.

(26). I Decree the full authority of All Holy Angels assigned to aid remembrance and giving of additional opportunities to all children of man to elicit gentleness, awareness and peaceable actions toward the air, water and land and all living creation in relationship to man and the earth.

(27). I Decree this as binding on earth as it is in Heaven by the alignment of the will of God and man, bridging all past, present or future events until the fullness of the shift of transformation arrives and The Master Caretaker of the Kingdom of God assumes full authority by the order of the Purification Act as ordained by the Blood of the Covenant as witnessed and given through the Holy Spirit by the Love of God, Amen.

(Visualization: A cloud forming a raindrop, falling onto earth which then turns from brown to green and full. Color: Blue
Duration: 10 days. Repeat the entire Purification Act in 10 days).

Understanding the Transformation Act:

(24)…full cleansing of the air, water and land and all living creation in relationship to man and the earth…The Purification Act is to return, heal, prevent and harmonize man's relationship with the world around him. Long have we known of the importance of man's relationship to the environment, and in this age of instant communication, we can see and feel the impact of storms, disturbances and imbalances even more than ever before. What a wonderful thing that we are given the perfect words to participate with bringing assistance, protection and cleansing to the earth. The unHoly Angels seek to pervert what is natural and to turn it into something unnatural, to twist and manipulate it into something it's not. We know that storms are not supposed dump millions of gallons of water at a time, thus causing flooding, severe mud slides and loss of life and property. We know that clouds not raining for months or even years at a time and thereby causing drought, starvation and disease are not how it is supposed to be. It is not only the quickness of worldwide communication that let's us see the amount of destruction going on – it is also because this amount of destruction has never been seen at this intensity before.

During this time of transition of shifting into light, we were told to expect this attack upon the earth, and also to know that it will NOT go to a conclusion resulting in annihilation of the earth. Yes, we are going to see many things that may try to stimulate us to fear. But, we can also see these things as an opportunity for our participation in easing the change into great radiance. So as we see the things that are not of Love, we are called to participate in the shifting of things, we are called to be men and women of action, prayer warriors of faith.

Some people have been taught that this transition is a bad thing, that Armageddon is an act of vengeance by God on an ungodly world and ends with total annihilation of the earth and everything upon it.

84

That is not the truth. The word "Armageddon" literally means "God's war." It is not like the wars of mankind, but a cleansing and transitioning time into Love's original purpose as set out at the Garden of Eden. The earth is a beautiful creation that God is well pleased with. *"God saw all that he had made, and it was very good." (Genesis 1:31)*

The word "world" comes from the same word "cosmos" where we get the word "cosmetics" from. It means "surface arrangement of things." In many Bibles the word "earth" and "world" are used interchangeably, but that is not the case in the original writings. This is why some people are confused about God's plan for the earth, and may have even thought the scriptures were saying two different things. For example: *"Blessed are the meek, for they will inherit the earth," (Matthew 5:5) "the world is passing away and so is its desire." (1 Corinthians 7:31)*

So we see that the earth will not be destroyed, just the surface arrangement of it will be drastically changed, including new heavenly governmental rule, and not the rule of mankind. Government is often represented in the scriptures as a "heaven" over the earth, so we are also shown in many places that there will be a "new heaven." Even with using our human common sense, we would not accuse God of wanting to destroy the earth. For example, if we were a landlord and had built a beautiful apartment house and had some tenants that broke the rules, threw wild parties, destroyed and defaced the property, and made it unbearable for all the other tenants, what would you do? Would you burn down the apartment house? Or just oust the bad tenants? Do you think God would do any less? And to aid the illustration, timing wise, we are here at the time the bad tenants (the unHoly Angels) have been served notice and has a limited number of days to move out or be forced to. So we are witnessing the last desperate actions of the tenant's bad choices. And as the countdown continues, they are really upset now, so are trying to cause as much commotion as possible.

...including rendering harmless any and all harmful choices made by the conscious or unconscious mind of the children of man... It is obvious there are ripple effects of mankind's own cause and effect of bad choices, whether conscious or unconscious.

85

It has been granted to mankind to freely choose what they want to do, the good things or the bad. Many have chosen the bad. As a representative of the children of man, we are asking to change the ripple effect.

(25)…purify and sanctify any and all movements of elements beyond normal measures and to return all unHoly manipulations to the original parameters as first ordained by The Word of God, including peaceful and respectful interaction of man within the environment and man's transformation and balance of good and natural for all living creation in relationship to man and the earth in God's perfect plan of perpetual abundance as first ordained and commissioned… Now add to man's bad choices the manipulation of the unHoly Angels and we see horrible occurrences through nature. We see giant tsunamis waves killing; huge storms and tornados devastating; rising water temperatures; polar ice caps melting; ozone deterioration; deforestation; flooding and drought. We assume that it is from fuel emissions, pollution, chemical waste dumping and poor environmental decisions by those in power - but it goes much further than this! The unHoly Angels take these things and twist them even further, causing even more destruction, causing fear and creating areas of panic and desperation.

The 25th Decree covers a lot of things. Right from the beginning, we are looking to purify and sanctify; to bring things back to their former state without manipulation, back to their movement and interaction within normal measures (the original parameters set by The Word of God). As for God's *perfect plan of perpetual abundance as first ordained and commissioned,* it is clear that it was never meant for some to starve from paltry crops due to lack of rain, and for others to lose all because of too much. God's perfect plan is one of perpetual abundance in perfect balance.

(26)…aid remembrance and giving of additional opportunities to all children of man to elicit gentleness, awareness and peaceable actions toward the air, water and land and all living creation in relationship to man and the earth… This Decree speaks of reminding us towards gentleness, awareness and peaceable actions to the animals and earth, and giving us additional opportunities to do this.

86

These opportunities might be in the form of new information, or even new inventions. We were originally made to be caretakers for the earth, and to extend the first garden beyond any borders. We were created to interact with the animals peacefully and with joy, knowing and nurturing their abilities and qualities. We were created to transform things even then, with our mind and with our body. This Decree helps us remember who we are in relation to the earth and its environment and inhabitants, and encourage the power that we have to illicit change, always in conjunction with God and his Holy Angels.

(27)...until the fullness of the shift of transformation arrives and The Master Caretaker of the Kingdom of God assumes full authority... And we wrap the Purification Act up with our seal, binding this word through the Master Caretaker, the one who worked alongside his Father in creating the earth and all things upon it, Christ.

CHAPTER 12

BOOK EIGHT – The Awareness Act
Conscious Connection, Expansion and Lifting of the Veil

(28). I Decree as a Spirit of God born as a child of man full ability of discernment between Holy and unHoly. By free will,

(29). I Decree Guides assigned and All Holy Angels assigned full access, ability and free will interaction to consistently communicate with this soul in a manner conducive to the allowance of the veil and the full potential of connection allowed at the present time of understanding. By free will this soul asks for additional opportunities of awareness of conscious or unconscious choices of cause and effect even before any decision or action is made, and clear discernment and ability to choose without manipulations or unHoly intentions sent toward this soul.

(30). I Decree this soul's free will ability to immediately recognize and call in All Holy Angels assigned in all potential events of protection or harm to this soul (or to my husband/wife and those under my care) and for continuing expansion of awareness and acting in accordance with Holy signs and wonders and God-given methods of interaction and aiding personal connection, amplification, frequency and brightening of prayer.

(31). I Decree this soul's free will to remember and act upon God's Will and agreed-upon purpose and commission for this life and to easily recognize all God-given opportunities and realizations, and to resist opportunities for unHoly actions and turn away from unHoly manifestations and to act without doubt, hesitation or fear upon every God-given opportunity and transform dark to light, and fear to Love and I ask Guides assigned and All Holy Angels assigned in assisting this soul with this, and assisting all children of man to full faith and trust in God and his Word.

(32). I Decree this as binding on earth as it is in heaven by the alignment of the will of God and man, bridging all past, present or future events until the veil is fully lifted and the Holy One of the Kingdom of God assumes full authority by order of the Awareness Act as ordained by the Blood of the Covenant as witnessed and given through the Holy Spirit by the Love of God, Amen.

(Visualization: A supernova expansion, starburst in the sky, a light turned on in the darkness Color: Purple
Duration: 7 days. Repeat the entire Awareness act in 7 days).

Understanding the Awareness Act:

(28)...full ability of discernment between Holy and unHoly... The Awareness Act is a beautiful testimony to what this is all about, unity with God and committing to action with God and his will for us. We start off with asking for discernment of what is Holy and of God and what is unHoly and not of God. This awareness plays a vital role in doing our work and leading joyful and successful lives. Really, knowing the difference between right and wrong is at the core of our soul's journey into the light of Love and remembering who we are in the process.

"Who is wise? He will realize these things. Who is discerning? He will understand them. The ways of the LORD are right; the righteous walk in them, but the rebellious stumble in them." (Hosea 14:9) This is the recognition of what discernment does to help us in this time of transition. There are many who are confused in their search for God, many open to a few things and many open themselves to all things. This is why discernment is so important. There is a comical saying about a person whose "mind is so open his brains fell out!" Not all things can exist in a "gray area." For example, God either cares about his creation or he doesn't; the earth either stands forever or it doesn't; the human spirit either exists after death or it doesn't; etc. We need to recognize what is true and what is not. To do this, we need to recognize what is of Love and what is not. This is why we were given analytical thought.

The analytical mind in its pure form is not a bad thing, but is actually made to process, sort and sieve out the real from the fake, and to make choices based on that. Not everything can be true, so some things are false.

As simple humans, we can see and understand the need for discernment for making the right choices. Would you rather have a child that obeyed you out of restriction and limitation or would you rather have one that wanted to be with you simply out of love? Recognizing the gift of free will is powerful, but *applying* our free will in a beneficial way is even more powerful. Many apply their free will to things that are harmful to themselves or others, and then blame God for the bad consequences, when he had nothing to do with it at all!

The most favorable use of free will is to recognize the things that are fully beneficial; that is, to recognize the choices of love. But first we have to agree that Love *is* the right choice. This is at the core of the original issues, where the unHoly Angels have questioned the authority of Love's right to rule. God says love is the best way, and he can help us learn everything about it. Everyday our lives are an answer to "is love the best way" by the consequences that occur from our good or bad choices. God trusts us to ultimately make the choices of love, and recognize the benefits of it. He knows our innermost desires, our passions and our convictions. He knows anything other than the way of love leads to pain, suffering, and negative consequences. In fact, God is the one who first taught us about love. *"Whoever does not love does not know God, for God is love. (1 John 4:8) "Dear friends, since God so loved us, we also ought to love one another." (1 John 4:11)*

Then how do we gain discernment and see what is of love and what is not? And after that, can we go further to tell the difference between what is good and what is the *greater* good? Sometimes there is more than one answer of love; can we recognize the greater good for all, harming none?

(29)…to consistently communicate with this soul in a manner conducive to the allowance of the veil and the full potential of connection allowed at the present time of understanding…We have first asked for discernment.

Next, we are asking for consistent communication "in a manner conducive to the allowance of the veil and the full potential of connection allowed at the present time of understanding." We have agreed with an interaction that can help us tremendously with discernment, guidance, protection, understanding, and love. And all this is done in accordance with where we are in our own stage of development.

As we have been shown previously, the veil is a covering of the full recollection of things; who we truly are, what we have come here to do and the facets of love we have already polished. These things are covered according to God's Will for us, that we may be able to recognize, each time, each life the things of love. The veil is also in place to help keep us focused on the life at hand.

There are many that would argue against this and say: "why doesn't God just lift this veil so we can see for ourselves the truth of things and remember it now?" The answer is that we have to learn how to crawl and balance before we can walk, and how to walk before we run, and we do this step by step. Such is God's pacing and timing for us. We are not to be so arrogant as to think that we know better for ourselves than God does for us, God is the Almighty. Do you have any memories of bad choices made in the past? Have you *always* done and said the right thing in *this* life? Have you *always* had the best things happen to you by the hands of others in *this* life? No, of course not. We are imperfect and live among other imperfect people, and where many can be used as puppets by unseen forces. So, how easy has it been to not let any of these previous things cloud your perception of how you view your life presently and how things might proceed in the future? Even in this life, if we live in the past, we have difficulty seeing a new future. Now, are you sure you want to have *all* the details of *all* your lives open to you *right now?* Truly as we have seen, when God opens the veil, it is at the right time, and opened to the right things that keep us encouraged and confident.

...additional opportunities of awareness of conscious or unconscious choices of cause and effect even before any decision or action is made... This Decree helps us to be aware of the ripple effect before we even make a move.

This helps us make a better choice in the beginning of a matter rather than racing to fix it afterwards.

(30)...ability to immediately recognize and call in All Holy Angels assigned in all potential events of protection or harm... Our Loving God protects us, whenever we ask we can call in a Holy Angel. Because of free will he cannot automatically protect us unless we request it. This is the reason why we are given The Divine Decrees, to share them with all our brothers and sisters and to have them protected in God's Love. God looks to assist his children in their time of need. We are given these Decrees to add with our prayers that we may be able to withstand all that comes against us and remain faithful and true to God, even when we see the unHoly cause more and more destruction. The unHoly Angels try to convince us that we are not heard by God and that our prayers don't matter. They try to disguise any places of attack so we will not pray for the warrior Holy Angels to stop them from producing harm. God tells us, "Do not be afraid" 65 times in scripture. We are constantly told we are not to fear, and are asked to *"Be strong in the Lord." (Ephesians 6:10) With* God on our side, who can be against us? *"For I am convinced that neither death nor life, neither Angels nor demons, neither the present nor the future, nor any power, neither heights nor depth, nor anything else in all creation, will be able to separate us from the love of God that is in Christ Jesus our Lord."(Romans 8:35-39)*

...for continuing expansion of awareness and acting in accordance with Holy signs and wonders and God-given methods of interaction and aiding personal connection, amplification, frequency and brightening of prayer... We are not only asking for ability to increase our awareness, but also to act upon it. Remember we are responsible for the brightness of our candle. Are we doing the dirty work of the unHoly Angels for them, are we dimming and extinguishing our own flame? This would take us out of the game and keep us from helping at this precious time.

Look at the beauty that is inherent in this Act, and notice the vital importance of prayer. WE are the ones in charge of our brightness. WE are able to be bright for God.

And we are asking not only for continuing expansion of awareness, but also to proceed in accordance with how Love interacts with mankind. This includes the expanding signs and wonders given as proof of his Presence, which we may individually be partakers of. God has used signs and wonders all through history to testify to his intentions and connection with mankind. And we are told more and more gifts will be given and shown. *"God also testified to it by signs, wonders and various miracles, and gifts of the Holy Spirit distributed according to his will." (Hebrews 2:3,4)* In this Decree, you are asking to act in accord with *his plan for you in reference to these signs!*

(31)...and to resist opportunities for unHoly actions and turn away from unHoly manifestations and to act without doubt, hesitation or fear upon every God-given opportunity and transform dark to light, and fear to Love... In this Decree we are asking for help to resist unHoly actions and to turn away from unHoly manifestations, acting without doubt, hesitation or fear with every God-given opportunity to transform dark to light and fear to love. The unHoly manifestations are things that appear to be good, but are not. Many times Jesus showed the difference between outward appearances and what the truth really was. *"Woe to you, teachers of the law and Pharisees, you hypocrites! You are like whitewashed tombs, which look beautiful on the outside but on the inside are full of dead men's bones and everything unclean. In the same way, on the outside you appear to people as righteous but on the inside you are full of hypocrisy and wickedness." (Matthew 23:27, 28) "...you give God a tenth of your mint, rue and all other kinds of garden herbs, but you neglect justice and the love of God." (Luke 11:42, see also 11:39)*

...and assisting all children of man to full faith and trust in God and his Word... Many uninformed people will see this time of transition through only eyes of fear, hopelessness and misunderstanding. Now you are learning the real truth of why things are, and how individuals can participate in their personal journey through it. Will you help calm the fear and share what you have learned? By stating this Decree, you are asking for this opportunity.

(32)...until the veil is fully lifted and the Holy One of the Kingdom of God assumes full authority... Soon there will be a time of the veil being fully lifted for each one of us. Blessed Tiffany was also shown that not only will we individually know all of our past experiences and be OK with it, but the story of each our lives will also be on display for one another. This helps each of us see the justice and love of God and how it played out from the bigger picture, almost like a "reality TV show" God-style, with "behind the scenes footage" included! This will help for training purposes for all, and will be a delight and real mind-opener for all to see what was *really* going on during many of the struggles and blessings that mankind has had.

Won't it be beautiful to see the story of Christ unfold, the stories of the saints, the stories of our friends, family and neighbors, progressing in love through each life time? We are told this learning only happens during the first thousand years of the Kingdom of God. Not long after that, *any* unHoly actions will never be brought to mind again. Praise be to God! All indents to unHoly and pain will be cleansed away, and only the beauty will remain, as God is vindicated that Love is the best way for all. *"I will pour our my Spirit on all people, your sons and daughters will prophesy, your old men will dream dreams, your young men will see visions. Even on my servants, both men and women, I will pour out my Spirit in those days. I will show wonders in the heavens and on the earth..." (Joel 2:28-30)*

CHAPTER 13

BOOK NINE – The Representation Act
The Power to Influence Government Around the World

(33). I Decree as a Spirit of God born as a child of man this soul's free will Holy Prayers and Holy Intentions that all those in designations of authority and divisions of government act for the betterment of the children of man.

(34). I Decree full authority and free will interaction of All Holy Angels assigned to render harmless any and all manipulations or unHoly intentions sent toward these representatives, and I further ask for additional opportunities of awareness of conscious or unconscious choices of cause and effect for each decision and action where it impacts the children of man and all living creation in relationship to man, by free will this soul asks for the consistent free will interaction of All Holy Angels assigned to expand the justice, support and protection for those under the greatest attack and to give additional opportunities to each representative to elicit peace and harmony between all people and nations, to assist with abundance for any and all in need, and to enact any and all laws and policies that will only benefit and serve the people in the highest good as a reflection of the recognition of the sovereignty of the God of Love and his justice, mercy, support and protection.

(35). I Decree full authority and free will interaction of All Holy Angels assigned to aid the protection of all children and any and all vulnerable children of man who are in need in body, mind, soul and spirit and rendering harmless any and all manipulations or unHoly intentions sent toward these vulnerable ones, and giving them additional opportunities to communicate with God, the Holy Ones, their Guides assigned and one another without restraint or fear.

(36). I Decree this as binding on earth as it is in heaven by the alignment of the will of God and man, bridging all past, present or future events until the King of Kings and True Ruler of the Kingdom of God assumes full authority by order of the Representation Act as ordained by the Blood of the Covenant as witnessed and given through the Holy Spirit by the Love of God, Amen.

(Visualization: A pebble being cast into a pond, the ripples going out to distant shores. Color: Black
Duration:10 days. Repeat the entire Representation Act in 10 days).

Understanding the Representation Act:

(33)…this soul's free will Holy Prayers and Holy Intentions that all those in designations of authority and divisions of government act for the betterment of the children of man…This Representation Act is a welcome relief for all those that have struggled with the rulers of this world. Right from the beginning we are asking that those in power act for the betterment of the children of man. This covers all those in designations of authority and divisions of government. This covers from the top ruler of a country all the way to the ones who enforce the laws and protect us daily. All are in designations of authority.

Many have noticed that elected officials often promise one thing while running for election, and do another after they are in office. Do you feel your government doesn't adequately reflect your view of justice, peace or even kindness? Have you seen laws and policies too strict in some areas and too lenient in others? Have you felt the need for change even in your town or community government where you live? This is the behind the scenes look at what happens with the rulers of this world, the many governments throughout and why.

(34)…render harmless any and all manipulations or unHoly intentions sent toward these representatives, and I further ask for additional opportunities of awareness of conscious or unconscious choices of cause and effect for each decision and action where it impacts the children of man and all living creation in relationship to man…Many people think that this Holy work is about being passive. But it is just the opposite. It is about being active, and transforming the darkness into light and fear into love. In this Decree, we are asking to bring in the heavy hitters to enlist their service in battle to protect our leaders in power. Those in power are under attack by the unHoly Angels, and it is a greater attack than they have ever faced before. They are in a spiritual battle every day.

Notice that we are also asking that all these representatives have greater awareness of their conscious and unconscious choices of cause and effect for each decision and action they make. First, there must be awareness so one can sense and recognize what is happening, and then there must be appropriate action to do something about it. In this Decree we are asking that the Holy Angels give these in the positions of authority the ability to make these choices without being manipulated by the unHoly Angels.

Those who are in positions of power have influence over a great many people. Their decisions can benefit or cause strife. They can elect to do the best for the greatest amount of citizens or to influence the well-being of a select few. Or they can be manipulated to do the very worst things, and the ripple effects carry through to not only in their own region and environment, but also the world.

This does not mean all people who get into office do it for the wrong reasons. There are many have truly wanted to change things, right the wrongs that have been done, and want the best for all involved. But the unHoly Angels are a powerful force, and *man's inability to rule himself successfully* (one of the original issues) plays a part too. Recognizing that those who represent us are under great attack and should be prayed for helps us understand that we are as much a part of the change that can take place in government as they are. And the difference is, we aren't going to try to figure it out on our own, but we place it in God's hands.

We call in the Holy Angels to render harmless not only the unHoly manipulations, but also the unHoly intentions sent by mankind themselves to one another.

How many people do you know who are seething angry at certain representatives and presidents, and are wishing them demise and destruction? It is similar to us creating a curse or hex upon someone when we send ill-will to them. It creates a problem for us too, and anger in what ever form it takes makes a problem in our bubble of free will, and it is self-induced. Then you know what happens: we get attacked through those holes by unHoly Angels, and a series of events can happen unless we follow Divine steps to change it.

...expand the justice, support and protection for those under the greatest attack and to give additional opportunities to each representative to elicit peace and harmony between all people and nations, to assist with abundance for any and all in need... Injustice and lack of support (food, finances, etc) and lack of protection are stimulators that the unHoly Angels use to create conflicts and wars between peoples and nations. They seek death and destruction and the shedding of blood. But no amount of evil bloodshed could take away the fact that Jesus shattered death for us. And remember, this was done *not only* for those who believe in Christ but for *all* of mankind, beyond religion, culture or political agenda.

The unHoly Angels seek to destroy not only the body, but to try to destroy the connection of mankind to God. They seek to create anger, doubt, pain and fear. So, if the unHoly Angels can manipulate someone in power to make a choice that will lead to greater death, conflict and bloodshed, the unHoly Angels will certainly go for as much damage as they can to cause as much disruption as possible. Now is it easier to understand that these people in governmental authority are the targets of great manipulation? All those in positions of power are like a prized commodity to the unHoly Angels.

…and to enact any and all laws and policies that will only benefit and serve the people in the highest good as a reflection of the recognition of the sovereignty of the God of Love and his justice, mercy, support and protection…The highest good is about making choices that reflect the one who is the highest good, the God of unconditional and abundant Love. This source is where perfect justice, mercy, support and protection come from. Even in whatever small part we can imitate this, wonderful events will happen. Remember it is not by our own power, for our own energy can only sustain so much, even if we do it with the greatest of desired good. But, by reaching beyond our own energy and asking for the participation and guidance of Love, all things are made possible, and the energy to sustain and bring into fruition then becomes limitless.

(35)…aid the protection of all children and any and all vulnerable children of man who are in need in body, mind, soul and spirit and rendering harmless any and all manipulations or unHoly intentions sent toward these vulnerable ones, and giving them additional opportunities to communicate with God, the Holy Ones, their Guides assigned and one another without restraint or fear…In the 35th Decree we see God's love made manifest for any one who is vulnerable. This means a person of any age who cannot take care of themselves. Some examples of this are those who have developmental challenges, or those who have dementia or Alzheimer's. The automatic protection that God gives during these times of struggle is a precious gift. When they cannot make connection on their own, he does it for them, and no molestation by the plots of unHoly Angels can harm them!

(36)…until the King of Kings and True Ruler of the Kingdom of God assumes full authority…In this Decree we conclude with the binding statement and see yet another name for Christ; the True Ruler, the King of Kings. This is also where we are agreeing that it is evident that we cannot rule on our own, that man needs the help of someone much smarter and kinder than himself. We only have to look at the current state of affairs in the world to see that we need God to get us through all this!

CHAPTER 14

BOOK TEN – The Salvation Act
Freedom in Our Birthright as a Child of God

(37). I Decree as a Spirit of God born as a child of man full surrender of my spirit and all attending delegates to the sanctity of baptism of Blood and Water, and I acknowledge that which was created pure became unclean unto itself, and was made clean and Holy once more by the Redemption of Grace, and through this Grace this soul stands in the light once more, and darkness has no authority.

(38). I Decree by free will my bending of knee in humility and spirit aligned with the Spirit and Will of God, now and through timelessness.

(39). I Decree by free will my full awareness of the Original Issues and I offer this soul's testimony to the rightness and truth of God's right to rule over his creation and that it has not been possible for the sons of man to successfully choose for themselves what is right or wrong and that the children of man call for the interaction of God and continue to seek for God and desire to learn and accomplish God's Will even when manipulations occur to their body's destruction or when their soul is not satisfied by gifts.

(40). I Decree by free will the complete fullness of Love even in suffering by the Son of God's Love, as testified to and witnessed in the life of his Life, Death and Life Again while maintaining fullness of purity and rebuking darkness, thereby breaking the bondage upon pure creation forevermore and freeing this soul and all children of man to continue the experience and expansion of Love. I receive by free will my birthright as a Child of God created by Love, in Love and for Love.

(41). I Decree this as binding on earth as it is in heaven by the alignment of the will of God and man, bridging all past, present and future events until the Savior of the World and King of the Kingdom of God assumes full authority by order of the Salvation Act as ordained by the Blood of the Covenant as witnessed and given through the Holy Spirit by the Love of God, Amen.

(Visualization: Golden light falling like raindrops from Heaven, covering all, body levitating on gold light, lifting to God. Color: Gold
Duration: 7 days. Repeat the entire Salvation Act in 7 days).

Understanding the Salvation Act:

(37)…full surrender of my spirit and all attending delegates to the sanctity of baptism of Blood and Water, and I acknowledge that which was created pure became unclean unto itself…The Salvation Act tells the whole story of what has happened and is happening now. It starts off by recognizing the fall of man from the Grace of God, the fallout from the choices of Adam and Eve. This is what is meant by "that which was created pure became unclean unto itself." Mankind through Adam became unclean unto itself (succumbing to temptation to disobey God and turn away from love), and was made pure and clean again through the redemption (Christ as a man choosing to turn back to Love). This is what the sanctity through the Blood of Christ brings, and this is what purifies and allows our soul to stand in the Light once again. It breaks the original generational bondage of our first parent's choices over us.

…and was made clean and Holy once more by the Redemption of Grace, and through this Grace this soul stands in the light once more, and darkness has no authority…This is a powerful statement, that we stand in the light once more not by our own merit, but "through this Grace" bestowed upon us. And when we comprehend that we truly are these beloved children of Light, darkness has no more authority to coerce us to think any differently, and we will not allow ourselves to be manipulated away from God. We are each sparks off the Original Flame, and the alignment of our will and Love's Will together guarantees that nothing can blow our candle out.

"You, O Lord, keep my lamp burning; my God turns my darkness into light." *(Psalm 18:28)*

(38)...my bending of knee in humility and spirit aligned with the Spirit and Will of God, now and through timelessness... In the 38th Decree we are reminded that free will is given a lot of respect, and when we freely state that we are "bending our knee in humility," we demonstrate our agreement that his ways are a better choice than doing things our own way. As humans, we can be proud of two things: him, and our choice of him. *"Not by might nor by power but by my Spirit, says the Lord Almighty." (Zechariah 4:6)* Kneeling in humility shows our submission to Love. When we are vulnerable to Love and surrender into it, all things flourish and transform in our lives not only each day, but into timelessness when the days are not even counted.

(39)...full awareness of the Original Issues and I offer this soul's testimony to the rightness and truth of God's right to rule over his creation and that it has not been possible for the sons of man to successfully choose for themselves what is right or wrong and that the children of man call for the interaction of God and continue to seek for God and desire to learn and accomplish God's Will even when manipulations occur to their body's destruction or when their soul is not satisfied by gifts... The 39th Decree addresses the original issues brought against God by the unHoly Angels. By stating this Decree, we are acknowledging that we know what the original issues are, and on whose side we have chosen. The original issues are:

#1. That mankind can rule himself successfully, without God.

#2. That mankind only comes to God for what man can get out of God.

#3. That mankind will do everything he can to save his skin, including curse God.

Through the several thousands of years since these issues were brought up, mankind and all creation has witnessed that these three issues have been proven false.

105

Man loves God and continues to seek him and his ways no matter if they receive something back for it or not. The children of mankind have also shown their integrity to God's love and his ways even to their own death many, many times. This is not just in the past, such as people being thrown to the lions – but also today in many lands with a gun pointed towards them or the ones they love. All of these who are put to death for their belief in God have stood as evidence that man believe their spiritual relationship with Love is more important than even their own tangible skin. And finally, we see all over the world that mankind has done a horrible job of trying to rule on his own, no matter what kind of government they may try. Just like a court case gathering evidence, these original issues addressing the sovereignty of God and God's right to rule have now been answered.

(40)...the complete fullness of Love even in suffering by the Son of God's Love, as testified to and witnessed in the life of his Life, Death and Life Again while maintaining fullness of purity and rebuking darkness... This Decree continues to describe the fullness of the love of God's son, and how Christ not only succeeded in remaining pure and rebuking the darkness, but also by dying with no sin upon him. All of his life was one without blemish. There are many things not written in the scriptures that also show Christ was truly loving and kind even from an early age. Blessed Tiffany was shown that as a child how he had picked up and healed a dead bird, cupping it in his hands and blowing upon it. He then tossed it up into the air where it flew away! Even as a grown man, when he sat upon a young donkey and was being led into Jerusalem (as was the people's custom when a new king was coming into his Kingdom), Blessed Tiffany was shown that Jesus felt sorry for the animal and prayed that his weight would be light upon the donkey!

...thereby breaking the bondage upon pure creation forevermore and freeing this soul and all children of man to continue the experience and expansion of Love... As we have seen, imperfect mankind was in a state of darkness, cut off from the Father of Light. No matter how many lives we had lived, or how good we were to try to earn it ourselves, none of us could brighten ourselves beyond the dent in the mold that was passed down to us from Adam and Eve.

106

All of mankind has been freed from this bondage, whether they recognize how it happened or not. But how wonderful it is to be able to give thanks where it is due, and to know the deeper things.

Jesus is the one who set us free from bondage. Prior to Jesus' surrender of his life for all our lives, all those that died with sin upon them would be reborn to cleanse and purify, to polish the facets of love to become brighter and brighter, but none could ever do it. We could never have polished enough no matter how many lives we lived, no matter how many times we came back. The dent in the mold from the beginning, the fall of man through Adam, one man created perfectly who chose to go apart from love had to have the karmic redemption through one man made perfectly, Christ, who chose the way of love and brought us all back before God through Grace. This is what is meant by the shattering the shackles of death, Christ freed the slaves from the bondage of constantly working at polishing the facets of love but not being able to overcome the sins of man. The one who was put to death yet had no sin upon him shattered this law and gave us all the ability to polish and be before God by Grace. Christ is the one who chose to do this for the sons of man and offered up himself as a willing sacrifice.

This is why we could never earn salvation, it was something given to us. We could never do enough to polish our facets of love, we could never do enough to become brighter than the shadow placed upon us through Adam's disobedience. We could however have a Savior, one who could do this for us. Christ Jesus was the first-born creation of God, the one formerly known as Michael the Archangel. This is why all the Angels know him, and why the mention of his name, now since his fulfillment of redeeming mankind, carries even greater weight and authority. This is why we ask all Angels that visit us, "Do you love Jesus now?" Because at one time they all did, but now only the Holy Angels are able to continue to say "Yes!"

We see this in Hebrews 4:14-16, *"Therefore, since we have a great high priest who has gone through the heavens, Jesus the Son of God, let us hold firmly to the faith we profess. For we do not have a high priest who is unable to sympathize with our weaknesses, but we have one who has been tempted in every way, just as we are - yet was without sin.*

107

Let us then approach the throne of Grace with confidence, so that we may receive mercy and find Grace to help us in our time of need."

...I receive by free will my birthright as a Child of God created by Love, in Love and for Love... God calls to all to know more about love. And the expansion of Love has just begun, there is much more to experience. Really, have you experienced all the love you want? Have you given or received your fill? Have you seen enough ripple effects of love through the works of your hands through creating music, art, writing, or other expressions? Do you know how to respond in love in every situation, and to select only the ways of love in every choice? We are only at the beginning of learning what there is to know!

In this Decree we are stating that we receive by free will our birthright as a child of God, created by Love, in Love and for Love. Love is the main reason why we are here. In the Bible, there was a time in the Old Testament when there were hundreds of laws that man tried to fulfill to "earn" love. This is what mankind asked for. But no one could do it, since love is a free gift, and mankind wasn't understanding that simply acting in love covered all the things covered by law that a person was meant to do. Mankind wanted the details of what that meant, and mostly it became a place of people even adding more laws by their own tradition. That is why Jesus took everyone back to the basics. *"Love the Lord your God with all your heart and with all your soul and with all your strength and with all your mind; and Love your neighbor as yourself."(Luke 10:27)*

God is not a prison warden or a strict high school principal, this law of love is what God is talking about when he says: *"I will put my laws in their minds and write them on their hearts. I will be their God, and they will be my people. No longer will a man teach his neighbor, or a man his brother, saying 'Know the Lord,' because they will all know me, from the least of them to the greatest."* (Hebrews 8:10,11) God wants this one-on-one relationship between you and him. Love wants all to become the mystic.

(41)...until the Savior of the World and King of the Kingdom of God assumes full authority... Here in the sealing of the Salvation Act we see a familiar name for Christ, as the "Savior of the World." As well, the gold visualization and seeing oneself as being lifted up and surrounded in the golden light of God once again sums up the heart of the deep message of love he has for his children, who are fully redeemed from darkness.

CHAPTER 15

BOOK ELEVEN - The Hierarchy Act
The Power to Influence Religion around the World

(42). I Decree as a Spirit of God born as a child of man this soul's free will Holy Prayers and Holy Intentions that all those in designations of sacred office and Holy Orders by vows given before God remain faithful and true in submission and humility for the consistent disbursement of acts of ministry to children of man as though ministering to God.

(43). I Decree full authority and free will interaction of All Holy Angels assigned to render harmless any and all manipulations or unHoly intentions sent toward these servants, and I further ask for additional opportunities of awareness of conscious or unconscious choices of cause and effect for each decision and action where it impacts the spirit and soul of the children of man and their delegates and all living creation in relationship to man. By free will this soul asks for the consistent free will interaction of All Holy Angels assigned to expand the houses of prayer and fellowship to all children of man throughout all the nations, granting Divine guidance, protection and discernment in teaching and reaching the hearts of man through Love and unification of those Holy in reflection of the Love of God and the magnification and sanctification of the fullness of the Name of God.

(44). I Decree this soul's free will Holy Prayers and Holy Intentions for all religions and faiths to serve as ambassadors of peace and unity under One God of Love, and that all these may shelter, feed, nurture, encourage, counsel, protect, defend, guide and give service by God's Words and Authority and not their own.

(45). I Decree this as binding on earth as it is in heaven by the alignment of the will of God and man, bridging all past, present or future events until the Anointed High Priest of the Kingdom of God assumes full authority by order of the Hierarchy Act as ordained by the Blood of the Covenant as witnessed and given through the Holy Spirit by the Love of God, Amen.

(Visualization: Succession of shepherd's staff being given from one to the other from God, through mankind and mankind giving it back to God, row of hundreds of people. Color: Silver
Duration: 10 days. Repeat the entire Hierarchy Act in 10 days).

Understanding the Hierarchy Act:

(42)...this soul's free will Holy Prayers and Holy Intentions that all those in designations of sacred office and Holy Orders by vows given before God remain faithful and true in submission and humility for the consistent disbursement of acts of ministry to children of man... The Hierarchy Act starts out with a supportive statement exercising our free will that all those who have made a commitment before God remain faithful and true, and humbly submissive so that they may be an instrument that God can use. Notice it says "vows given before God," it *does not* say "and before man." The spiritual journey is one that we make on our own with God, and is always a personal vow.

Now, when we choose to take on additional responsibility so that he can use us even more, there is a promise and a blessing in effect that God set up long ago, which includes stating our intentions in front of people and receiving a laying on of hands through those ordained in the ministry. This act shows the individual's desire to have additional spiritual responsibilities and is not reliant at all upon any imperfections of the one doing the laying on of hands, for it is God who disperses the gifts.

There are many examples of this passing down of anointing throughout scripture, but here is one of my favorites: *"For this reason I remind you to fan into flame the gift of God, which is in you through the laying on of my hands, For God did not give us a spirit of timidity, but a spirit of power, of love and of self-discipline."* *(2 Timothy 1:6,7)*

Blessed Tiffany was shown that when a person asks for more ability in God's work, greater blessings come with the greater responsibilities. Along with this are Holy Angels sent with specific abilities to help. All those who seek to do good in this world are going to come under attack. Those who seek to do even greater good come under even more attack – but are also given much greater protection. We never have to be fearful, for God protects and defends, and we are given the tools to accomplish what is needed. Whether this be in the deliverance and exorcism work, the blessing of homes and land, the cleansing of air or water, transformation of unnatural things back into natural, or numerous other things that we may be called to do. We are never given greater work without also being given the ability to do it. But sadly, mankind has placed many restrictions upon themselves that God never did, so many of the tools and gifts are never used.

…as though ministering to God… This Decree demonstrates how important it is to do our job well, the ripple effect of caring for our brothers and sisters is as if we were caring for God himself. We are asking that all those in ministry continue on a consistent basis to care for the children of man, giving them the same compassion, suspension of judgment, hope, faith and love as if they were ministering personally to God. *"Whatever you did to the least of these brothers of mine, you did to me…whatever you did not do to the least of these brothers of mine, you did not do for me."* *(Matthew 25:40,45)*

(43)…render harmless any and all manipulations or unHoly intentions sent toward these servants, and I further ask for additional opportunities of awareness of conscious or unconscious choices of cause and effect for each decision and action where it impacts the spirit and soul of the children of man and their delegates and all living creation in relationship to man… This Decree follows up with asking for protection for these individuals who have taken these vows of service.

As with those in government and representation, these in the hierarchy are in a spiritual battle every day, more so than most realize. In this Decree we are asking that the Holy Angels render harmless any machinations of the unHoly Angels or unHoly Angels intentions sent toward them by others. We are also asking that these in positions of spiritual direction are given more opportunities to be aware of the impact of their choices.

We have seen all throughout time how the natural spiritual journey toward love has instead been manipulated towards fear. Many atrocious things have been done in the name of God, which God has nothing to do with at all. All our choices have cause and effect. One who works for God needs to be especially aware of their choices that they may reflect the love and brightness of the one who made them.

As with those in government and representation, this does not mean all people who take on the job of spiritual direction do it for the wrong reasons. Many have recognized the comfort, joy and fulfillment of choosing a spiritual path, and the desire to help others in their journey as well. There is not going to be perfect spiritual direction or an ideal church or place of worship, since God only has imperfect men to deal with and each one is clouded in their understanding by their own inherent imperfections. *Man's inability to rule himself successfully* is also about spiritual guidance. No matter what differences of faith, or arguments that some might make about theology, it simply comes down to recognizing what is of Love, and what is not, and following through accordingly. God doesn't make divisions, people do. Some people are going to feel more comfortable on a stricter path than others, because that is what they are used to or feel they need. Others won't. This is why God meets people wherever they are at on their journey. And he continues to give opportunities for greater freedom and love all along the way.

…By free will this soul asks for the consistent free will interaction of All Holy Angels assigned to expand the houses of prayer and fellowship to all children of man throughout all the nations, granting Divine guidance, protection and discernment in teaching and reaching the hearts of man through Love and unification of those Holy in reflection of the Love of God … This Decree goes on to ask for an expansion of the houses of prayer and fellowship to all children of man throughout all the nations. Houses of prayer give an opportunity for coming together to focus on spiritual things, to encourage one another and share, for learning and teaching, for spending time in prayer, meditation and communion with God, and can serve as a place of protection for us spiritually and at times even physically. All of this is a strengthening for mankind. *"Let us not give up meeting together, as some are in the habit of doing, but let us encourage one another – and all the more as you see the Day approaching." (Hebrews 10:25)* We are also asking for Divine guidance, protection and discernment for those teaching and reaching the hearts of man. As well, we see that it is not only through love but through the unification of those Holy in reflection of the Love of God and his name that will give strength and support for this to occur.

…and the magnification and sanctification of the fullness of the Name of God… God is called by many names – Father, LORD, Ancient of Days, Lord Almighty, Yahweh, Divine Love, I Am that I Am, Jehovah, Most High, etc. God's son Jesus is also called by many names: Lord, Great Teacher, Messiah, Christ, Prince of Peace. "God" is just a title, like "president" is just a title, but both the president and God have personal names. And each know what they are. This Decree is talking about the fullness of the name of God, which is more than a personal name, but also all that the name carries with it. *"A good name is better than fine perfume…"(Ecclesiastes 7:1)* There is an acknowledgement of the sanctification of all the things that God has done, which is represented by his name, and we see it is listed as first priority in The Lord's Prayer when Jesus gives us an example of how to pray, he first says: *"Our Father who art in heaven, hallowed be your name, your Kingdom come, your will be done on earth as it is in heaven…" (Matthew 6:9,10).*

The name of a person represents all who he is. So a person or a place can get a bad name by the actions or events related to it. Remember that Blessed Tiffany was shown that if his Holy name was given to us just as represented by numbers, by the time we were told it and then repeated it, it would be wrong because Father continues to expand who he is. God knows who you are talking to, and at this time of our ability to understand, allows the many titles. Here is the title that certainly sums him up quickly: *"...God is Love." (1 John 4:8)*

(44)...Holy Prayers and Holy Intentions for all religions and faiths to serve as ambassadors of peace and unity under One God of Love... This is what religion and faith are supposed to be - a place of peace and unity, not war and division. Religion was and is to be a touchstone to faith, where man can seek out God, delving through the veil to where the Holiest of Holies resides and beckons us to come to him. Religion wasn't meant to be perverted and manipulated as a place of power dictating who can participate and who cannot. Religion is meant to be a place where all are welcome, a mirror of God's Love, a demonstration of the peace and unity that we all have through the one who made us all. It is to serve as an ambassador of peace and unity, not excluding or judging, not condemning and isolating and certainly not killing. Do not be fooled, God's acceptance and love for us will not come through the earning of it by works, but by the receiving of Grace of unconditional love given by Father. How wonderful when we can faithfully walk in his path of peace and unity when seeking to deliver his messages of love, hope, trust and discernment. In this way, though we may see the details of God differently than others do, submission to serve as ambassadors of peace and unity bring all of us under the banner of one God of Love.

...and that all these may shelter, feed, nurture, encourage, counsel, protect, defend, guide and give service by God's Words and Authority and not their own... How beautiful to have this reminder of the kind of practical service that God wants, especially at this time when it is most needed. All religions and faiths are encouraged to remember that it is through his Will and Word that all is accomplished.

This is why we share this information as it was given to us through the Divine guidance and channel of Holy Stigmata, for these Decrees are by God's authority and is meant to be available for all to have access to it. It is a true blessing to be able to share this information that creates so many wonderful opportunities to ease the suffering of the children of mankind during this time of shift upon the earth. These who state that they serve God must always remember to serve him through his Will. And here in this 44th Decree we have the more practical aspects of how that is done: sheltering, feeding, nurturing, encouraging, counseling, protecting, defending, guiding and giving service…and all by God's words and authority *and not their own!*

(45)…until the Anointed High Priest of the Kingdom of God assumes full authority…Christ is the chosen High Priest of the Kingdom, anointed for the job by God himself. In the days to come, he will assume full authority. There will be no better teacher than this, no better example to follow as the reflection of God's love to help us help one another, for all of us are called to minister love.

CHAPTER 16

BOOK TWELVE – The Rainbow Act
Love Wins - The Shift into Timelessness

(46). I Decree as a Spirit of God born as a child of man full agreement and free will alignment to the completion and fulfillment of the Will of God as originally ordained, including the perfection of the children of man and all living creation in relationship to man and the earth, including the air, water and land.

(47). I Decree this soul's full agreement and free will alignment of full unity and communication through sacred interactions and sharing of experiences of Love's expansion and validation of answered questions in the Original Issues of the Sovereignty of God's Love over this soul and all creation as was commissioned and comes to be in perfect fruition.

(48). I Decree this soul's full agreement and free will alignment of the end and fulfillment of time and the never-ending expansion of timelessness and the full availability of mobility, unity, communication and interaction between all Spirit Beings and creations of the Love of God.

(49). I Decree this soul's full agreement and free will alignment to utilize all Divine Decrees and the Twelve Books of Acts of the Love of God to ease the manipulations and unHoly intentions toward the children of man during the end of time and the shift into timelessness, and to call in All Holy Angels assigned and give full authority and free will interaction to render harmless these manipulations and unHoly intentions toward this soul (and that of my husband/wife and those under my care) and to transform any unnatural manifestations and to purify and sanctify any and all movements of elements beyond normal measures and decommission, bind and encapsulate all unHoly Angels until the fulfillment of the Word of God is satisfied through the Warrior Son and his Holy Army.

(50). I Decree this as Binding on Earth as it is in Heaven by the alignment of the Will of God and man, bridging all past, present or future events, and the Prince of Peace of the Kingdom of God and his Holy Army will assume full authority and triumph victorious and return timelessness and rightful sovereignty of the Kingdom of God by the order of the Rainbow Act as ordained by the Blood of the Covenant as witnessed and given through the Holy Spirit by the Love of God, Amen.

(Visualization: Arrows like comets racing across the sky, all heading to a purified and sparkling earth. The sound of myriads of Angels singing. Colors: All the colors of the previous 11 Acts: white, yellow, orange, red, brown, green, blue, purple, black, gold, silver in a beautiful rainbow! Duration:12 days. Repeat the entire Rainbow Act in 12 days).

Understanding the Rainbow Act:

(46)…alignment to the completion and fulfillment of the Will of God as originally ordained, including the perfection of the children of man and all living creation in relationship to man and the earth, including the air, water and land…The Rainbow Act is a beautiful summary of what is happening now and what will be happening. This outlines several things; first, that we agree with God's Will for us and the original ordination of the purpose of mankind. Second, that it includes man's attainment of perfection. How about that! We will be in the place of perfection and we will be in a perfect relationship with the air, water and land. How many of us have longed for harmony with our environment? How many of us seek the serenity of nature unencumbered by the pollution resulting from man's poor choices and the manipulation of the unHoly Angels seeking to pervert nature? It will all be as Love originally ordained, as God had planned for us from the beginning. It will be paradise!

(47)...alignment of full unity and communication through sacred interactions and sharing of experiences of Love's expansion and validation of answered questions in the Original Issues of the Sovereignty of God's Love over this soul and all creation... In God's Kingdom there will be a oneness between God, his creation and one another that mankind has never known. In that place of full acceptance and encouragement, there will be cherished and sacred interactions and sharing of experiences between us all. In all of these, the ripple effects will be seen of what choices have been good, and which ones bad, and how God's love is always the best way to do things, and this answers without any doubt the original issues.

All the way through we have seen that these Divine Decrees are for the alignment of our will with God's Will for us. The unHoly Angels have been proven wrong by the sons of man through their many choices of love even in the midst of struggle. We have demonstrated throughout time that we come to God out of love and desire to do God's Will for us, and not just for what we can get out of God. We have demonstrated that man will face fear successfully and will give up the body even to the point of death instead of turning against God. This is yet another example that comes through those who are sharing with Love in the Holy Stigmata, turning their bodies over in surrender, to brighten and deliver his messages to the sons of man. Even in the midst of pain, though it may not go to death, it is experienced entirely yet the person experiencing it does not ask for it to stop. We have also seen how mankind cannot guide themselves successfully separate from God. Over and over we show that we need God! We cannot do it effectively apart from Love, but only with him. God in his eternal wisdom is once again proven victorious!

...as was commissioned and comes to be in perfect fruition... This is an underlying message throughout the Rainbow Act, we see glimpses of how things are to be, harmony, peace, unity, love. All of it will be the way God commissioned it to be, and it will be in perfect fruition. And these Divine Decrees are a gift from God to help us in the transition time, the time of shift until all these things have taken place. They help tremendously to ease the suffering of the children of mankind.

Many of us who long to do the greatest good for the greatest amount of people do so through these Divine Decrees, through the alignment of our will and God's, and through God's pronouncement, all those he asks, such as the Holy Angels, make it so.

(48)...I Decree this soul's full agreement and free will alignment of the end and fulfillment of time and the never-ending expansion of timelessness and the full availability of mobility, unity, communication and interaction between all Spirit Beings and creations of the Love of God... In this Decree we are agreeing for the end of this time of man's rule upon the earth and for the never-ending rule of God to be fully established. It is actually referred to as "the end of time," but only because we are moving into a greater expansion beyond time, and into "timelessness." Perhaps it could be compared to when you go on a vacation, and lose track of what day or even what hour it is, because it simply does not matter. In timelessness, we will have a tracking of the movement of experiences, but it will be totally different than how we view life right now. It will not be based on our limited perception of even the average lifespan of 70 years, of segments of time of growing up, maturity, and growing old. We are coming shortly to the end of time, but simply moving into timelessness – which is what we need to know and experience the giving and receiving of Love, of God and his continuing expansion.

In reference to the term "Spirit Beings," many people have questions regarding the existence of other beings, aliens, or extra-terrestrial life. It is critical to understand that yes, there are in fact other Spirit Beings (Angels are one form of Spirit Beings) and even more critical to understand that they are all under God's orders not to interfere with what is happening here on earth. The original issues put earth in a "holding pattern" until the issues were solved, and since the issues were presented about mankind and his choices on earth, the issues had to be solved here. The unHoly Angels know this rule is in effect, and have also been limited to the area of earth as well. (Revelation 12:12) They also know mankind has sought out evidence regarding life on other planets throughout much of recorded history. The unHoly Angels once again seek to pervert what is natural (such as the fact that other Spirit Beings do exist) and twist it to something unnatural that creates fear.

What most people think of as UFOs are manifestations that the unHoly Angels create to cause fear. The unHoly Angels prey on those who are afraid and who make their choices out of fear rather than love. The unHoly Angels seek to twist and pervert the information that yes, there are other Spirit Beings out there. The unHoly Angels want to make us question even the existence of God, and use these manifestations as a place to create all kinds of unnatural questions about how mankind has come to be upon earth, etc. As for the Spirit Beings, all of mankind will be able to share with them freely after this shift into timelessness, and not before. This time will come! This is one of the more precious parts of the Rainbow Act, the peeking into what is to be here on earth. This includes full mobility, unity, communication and interaction with all his children, whether originally created as Spirits of God born as a child of man, or Spirits of God born elsewhere.

(49)...alignment to utilize all Divine Decrees and the Twelve Books of Acts of the Love of God to ease the manipulations and unHoly intentions toward the children of man during the end of time and the shift into timelessness... The 49th Decree give us a look at the fullness of what we are actually doing through the Twelve Books of Acts of the Love of God – participating in easing the trauma upon the children of man during this shift. Calling in the Holy Angels is a huge part of what we are to do, and because of free will, our wording is important in this participation. We are not to do this on our own energy, for we are never alone and have energy beyond ourselves to accomplish great and Godly things. As for Holy Angels, our participation with them is crucial; we even start out with one assigned to be our personal Guardian Angel. The Holy Angels have many jobs, and we are to give them the opportunity to do even more with and for us: to assist, defend, guide and protect us. They are here to help us. Remember it is written, *"For he will command his Angels concerning you to guard you in all of your ways."(Psalm 91:11)* His Holy Angels are here to help us. Never be afraid to call in his Holy Angels, even stating "Father, send your Angels to help me," is sufficient. God is kind and merciful. God knows what we need and when we, through our own free will, ask for help. It will always be there!

...and to transform any unnatural manifestations and to purify and sanctify any and all movements of elements beyond normal measures and decommission, bind and encapsulate all unHoly Angels until the fulfillment of the Word of God is satisfied through the Warrior Son and his Holy Army... We continue on in this 49th Decree to say the main words found in a deliverance prayer. When we say this, we demonstrate our agreement of how Love handles the unHoly Angels. God is the one who is in charge. God wants all of his creation with him in the timelessness of love, and we are to trust in his timing no matter what. We demonstrate our faithfulness in the one who made us, the one who sent his son for us, the one who calls to us from behind the veil, our loving and true God.

God has allowed much to happen – the allowance of time so that the original issues may be answered for mankind, the Angels and all other creation now and to come. Also the allowance of time is further opportunity for more of the unHoly Angels to turn back to God, ask for his forgiveness and receive a new name. God is so loving. We, the sons of mankind have been saved by his son, the ransom sacrifice has been paid. It has been a different story regarding the choices of Angels, but the answer has been the same – God forgives and wants his children plugged back in to the power of love. He rescues all of us. And if we choose to align our will with his in The Divine Decrees, we get to participate in the rescue operation taking place even as we speak, of ourselves, all others, and the environment. All we have to do is ask. *"Because he loves me," says the LORD, "I will rescue him; I will protect him, for he acknowledges my name, he will call upon me, and I will answer him; I will be with him in trouble, I will deliver him and honor him. With long life will I satisfy him and show him my salvation." (Psalm 91:14)*

(50)...and the Prince of Peace of the Kingdom of God and his Holy Army will assume full authority and triumph victorious and return timelessness and rightful sovereignty of the Kingdom of God... The 50th Decree wraps up The Divine Decrees as they were given for the sons of man. Many will see and recognize another name for Christ, Prince of Peace. He has succeeded in the past and Christ will triumph victorious!

God's Workbook
Introduction to the Classes for Teachers and Students

This is a layout that we were given that will be helpful specifically for those teaching the classes. (1). We have outlined the purpose for the classes, (2). given some deeper information in regards to the classes, (3). then proceeded to the classes themselves. You can suggest to your students to read the lesson ahead of time, and the chapters on the specific Divine Decrees cited in the class as well. Then just use the basic outline to cover the information in class.

We always start with opening prayer to invite Love in, asking for assistance to open our hearts and minds, asking for assistance from the Holy Angels throughout the class to help us in our brightening. General statement as to this being a safe place, free of judgment where people can share openly without worry of how they will be perceived. A place for all to treat each other with love and respect.

Describing format, the one leading the class will speak on the topic for a period of time, then open it up for questions. Please hold all questions until it is time for sharing. In this way the necessary information is given without interruption. Suggested time format, speaking for 30-40 minutes, questions for 10-20 minutes, then break. During the question and answer period it is recommended that you (the teacher) remain conscious of time devoted to each question. You are responsible for keeping everyone on topic and helping them with relevancy. Always do this with love and kindness. Redirecting them back to the theme and helping them to integrate it is a wonderful way to build momentum. After the Q&A, a break of 15-20 minutes is suggested.

Remember that much more is happening here than simple sharing of information. We have invited God in and his interaction with our spirit has an effect upon us as well. We will be going through expansion, and the classes will feel like a healing time for many. Allowing break time assists the body in assimilation of the information.

You as a leader are to take a break as well during break time. This is not a time for one on one (though it can be done when necessary), it is suggested that you take your break, get some water, pray and listen for what Father has for you next. When you return and check in, ask how everyone is doing so far. Repeat that you will talk first and then open for questions. Keep aware of the overall structure and design: to build on their current strengths, encourage, love and guide. These classes are about aligning our will with God's Will and learning to hear Love's voice! They will be taught with love and respect for one another as well as for you and the information given. This is a supportive class and you will be required to balance these issues.

This is not a critiquing of where someone has been or what they have done in their lives. It is about meeting them where they are at, building their confidence and helping them to strengthen their connection with God, always through love, and never harshly or uncaring. We teach love through showing and being the place of love. This is not about tearing down or converting.

In going over the topic for the class, it is suggested to use illustrations to assist people with understanding. If you are comfortable with it, referring to scriptural examples will be helpful as well, *but* this is not a place to argue about interpretation. This is not about religion or controversy, but about Love, and it is important to bring students back to topic. Suggested format: topic; introspection; back to topic; showing relevance in our lives now. It is not just about sharing the information but helping everyone to see the importance of it, the usefulness of it and the strengthening it provides.

When possible, share relevant stories and examples that touch the heart of mankind; persuasive, compassionate and powerful experiences of love wrapped in hope – whether they be your own, ones you have read about, or the sharing of the students themselves. This also helps to touch their hearts and make them feel more comfortable about sharing their stories of love.

When reading The Divine Decrees, say them out-loud as a group, and have copies of them to pass out if they have not brought their own copy of _God's Workbook – Shifting into Light_. Giving students a copy of the each class outline helps them follow along too.

Throughout the nine classes you will be given time to utilize your interpersonal skills, drawing people in, using their names, making eye contact, using appropriate touch and having consideration for people in this safe space and their experience. It is about helping everyone to feel comfortable in sharing and referring back to their questions and the points they have made throughout the classes. For example, *"Bob made an excellent point with his question last class and we can see how it is important to remember that God loves us and actively seeks to help us receive that love"* or *"Georgia shared about what moves her, what motivates her heart to greater compassion and now we can see the importance of passion in this work."*

This helps them to feel confident about their contribution and see the importance of what they had to share. God is working on and through us all, and you will hear some beautiful gems spoken in these classes; God sharing in simple ways, opening us even more to his Holy love. In these classes, we are a microcosm of the macrocosm of love. All are worthy; all are given opportunity to see the love, to recognize Father and listen to what he gives to them in their hearts. We hope to touch their hearts, moving in love, directing a ship of love among life's stormy seas toward the port of safety we ourselves have found.

Throughout these classes it is suggested to pay attention to the overall attitude of the group, keeping your fingers on the pulse of those you share with, evaluating their comprehension and assimilation of what has been shared. See what stirs their emotions, what is helping and what isn't working as well. Address their concerns and questions, illustrating and refocusing when needed. Remembering as well that all are different, just as Father has blessed us with different gifts, we are also given different abilities to take in the information. Some will be strong visual learners and like to have visual cues, some will be auditory learners and do well with lecture/sharing and some will be kinesthetic learners and do well with movement and feeling, stretching and walking around. Pay attention to where everyone is at, trust in your ability to reach and touch their hearts.

Know that God is working with you seeking to share all that has been passed to us to share with *"all those who have ears to hear."* The information shared is like an electrical storm that strikes the sky of our spirit and must ground into our body. When we break and rest, stretch, eat and drink water, play and balance we place lightning rods in the brain giving the new energy opportunity to ground within our bodies.

Remember the difference between spirit and soul. Your spirit is who you truly are and can be used with or without a body. Your spirit is like a golf tee, stemming from your brain down your spinal cord. Many cultures have recognized the significance of these areas and treated them with respect. Your soul is the combination of your spirit and a body. We are allowed to be here at this time, specifically to assist all of humanity, easing the suffering of mankind in this time of shift. This is deep work we do! Those who repeat The Twelve Books of the Acts of the Love of God will feel the depth of this work. Those who take these classes recognizing the calling they feel to help at this crucial time will need to balance. Letting the body balance with the heavy duty spiritual work will be extremely beneficial. This will be mentioned specifically in the first class and it is good to remind of this throughout the classes that all may check in with themselves.

If we take the example of a teacher and a student as an illustration; the teacher takes information that is not easy to learn, simplifies the information so it can be more easily received and presents it to the student. The student now has the opportunity to assimilate it. It is the student's free will choice of learning or not, participating or not. The teacher has many students and knowledge will be given. It is a question of who is open to receive, apply and share the knowledge. What joy there is when a student understands! The student feels the success from having chosen to participate and follow through and the teacher feels the success for taking what was not, and transforming it so it is.

Do you remember your favorite teacher in school? How easily it comes to mind the one who cared enough to take time with you, to give you what you needed to understand, the one who supported you and encouraged you, believed in you and loved you.

We as the student are congratulated on our choice to participate but the teacher is glorified in the success of the student as well! This is how it is with Love. We do not do this Holy work for self glorification but for the Glory to be given to God. God is the one worthy of all Glory, honor and praise. Love is the ultimate teacher! We are blessed that God calls upon us to be his students, to pay attention to love and practice it, doing our homework. And the best part is - God doesn't grade us! He loves us perfectly and is joyful whenever we choose to recognize the way of love and choose the way of love, for in doing so, we choose God.

Illustrations are wonderful teaching tools, and what we just did is an example to help people to see the bigger picture (God and his Will being accomplished), draw upon their own experiences (thinking of their favorite teacher), see it all perfected through God as an opportunity (free will choices as a student) and the culmination of their efforts through his Holy Will in success! Many people will understand that you are teaching much more easily if you use illustrations. This is what Christ did as well. He used stories and parables illustrating the simple, common, everyday ideas and interactions of the time. Christ met people where they were at; we are to do the same. Christ taught through love; we are to do the same. Christ loved and offered opportunity for all those God brought before him; we are to do the same. By teaching in this example, we demonstrate our desire to love and honor God just as Christ did, in touching the heart of humanity in a way that is easy to understand and relevant to their everyday life and future life as well.

Another example of an illustration that can be shared in the classes is that of God being the ultimate romantic. Even if a person is not in a relationship at the time, each person has experienced love in some way. Drawing upon love and thoughts of love, especially romantic passionate love, helps people to relate. So we can understand God being in the role of the ultimate pursuer of our heart. How God calls us, asks us to share our day, seeks to hear what is important to us, to listen and be with us and to take care of things for us, leaving love notes everywhere in the hopes that we see them, a bird that flies to your window or a butterfly that lands on your leg. God can easily be recognized in the wonders of love. God as the ultimate, romantic lover of our souls, our spirits.

This is something that people can recognize and relate to, this is an example of bringing God through in a place of love so people can relate and grasp just how much he cares for us all, in human terms and experiences.

Throughout all the classes we will be underlining the awareness that although the dark is getting darker, the light is getting lighter and that Love Wins, and to have hope for the future, for the things to come are sure. Remember to illustrate the fullness of why all this is happening, what we are called to do, recognizing our purpose and making our conscious free will choice to participate and assist, in this story of God's Love. Free will is an extremely important issue that will come up many times in the classes.

Letting people understand the importance of not giving their power away, allowing that to be with God and no other, seeing the importance of saying The Twelve Acts of the Love of God according to the times recommended in The Divine Decrees, underlining our desire to align our will with God's Will. Using an illustration such as cleaning the dishes or cleaning our room. Do we do it just once? No, we keep using dishes, we keep using our rooms and through the use we have to take care of it to make it more functional and easier to be around. Explaining to people in simple terms like this is the same way we are needed to repeat the Decrees, we are still in a body, still here on earth, still making free will choices everyday.

Our focus with each class is that of love of God, and our neighbor as ourselves. We are to remember that in every class we can emphasize that this is about God and them. It is about *their* choices, *their* free will and *their* experiences with Love. Even if they fail to see the love in these classes, God will provide further opportunity for them in another way, at another time. You are offering a wonderful opportunity, but it is up to them to receive it.

Another teaching tool to share is the gift of discernment. Can we discern what is of God and what is not, what is of love and what is of fear? *"God is Love."* *(1John 4:16) The Divine Decrees* and these classes will help tremendously with discernment. Understanding that there is manipulation upon us from unHoly Angels can be a new idea for people, because most people acknowledge belief in Angels, but do not know there are two kinds.

Giving the information about unHoly Angels is simply for awareness, for when we know that we are under attack, we are then stimulated to utilize the tools to protect ourselves.

It is not necessary to know fear to know love or to know darkness to appreciate light. This is another falsehood placed upon mankind to keep us from the truth that we are loved and we are of love. An easy illustration to share about this is to picture ourselves as a baby in the middle of a circle of people, each one claiming to be our parent and yelling and screaming at us to crawl to them. These are all the unHoly Angels trying to confuse us. And there is our true Father, God, who simply smiles at us and knows that we will recognize him. He doesn't manipulate or try to out-scream the unHoly Angels; he just waits patiently, knowing we will remember his love and who he is. Our students are in the midst of it trying to figure it all out. You are helping them to discern who Love is. As soon they recognize him and freely make the choice to move towards him, he steps towards them, puts his arms around them and picks them up. He rescues all of us from false parents and false security. He brings us into the place of love and teaches us who he truly is and what he has for us. It is our job to discern what is of God and choose that love. God is patient. You as the teacher must be too, and help your students, even in their infancy, discern Love over fear. (2 Peter 3:7)

There are 9 classes to be taught over a 3 week period. It is recommended that there be a break of at least one day between classes. For example, a schedule might be Sunday 2-6 pm, Tuesday 6-9 pm, and Thursday 6-9 pm. Find a schedule that you can work with and one that helps as many people as possible to be there. Pacing and patience are essential. Remember this information is not just about learning, this information is also about your spirit and the expansion that takes places with this knowledge.

The classes are to be taught consecutively, since they build a foundation upon each other. The first class is a crucial part of laying the foundation for the others. In fact, if a person misses the first class, they are not to continue the rest of the classes. They must wait until another time. However, if they have taken the first class, they may miss a class or even two among the others and still continue.

131

It is highly recommended that they come to every class, since they are building a foundation for the further information. We start children with milk, and then the solid food comes later, we do not want them to choke by eating something they are not ready to assimilate. The pattern for these classes is not to be changed. It is easy to see that if we are open to receiving more fully of his work and blessings, we must first start with what is given and follow that.

*Teacher: <u>In the Layout of the 1st Class</u> we will be very specific with you, and from here we will just basically state the focus of each class. If you incorporate this outline and use this for the flow of the other classes, you will see great benefits. Here are suggestions for 2 other items unique to class 1:

<u>Write and Release:</u> Pass out a lot of paper and pens. Teacher and students write down all of their fears and worries, spending no longer than five minutes. When time is up, bring a trash can into the room, and have each loudly crumple the pages and throw away, and congratulate student's ability to bring out hidden fears and dispose of them. For all these things are not needed in this class. Now ask students to draw a big heart on another piece of paper, with their name in it. This class is about getting rid of fears, and transforming ourselves through love. You have just shown a literal example of this. Ask each to take this home, to color it and make it pretty, and to place it somewhere in their house or on their refrigerator to remind.

<u>Names:</u> Who you are and leading them in sharing their names. This can be done in a fun way, lightening up the first day, maybe by including their hobbies, pastimes or favorite things to do. A lighthearted introduction helps set the tone for people becoming more comfortable with each other.

At the end of the 1st class students will be given the opportunity to choose whether they would like to continue on or not. Those that are easily recognized by you as being of the 1/3 will not be allowed to continue and any remaining funds that covered beyond the 1st class will be refunded. Remember, these classes are being offered to those that are thirsting for the knowledge, hungry for God, and will not distract others from learning.

132

The First Class

Physical Healing and Breaking Generational Bondage

Focus: What are we doing today? This first class is all about personal strengthening. This is about you, your self, here and now, your body, physical healing and being open to cleansing off anything not of light and love.

Outline
I.   Introduction and Opening Prayer
II.   Write and Release
III.   Who are you? Names…
        Focus: confidence, personal strength
        Sharing importance of balance, what is spirit/soul
        Comments/Break
IV.   Today's topic, healing prayer and miracles
        The Divine Decrees
                The Transformation Act
                The Awareness Act
        Teacher Shares about Decrees
        Comments/Break
V.   Original Issues, Specialty Prayers
VI.   Teacher shares
        Comments/Break
VII.   Review
VIII.   Questions and Answers, students share
IX.   How this builds, synopsis on all classes to come
X.   Next class info… Closing Prayer

Opening Prayer: inviting Love in to help us, guide us, teach us and lead us. This will be the model every time, starting class asking for direction and to be open to Love. Remember this is not about religion, but an open expression of our heart-felt desire to connect and be guided together by the Spirit of God.

<u>Focus:</u> Outlining what the class will be about: clarifying structure and layout. Then opening with our first topic, healing of self. Before we teach this section of the 1st class on The Divine Decrees, we remind them that this is a personal journey, between them and God. They are to hold all things up and ask "is this of you, Lord?" This is about personal strengthening, their discernment of what is of love and what is of God. This is about their understanding of connection, the brightness of their prayers, their faith, the frequency and amplification of their prayers. *So much of this work has to do with confidence.*

In this first class we will address the issues surrounding confidence and help them to see themselves how God sees them, through the eyes of love and compassion, reminding them that God only sees the things of love that they have done, nothing else. God is there for them as a best friend, a confidant, a true love and perfect Friend and Father that will never disappoint. Building their confidence and reminding them that God hears their prayers. We remind them that God answers prayers in 3 ways: "yes," "not just yet," and "I have a better idea." This is an excellent tool to strengthen their relationship with Love. Helping students to recognize that we are each a spark off the Divine Flame, made in the image of God. We are more than what meets the eye. We are much greater, capable of fantastic things through love. Talking about how we were made by Love, through Love and for Love, and this is a time of being able to actively participate in seeing Love's transformation of ourselves, in even a physical way.

Interacting with Love is what heals us. This is an excellent place to explain how many of us are very good at loving our neighbors but lousy at loving ourselves. The Golden Rule says, *"love the Lord your God with all your heart, with all your mind and all your soul and love your neighbor as yourself." (Matthew 22:37-39)* God will not stay in a house where there is not love! If we are loving and caring, tender and patient, accepting and forgiving of ourselves, God has a place of love to reside in. For light and dark cannot exist in the same place, so the dark must either transform into light to stay there, or move away.

Bring the light of love into our hearts and be the place of love for ourselves, allowing love to flow in who we are and everything we do. This will help people greatly when it comes to receiving for many are familiar with the scripture, *"it is better to give, than to receive." (Acts 20:35)* But few know the importance of having the fuel for the vehicle, the air for the candle to burn. To do his Holy work, we need to receive the love. Being able to receive love even through the imperfect people around us, being able to receive Love directly, knowing we are worthy to be loved and opening our hearts to receive. This is our charge, to be the place of love for ourselves and our brothers and sisters, all through the one who taught us Love to begin with.

Balance is essential for doing God's Work! Even more so as we step up to greater responsibility and greater power. These bodies being a combination of our spirit and flesh. How our spirit lays like a golf tee in the body, on the head and down the spine. Talk about the necessities of taking care of these bodies, how we have to eat, sleep, exercise and balance these bodies. Explaining the 3 parts to the day: 1st part, active in body and in spirit, awake and alert, both body and spirit actively working. 2nd part, the balance time, as the day starts to wind down - an opportunity for the spirit to play, the body to do simple, easy, fun, repetitive tasks such as gardening, walking the dog, playing games or hobbies. Allowing for the spirit to relax and be playful, like a child. 3rd part, our body is at rest, sleeping and our spirit is in high active mode. This is a time when our spirit is working very hard, we are learning in night school, being taught how to handle things better and also helping other people. This is why it is extremely important to play during the day and have balancing time, for if we do not, our spirit is constantly working, day and night and we quickly burn out, feeling exhausted no matter how much we sleep we get, and feel overworked. We must let our spirit play during the day, or else it doesn't play at all. Comments/Break: of 15-20 minutes is suggested.

Today's topic: healing prayer and miracles. Sharing about physical healing, modern miracles, either sharing stories or testimonies of healings by Blessed Tiffany or other healers (either from books or websites) and then inviting experiences from students. More about balance, opening up to receive more that we may give more. It is not just about giving and giving and giving.

135

We are to fill from God, receive God's Love and his Holy Spirit, open ourselves to Love's blessings. Many have the desire to give and give but do it by their own power. It is essential, if we want to give, we must receive.

In receiving, sharing about how we are to receive openly, not to grieve the giver of all good things by not fully receiving the gifts. We are building a foundation that we may do the greater work, the bigger things, the things we dream about! In order to do this, we must have a solid foundation upon which to build our temple of love, we must have the pieces we need to step up to the greater things. This is a good time to do prayer for physical healing: have students place hands on themselves, where they want to be healed, or across their heart. Take a moment for their own silent prayer asking to receive healing Love, then teacher says out-loud prayer for healing for all. After, ask how many felt their hands get warm, or other sensations. Encourage them to heal themselves everyday, and it will get stronger for them as they brighten through the classes. Many examples of healing in *The Power of Divine: A Healer's Guide – Tapping into the Miracle* by Tiffany Snow (Blessed Tiffany).

In the bigger picture in relation to our self: the recognition that comes with our awareness that we are in charge of our choices, we are in charge of our responses and the speed we advance in our life journey. What blessings are upon us little ones to be given the opportunity to be present here on earth, especially at this time. Seeing how Love seeks to work with us, how God looks for us to be able to handle the amount of love needed to transform bigger things and even how God steps us through, bit by bit, step by step. We are given choices all along the way of how much we want to participate, how much we want to help and what we can do. All the while God is working with us to help us remember who we are.

The Divine Decrees: *The Transformation Act, The Awareness Act,* reading them out-loud together. Teacher Shares about Decrees. Letting them know as well that The Divine Decrees do not take the place of prayer, they are to be used with their prayers. Allowing those that are bright and of love to become stronger and create more love in the world!

Comments/Break: 15 - 20 min. Original Issues, Specialty Prayers: This will give everyone a foundation of understanding why there is evil in the world, what God is doing about it, what our part in this is, then we have the opportunity to help them to expand their awareness for what God has in mind for them. Three questions were raised: (1). Mankind can rule himself successfully without God. (Genesis 3:1-5) (2). Mankind only comes to God for what he can get out of God. (Job 2:1-10) (3). If threatened to his very life, man will always turn from his integrity and curse God. (Job 2:1-10)

Share about our free will choices, the bubble of protection that is our free will. Those who are helping God in this work, the Holy Angels. Why the deliverance prayer is necessary, attacks against health, finances and family/relationships. Speaking again on this work being active work, never passive. How we are to take action and not just write it off saying God will take care of it. As his children we have the opportunity to love, to share, to remember who we truly are and to bring about this love for all. Awareness for themselves of where they see this happening and letting them know that they have the tools needed to take care of themselves, those they love and many more. These tools include The Divine Decrees, and the specialty prayers.

Do the deliverance prayer, and the prayer for breaking generational bondage. Asking students to say "Amen" at the end is all that is needed for their agreement before God to receive these blessings: *Lord, I ask that any unHoly Angels in, on, near or around me be nailed, held fast and silenced. I decommission, bind and encapsulate them through the power of the Shed Blood of the Lamb and I bring them up to your Presence immediately to deal with as you see fit. May you fill any empty place or lonely space within me with your love and your light. Thank you Father, In Jesus' name, Amen.*

Lord, I ask that any generational bondage, all that is known, all that is stated here (state places of generational bondage-can be done internally without speaking it aloud), and all that is unknown as well, any curse, hex, spell, incantation, negative prayer or evil intent of any kind sent against me be null and void through the power of the Shed Blood of the Lamb and we send back love in return. Thank you Father, In Jesus' name, Amen.

137

Helping them to feel empowered, helping them to see their choices and the impact of their choices. This is a precious time for all these here to understand what they are actually being called to do, to be the place of God's Love here on earth. These prayers will help them with clarity as well. <u>Teacher shares, Comments/Break</u>: 15 - 20 minutes is suggested. Coming back with info on God knows it is difficult to see or hear him. Just as the leaves on the trees move, we know there is wind but we cannot see it. So it is with all of us. Love is the wind we cannot see. *"Faith is the belief of all things known but not yet seen" (Hebrews 11:1)* How will you let love and faith move you? How will your course be steered by Love, by God?

We are here as representatives of God, meeting people where they are at, accepting them without judgment, loving them, teaching them, encouraging them, strengthening them, preparing them and sharing with them as they brighten and transform. This is about our choices and the opportunities that God provides us with throughout our lives. This preparing that we do is like creating a sword. A metal sword is heated, removed from the heat, shaped, returned to the heat, removed, folded and shaped, heated again and so on. This is the process we go though in the classes, in doing his Holy Will, this is expansion and sharing in the opportunities that God has given to us as his children.

<u>Review:</u> Questions and answers, students share. <u>How this builds/ Next class info:</u> synopsis on all classes to come. Sometimes there will be simple and fun homework, but none today.

<u>Closing prayer</u> and congratulating everyone! You did it! Congratulate all for listening to spirit to be here. Encourage them to drink lots of water, rest, and play. Class will be like a strong healing, for much was covered, and much change will happen for them. Encourage bringing their own copy of <u>God's Workbook – Shifting into Light</u> into class with them. This will prepare them with more understanding and they will be able to read The Divine Decrees from their own book, and to write in any notes as well.

138

The Second Class

Healing and the Deeper Self, Emotions

Focus: *This class is about continuing to build upon the deeper self work. We are to receive so that we can give even more. We get to do this all through the eyes of love, compassion and forgiveness. From understanding the love upon ourselves and being open to receiving and building on our foundations. We learn to love and expand forth, love builds and grows. Concentric circles rippling forth, love ever expanding without end.*

Outline

I.   Opening Prayer, review of names
II.   Interests, self-benefit, motivation, worthiness
III.   How and why emotions affects everything,
        Why is this class so important?
        Comments/Break
IV.   Today's topic, healing the deeper self
        5 things to pray about for any situation:
        Discernment, Trust, Hope, Faith and Love
        The Divine Decrees
                The Arrival Act
        Teacher shares about Decree
        Comments/Break
V.   Superheroes and saving the world
VI.   Everyday heroes, confidence
        Comments/Break
VII.   Review
VIII.   Questions and Answers, students share
IX.   What do you see, what do you feel?
X.   Next class info...Homework: examining your relationships
XI.   Closing Prayer

Covering love and acceptance, why no one has the right to judge another, that is up to God.

"Who are you as a servant to judge another servant, that is the job of the Master!" (Romans 14:4) Explain the difference between having judgment and having discernment. This lays the foundation for the forgiveness class as well.

Confidence and reaffirming that they are loved and accepted by God just as they are. To have faith in themselves just as God has faith in them. For they are here on this earth because they have accepted a commission to be here, a specific purpose. Aligning their will with God's Will affords them the opportunity to hear his voice and know what he is asking of them. God indeed has a plan for them and seeks to share it with them, in their heart, opening them even further to his Love for them and their ability to choose his love. Reminding them to invite God into their day just as we invite God into every class.

Getting down to the issues of worthiness, acceptance of self and others. Contrast to earning acceptance in our jobs, education, etc. This is about God's unconditional love. We already have it. Example of a mother carrying a baby in her womb, baby is already and unconditionally loved, without having done anything at all. Go around the room and ask what is it that touches their hearts, what do they love, what would they like to see change the most in this world.

It is suggested in this class that some type of artwork experience be chosen, whether it is using colored pencils, markers, crayons or even finger paints! The key for this part is for people to draw themselves. Again, it is important to stress that all remember that this is not an art contest. This is a simple opportunity to see another view, to use another part of their brain and be creative. This is a great time for balancing with the work and an excellent way to pull people in. This is never to be forced upon anyone, just be presented as an opportunity. You as the teacher are to do this as well. Taking the time to go around and hear people describe their own pictures is listening them tell things that are precious to them about themselves. Suggested time for this depending on people there can be anywhere from 30min-40min. This is strongly recommended!

"Do not be anxious about anything but in everything through prayer and supplication, with thanksgiving, let your requests be known to God."(Philippians 4:6)

Now that people have opened a bit more, listening to where their may be weak spots in their armor of free will. It is detective work all the way through these classes but especially here, in this class, where we get to examine the deeper, emotional aspects of our lives. Where are their places without love or too little love? Where do people focus their energy? What do they spend their time worrying about? What else can they do to increase and utilize their faith?

This is what we will be polishing here in this class, aspects of self love that need to be strengthened. Seeking out the places in our free will, seeing it as a suit of armor, places where there may be gaps or holes. Strengthening our armor, *"Be strong in the Lord and in the power of his might. Put on the whole armor of God, that you may be able to stand against the wiles of the evil one. For we do not wrestle against flesh and blood but against principalities, against powers, against the rulers of the darkness of this age, against spiritual hosts of wickedness in the heavenly places. Therefore take up the whole armor of God, that you may be able to withstand in the evil day, and having done all, to stand. Stand therefore, having girded your waist with truth, having put on the breastplate of righteousness and having shod your feet with the preparation of the gospel of peace. Above all, taking the shield of faith with which you will be able to quench all the fiery arrows of the evil one. And take the helmet of salvation, and the sword of the Spirit, which is the word of God; praying always with all prayer and supplication in the Spirit, being watchful to this end with all perseverance and supplication for all the saints."* (Ephesians 6:10-18)

This scripture gives an overview of what is happening here in these classes. This is Holy Work we do. We recognize that this battle we are in is not against flesh and blood, not against ourselves, it is against the heavenly forces that fell, the unHoly Angels, those that seek to manipulate people in power, seeking to control and cause damage against mankind. This battle is against the darkness of this time.

141

We are clothed in his Light, protected in Love. Seeing our clothing as armor when it is of God, truth, righteousness, the gospel of peace, faith, salvation and the sword of the Spirit, which is the Word of God, Jesus Christ.

This is what we are called to do, to be the place of love, these are all aspects of Love: truth, righteousness, peace, faith, salvation and the Love of God through his Son. We are to understand the bigger picture and take steps to protect ourselves against the evil one and anything that is of him, which is anything that is not of love. This helps us to recognize as well that it is not by our power but by God's power. *"Not by power, nor by might, but by My Spirit sayeth the Lord of Hosts" (Zechariah 4:6)* Thus, we understand the importance that it is by God's hand we are given breath, life, love and the power to heal, assist, teach, guide, defend, protect, unite and be the fullness of what God has asked us to be.

Love has given us all gifts. God has blessed us with great abilities. We are given wonderful opportunities for participating, about using the gifts he has bestowed upon us. Read the Parable of the Talents. *(Matthew 25:14-30)*

This parable outlines talents/gifts/responsibilities that we are given. What do we do with them? Do we put them to use? Do we follow up on what we agreed to do? Do we be true to our commission? Can you see the importance of strengthening as a person? Can you see the importance of being the place of love? Can you see the importance of having discernment that you not be fooled, that you have the ability to hear God's voice and know his Will for you? Can you see the relevance of building your relationship with God, knowing you are worthy, and that you never have to earn this love, it is a free gift from a loving Dad? *"For we know love for he first loved us." (1John 4:19)* Can you see the necessary awareness of this love so we don't fall prey to damage from feelings of unworthiness?

We are all called to be the place of love. What is it about superheroes that is so exciting for us? Why does a child put on a towel and run around the room, jump off the furniture pretending to fly? Superheroes have gifts and powers. They can fight against evil and stop crime, making the world a better place. Here is something interesting to think about.

142

When a superhero first recognizes that they have a gift they are not that good at using it. We see in the movies and on TV how the superhero struggles when first learning but after patience and practice they strengthen their gifts. They literally become super-heroes. We are called to be a super hero everyday, using our powers for good rather than evil. We are all called to be the place of love. How do we do after recognizing our gifts and abilities? Do we doubt ourselves or our ability to wield the power of love? Do we doubt that we can be a hero to so many who are in need? Can we step up to the responsibilities that come with the gifts and power of love, the power of God that has been shared with us? Can we be an everyday hero?

This work takes confidence. We can be confident that we are worthy for we are made in love and for love. We can trust in the love that bestowed upon us love. This work takes recognition of the fact that we are already loved. Settling into God's Love. Now that we know that we are loved and that we never have to earn it (for no amount of good deeds could ever earn this love) we can move on to filling our cup at the wellspring of Love. We need not ever have fear in this work for *"Perfect love drives out fear." (1John 4:18)* This work is about receiving Love and offering ourselves as God's mobile sacred space where we can be placed as representatives of his love and light to dispel the darkness. Build confidence, congratulating for having come this far, and that Love is a pursuit that grows and builds, in excitement and joy.

Covering our connection and brightness in our prayers. When we have faith and confidence that our prayers are heard, we are bright! When we know that God seeks to communicate with us, when we trust in his love for us, when we see his patience with us and understand his forgiveness upon us and how as a perfect Father he continues to teach and guide us, then we are without fear and open to all that he can give us. Why is it that we love stories and movies about love winning no matter what? Why is it that we cheer to see love overcome adversity, to conquer struggle, to persevere and persist no matter the obstacle? It is because we all know that love wins. Have faith and confidence in yourself and God's ability to use you as a lighthouse of love shining on all!

The Third Class

Healing and the Family and Relationships

Focus: On our extended family, who we are, our connection and interaction. Distant healing work, compassion, quantum prayer and ripple effects, past, present and future.

Outline

I.   Opening Prayer
II.   How we interact with family, who is family?
III.   The facets of love we are polishing
       Comments/Break
IV.   Today's topic, healing the family and relationships
       Cosmic soup, indents and quantum mechanics
       Compassion and distant healing for family
       The Divine Decrees
           The Unification Act
       Teacher shares about Decree
       Comments/Break
V.   Community. Love and transformation
VI.   Difference between cry for help/transfer of responsibility
       Comments/Break
VII. Review
VIII. Questions and Answers, students share
IX.   Who are the 1/3, unpolished facets
X.   Next class info…Closing Prayer

We begin the 3rd class on family & relationships by speaking of love. In the first two classes we have gone over our own personal choices, our own health and the deeper aspects of our selves. We have focused on our physical and emotional healing laying the foundation for the greater things to come.

This 3rd class is an important class as it not only completes the process of building the foundation from the first 2 classes but when they understand free will and interactions on a personal level, in personal relationships and interactions it establishes the ability for greater comprehension and compassion for those whom they have never met and may never meet. Free will, how it works and the ripple effect of our choices upon our free will and the impact it has upon others is a powerful understanding.

It is essential for being able to do the greater work, to understand free will and how we interact with one another. We have discussed earlier how the unHoly Angels seek to attack a person in 3 places, health, finances and family & relationships. All throughout history, the unHoly Angels have sought to attack these 3 places to create manipulation, in an attempt to cause division, disharmony, fear, isolation, separation, doubt and anxiety. Family and relationships are something we all have in common. We can all relate to really trying to communicate well with another person, to establish good rapport and build a solid foundation of love to trust another and be able to share with them our hearts and what is precious to us. We can choose to experience life and share with it others, or we can choose pull away out of fear. We are in control of our choices. We are in control of our own free will. What do we choose, fear or love?

We continue with identifying who we consider family. Is it just our nuclear family? Are there others who are close enough to us that we consider them family? How about our close relationships? This is an excellent time to share the scripture that Christ spoke, *"who is my mother and who are my brothers?" (Matthew 12:48)* and Christ's reply in pointing to his disciples, *"Here are my mother and my brothers, for whoever does the Will of my Father in Heaven is my brother and sister and mother." (Matthew 12:49-50)*. Here we see the bigger picture about tying in peoples' free will choices and who we consider to be our family. This scripture shows the unity in all those who love and obey God, this is our Holy family.

Relationships, some of the deeper things…now is a great time to share more about facets of love. Who we truly are. Our name is much more than Jill or Bob.

146

We are all the facets of love that we have ever polished, throughout all our lifetimes! We are so much greater than we realize. In explaining the facets of love, start at the beginning, when we were first created. For God knew us from before the womb, just like when God spoke to Jeremiah *"Before I formed you in the womb I knew you" (Jeremiah 1:5)* We are all sparks off of the Divine Flame. We are here to learn about love and to reflect the love that God has for us to one another. We have lived different lifetimes, this is *not* our first time around. Before we came into the womb, we existed as a Spirit of God. We are now a Spirit of God born as a child of man. We come in with facets of love that we have already polished and some facets which still need polishing. We can work on these facets of love such as compassion, patience, kindness, tolerance, peace and so on through interactions with one another. How much opportunity we have to practice these facets of love through our family and those who are close to us! These are all good opportunities for us to polish these facets through interaction.

An illustration to understand this concept is rocks in a tumbler. The rocks get more polished as they have the friction of the equipment and other rocks around it. Our relationships serve one or more of these purposes: it is for *our* brightening; it is for *their* brightening; it is for *all involved* to have opportunity to brighten. When we are easily moved by Father it is a wonderful opportunity to be able to present love for one another that we can all know more about Love.

Today's topic, healing the family and relationships, how we have an indent to our family members, can use this for distant healing, laying hands on oneself for another to be healed, while keeping that person in mind. Teach about how we are all in this cosmic soup of God's love, but our indent is the compassion and connection we have to make change, and that connection to energy beyond ourselves. *Forward From the Mind – Distant Healing, Bilocation, Medical Intuition & Prayer in a Quantum World* by Tiffany Snow (Blessed Tiffany) tells in depth how this works, and gives a wonderful study of what happens during and after distant healing. Now follow as if for personal healing: have students place hands on themselves, where they want their loved one to be healed, or across their heart.

Take a moment for their own silent prayer asking to receive healing Love, then teacher says out-loud prayer for healing for all. After, ask how many felt their hands get warm, or other sensations. Remind them that receiving distant healing is a free will choice the spirit of the other person makes, so if their hands stayed cool, or they felt no sensation, that is OK too. We always make opportunity for Love.

Community. Sharing about the bigger family we are all in. Remembering that when one is harmed, all are harmed. When one is healed, all are healed. We are all in this together. Some will see love, some will not. We don't judge, just offer opportunity and continue to make our choices out of love. Our extended family is more than just our relatives; our extended family is all our brothers and sisters throughout the world.

Next, we lay the foundation asking people to remember any places of harm they have experienced through family, and to transform it transform it through prayer and to see it play out differently in their minds. Reminding them about holes in the free will and how to say Deliverance prayer whenever they feel heaviness and darkness. This is very much about each person in the class being able to heal and transform their own lives. But *we are not in control of is the free will of another person.* We cannot choose for them, even if they ask us to choose for them, even if they attempt to pass us the responsibility for their choices, they are still in charge of their own free will.

What about those who don't get it, who don't understand love and willingly depart from love? What happens with them? What are we called to do? We all have people in our lives that struggle with love, and it hits on one or more aspects: love of self, others or God. We are asked to show the way of love and be the place of love for one another – but we are not asked to do it for them, to make the choices for them. We all can benefit from recognizing the difference between a *call for help and a transfer of responsibility.* But we are called to be Christ-like. What does that mean?

An illustration to use: picture a person who is deep in muck and mire, surrounded by mud and filth. We are called to be at the edge, outside of the mud, with both hands open to them.

148

Like Christ, we are ready to offer assistance to those who recognize that they are swimming in muck and who want to get out. It is our job to offer help out of the filth, to give an opportunity of love. We are not asked by God to go down into the filth to help them out, for we would only get ourselves caught up in the grime, and this wouldn't help either of us. We are simply called to be at the edge, hands open, offering an opportunity. But there are many who are in the muck and mire who merely wish to pull us in rather than get themselves out. That is not what we are asked to do. Yes, we reach out our hands in love, but it is up to the person in need to reach up and put their hand in ours, there is a participation needed on their side. We are not to, and cannot, do everything for them.

It is also a demonstration of reflecting the perfect love of God by offering opportunity, but NOT by doing it all for them. There will be those that cry out saying "come in and save me, help me get out!" You cannot pull someone out, no matter how badly you want them out of it. They must make the effort to pull themselves out. It is not for us to do it for them. An honest cry for help is someone stuck in the mud, and when we offer, they willingly and with gratitude put their hand in yours, and come out of the mud. The transfer of responsibility is the one who cries, but doesn't want to do anything about it on their own, they want you to do it all for them.

Also, we must recognize that even if we want a person to "get it" and come out of the mud because they would be so much happier, etc, we cannot manipulate free will to try to force them. Just like God doesn't manipulate free will, and we can't either. We can only offer opportunity, and know that God will continue to offer opportunity to each one of these as well. We are each one of his kids, and he wants all of us to come up on his lap to be hugged. *But each one of us is responsible for our own choices.* No matter how great our desire, we can not manipulate another or use fear or intimidation to teach about love, it is contrary not only to the purpose of teaching through love but contrary to the message of love itself. We are to do only what our Heavenly Father does, offer opportunity for all to recognize the way of love, and then follow through on our responsibility of choosing it as well.

149

We are told that when we pray for another person that it is as if the path that they are walking on now has flowers. The more we pray, the more flowers there will be on their path. No matter how many flowers are on their path it will always be their choice of looking at the flowers and seeing the love or not seeing the flowers and continuing to struggle. We cannot walk on their path and push their heads into the flower; that is manipulation. We simply put more flowers that no matter where they look they may have opportunity to see flowers and see love! This is always a place people have questions, so take a break for questions here.

Reminding about the facets of love we have all had opportunity in each lifetime to polish. Talk about those who continually chose each time, fear over love, and they will not be able to learn about love in this one lifetime, especially with the greater manipulation that is upon all of us. These 1/3 are those who haven't chosen to polish the facets of love, those who are lazy in spirit, those who seek to have others do the brightening for them, and who want us to get down in the muck with them. These 1/3 are the ones who see themselves with this attitude: "me against the world, kill or be killed." They are easily manipulated and used like pawns by the unHoly Angels to create problems, cause disharmony, distrust, fear and suffering. Know that God loves these too, and we are to love and pray for them as well. God has shared that these will not be able to learn enough about love to brighten quickly at this time of world shift where things are speeding up, so we are to focus on those that recognize love and truly are crying for help. Not for us to do all things for them (transfer of responsibility) Right now we are not teaching people to have faith but what to do with their faith. There will be a great time for teaching these later, when there is no manipulation or distraction upon them.

This understanding of manipulation by the unHoly Angels also sets the stage for the next class about forgiveness and vulnerability. All have the opportunity to learn from God directly. Those who know love will recognize love, as Christ spoke: *"I am the good shepherd, I know my sheep and my sheep know me."(John 10:14)*.

150

The Fourth Class

Forgiveness and Vulnerability

Focus: Learning how to truly forgive ourselves, others, past experiences. A healthy, safe, open and trusting environment to receive and heal!

Outline
I.   Opening Prayer
II.   Why forgive?
III.   Manipulation, curses, perfection
        Comments/Break
IV.   Today's topic, forgiveness and vulnerability
        Forgiveness as a part of healing self, others, situations
        The Divine Decrees
                The Forgiveness Act
        Teacher shares about Decree
        Comments/Break
V.   Healing past experiences
VI.   Vulnerability in marriage and relationships
        Comments/Break
VII.   Review
VIII.   Questions and Answers, students share
IX.   Examples of forgiveness, vulnerability
X.   Next class info…Closing Prayer

This class is about learning how to truly forgive ourselves, others and situations. It is purposeful that this class follows the course on family and relationships.

After our opening prayer, we check in how everyone did with the last class on family and relationships. This feedback will be a direct link to what needs to be addressed in this class on forgiveness. Remind everyone this is a safe place to share and we are not to judge one another.

We are not to judge one another or our families and relationships. We simply teach about love and the way of love. Each of us has to choose how we apply this in our own lives. We remind each one of the fact that people have free will in forgiveness and vulnerability too, and that these choices have ripple effects for us, our free will and those around us. This puts the responsibility where it belongs, squarely upon our own shoulders. This class will examine the ripple effects that come with poor choices that we make, that are made toward us or with us, and what to do about it.

This work of love requires an awareness of others and their impact upon us. We are not asked to isolate ourselves on a mountain away from others to live a perfect life. We are asked to be the example of love in the midst of all that goes on around us. Since we are all imperfect, this requires forgiveness.

Forgiveness. Are any of us perfect? Do we all make perfect choices all the time? Do we always act out of love and treat ourselves and others with respect and care? No. Are we going to be perfect now in the midst of all this shift in the world where the dark is getting darker and the light is getting lighter? No. We don't have to be perfect! That is not what is being asked. We are asked to be the reflection of the love of God. It is up to us to polish the mirror, who we are, to reflect this love the best we can. The time for perfection will come.

Forgiving. Knowing that none are perfect and that we don't always make the best choices for ourselves or with others, we can have gentleness and compassion towards all. We can allow for healing to take place, for love to flow in. When we do not forgive, we hold this weight upon others and upon ourselves. It is like an energy spider-web that attaches from us to them or that situation, and whether we are aware of it or not, it drains us to keep it going. Unforgiveness is a big deal. Unforgiveness is just shy of a being considered a curse. This is how strongly it is viewed by God. When we don't forgive, we create a situation that doesn't allow for healing for us or the other party. We know we should forgive. When we hold unforgiveness, we know we are doing something we shouldn't be doing, and it is considered "willful sin."

152

This is shown as a huge place of manipulation through which the unHoly Angels can cause us great harm. It is written *"Forgive one another, as you are forgiven." (Colossians 3:13)* When we forgive, it allows for healing to flow in and close these holes.

We are given great examples in scripture about forgiveness. Jesus said *"Do not judge, and you will not be judged. Do not condemn, and you will not be condemned. Forgive, and you will be forgiven. (Luke 6:37)* See for more examples: *The parable of the unmerciful servant. (Matthew 18:21) The Lord's Prayer, "Forgive us our trespasses as we forgive those who trespass against us."(Matthew 6:12) "If he sins against you seven times in a day, and seven times comes back to you and says, "I repent" forgive him. (Luke 17:4)*

Remember the experience that Blessed Tiffany had when Christ was upon the cross, and Jesus said: *"Father, forgive them for they know not what they do." (Luke 23:24).* One of those who had tortured Christ was there at the foot of the cross, and he had an evil grimace on his face – then when Jesus prayed for forgiveness, a dark shadow moved out of the person, and a face of child-like innocence appeared in its place. We can forgive because we are aware of the puppeting and manipulation that occurs on people.

As Christ showed forgiveness for these people and asked that God do the same, the unHoly Angels left and the Holy Angels came and supported these people. That is the underlying beauty within forgiveness that we allow for healing, light and love to be sent in! Christ in speaking this phrase *"for they do not know what they do"* also gives information about manipulation and how people fall prey to it, sometimes without their knowledge. When we forgive, love flows in to heal. Whether a person knows or not that they were manipulated by the unHoly Angels to say or do something hateful or harmful, love still flows in! We can be a healer for ourselves and others through forgiveness. We have been given the power to forgive sins just as our sins are forgiven. *"Bear with each other and forgive whatever grievances you may have against one another. Forgive as the Lord forgave you." (Colossians 3:13)*

These examples are powerful and make it clear! We are to forgive. Now you know some of the deeper aspects as to why. Here is another, when you forgive and you know that you are forgiven, you recognize the redemption of mankind through God's Love and the passion, suffering and death of Christ. All our sins were nailed to the Cross. We have been forgiven. Can we recognize this, and not judge our neighbor and forgive, and allow for healing to take place for all involved? We have the ability to do so - do we have the courage as well? Without forgiveness, we will never heal; and this affects us physically, emotionally and spiritually.

We forgive 3 ways:
1. Forgiveness for all others involved
2. Forgiveness of self
3. Forgiveness of the situation

These are the basics for forgiveness. We have known about the first one, forgiveness of *others*. We add to that our forgiveness of our *own* missteps, our own erring. Asking God for forgiveness when we have sinned or missed the mark. And finally, forgiveness of the *situation* itself. The situation carries a charge, emotions and attachment. We are to let go of this and transform it by bringing love into the equation. We know that people can be manipulated, ourselves included. Whoever is making a choice out of fear rather than love can fall prey to being manipulated by the unHoly Angels. The unHoly Angels can attempt to manipulate us directly or use those we love.

An excellent example of this is to ask about a common theme we see in mafia movies. Who does the mafia send to do the hit, to kill? They send the one that is not going to draw suspicion; they send someone who is close and well loved. This is how the unHoly Angels seek to get us if they cannot get us directly, they come indirectly. The unHoly Angels will try to manipulate those around us and use them against us. This is another reason why we forgive, for when we do we close the door on past hurts and allow for a healing to take place for ourselves and all those involved. This is about being able to recognize any holes in ourselves and sealing them up through forgiveness and allowing for healing for not only ourselves but all others involved.

154

At any time, especially for those that have struggled with forgiveness, it is recommended that they do not do it on their own. We can ask God to be there with us, to help us to forgive. Many people ask "how do you forgive them if they are dead or if you cannot get in contact with them?" Asking God to step in and assist with the forgiveness is how! *"God alone knows the hearts of man." (2Chronicles 6:30)* God will help with this. After you ask, let it go.

To heal past experiences, having the courage to offer forgiveness to those who are still alive by speaking the words to them aloud is a powerful message. It is not just about the message of forgiveness but being able to say it, no matter how difficult. And it doesn't matter how the message is received, for that is not your job. We cannot make someone forgive us, we can only ask. As well, whether we ask for forgiveness or offer forgiveness we have chosen the way of Love. How or if it is received is up to the other person. The way of love is granting forgiveness as we are told to do. Asking God to help in the scenario that it may be received well can help tremendously. Remember that no matter what, we choose the way of love for that is the way of God.

Forgiving the situation is an important aspect to pay attention to as well. An analogy to use here is that of weeding a garden. If anyone has ever weeded a garden they will have seen more than one weed. Forgiving the situation is weeding the whole garden. The situation itself carries an emotional charge. If you feel yourself getting upset again by just thinking about the situation, there is more forgiveness that needs to be done; there are more weeds. If you think "I can forgive them but I will never forget what they did," then forgiveness of the situation needs to be done.

Can we see the choices of love amidst the confusion, amidst the anger, amidst the high emotion? Can we be the love that is needed to diffuse the situation, to bring love and healing to all those involved? Can we be the place of love and forgive one another as we are all forgiven by God? Remembering *"who is a God like you, who pardons sin and forgives the transgression of the remnant of his inheritance? You do not stay angry forever but delight to show mercy" (Micah 7:18)* and knowing that we are called to do the same.

155

Vulnerability. Being vulnerable to love, being able to be easily moved by God and his Holy Spirit. An illustration to use here is that of a leaf floating on the wind, carried and directed by the wind. It is okay to be vulnerable, to risk, to put ourselves out there and believe in Love. He will never let us drop.

Vulnerability to love is essential to our work for God. We must be able to be open to love even in imperfect relationships. God loves us in the midst of our imperfections, and asks us to love one another in their imperfections as well. We often think we have to be perfect to be loved. We have to look a certain way, dress this way or that, own or live here or there, have this kind of education, etc. Many people do all they can to hide any imperfections, for to them it is a vulnerability that may lead to not being approved of or loved.

Think of what it means being intimate with another person. How each lies naked next to another and shares what means the most to them, sharing who they are, their dreams, ambitions, thoughts, emotions and there own essence of self. This is vulnerability, being able to share this even though there is a risk that we may be rejected, even though our trust in sharing our deepest thoughts and feelings may be betrayed, choosing love no matter what. When we go into a relationship with this kind of trust, it can become a place of such great love that it will transform and heal our previous relationships as well, because we have learned to trust in love again. None of this happens without being vulnerable.

Can you love another who is imperfect like you? Can you allow yourself the vulnerability to open your heart to another, to trust another? To love even in the face of fear? This is what is asked of us everyday. Can we forgive? Can we trust even if we have been harmed in the past? In relationships, we have the opportunity to polish many facets of love, including forgiveness. Do we trust love enough to let another imperfect person close enough to us to experience this?

Here is a good place to mention that God never asks that we remain in an abusive relationship. It is not our job to fix another person. God wants us to be able to experience joy and love. Abuse is not a part of love.

In being able to recognize love and choose the way of love, this means showing love to ourselves as well, respecting the gift of life and not putting it in harms way.

Vulnerability and surrender to love is what being a mystic is all about. Think about others throughout time that have been vulnerable. How about Mary, the Mother of Jesus? Can you imagine being a very young girl and having an Angel of the Lord come to you to announce that you will carry the Savior of the World? She was living in a time when people were stoned to death for having sex before getting married. She was promised in engagement to an honest and upright man, and he knew they hadn't been intimate yet, so Mary would come under disfavor in his eyes. All her family members would be confused and upset. Can you imagine the vulnerability to answer "yes!" to God knowing that you will undergo such persecution? Yet she still surrendered herself to Love and continued to be vulnerable and follow his commands. Many are called to do great things. Many throughout time have answered "yes!" to God no matter what others may say. *Can we do the same? Can we open our hearts to love no matter what?*

Some will want to hold onto unforgiveness and will encourage you to do the same. Some feel that they must remember and hold on tightly so that the hurt doesn't happen to them again. It is as though they are putting up bricks around their heart, to protect themselves. But what really happens when we do this is that we don't end up protecting ourselves at all, but we end up isolating ourselves in a prison of our own making. Let down the bricks, be vulnerable in love, forgive and know you are forgiven, and don't have to be perfect either. Then you will know the true strength that comes in being vulnerable, in being humble, in being able to love, to forgive, to answer yes to God and to do what you came here to do. And you will see the ripple effect in your physical, emotional and spiritual health, and in your increased ability to hear clearly the words of God in your life.

Here is a visual aid to work on forgiveness. Get a drinking glass and turn on the faucet to a slow drip. Place the glace under the faucet and say all the things you experienced from a hurtful situation as if the person was there.

157

When you have filled the glass, turn it over, pour out the water and say the words, "I forgive you, and I forgive myself." Repeat this as many times as you wish. This is another example of forgiveness and the rinsing clean that comes with being able to forgive.

The Fifth Class

Angelic Protection in Past, Present, Future Events

Focus: How to protect ourselves, calling in the Holy Angels for past, present and future situations, listening to Divine intuition.

Outline
I.   Opening Prayer
II.   Forgiving our enemies, God's forgiveness
III.   Sounding the battle call, Divine intuition
        Comments/Break
IV.   Today's topic, protection of self, family and relationships
        Responsibilities of Holy Angels and you
        The Divine Decrees
                The Protection Act
        Teacher shares about Decree
        Comments/Break
V.   The story of God's love and the Angelic brotherhood
VI.   What happens to the unHoly Angels
        Comments/Break
VII.   Review
VIII.   Questions and Answers, students share
IX.   Additional information on Deliverance Prayer
X.   Next class info…Ongoing homework: anytime anything
        comes against, do the deliverance prayer. Closing Prayer

Recap from last class. How did everyone do with forgiveness? How do we all feel about vulnerability? How did it go for everyone? This will be a time for people to be able to see why the previous classes were essential in helping us to build to this place. In this class, we are asked to forgive those that we do not know, those that have committed atrocities upon mankind, and those who have done heinous crimes against humanity. We must be in the place to love without judgment, to strengthen one another and encourage one another in love and through love.

159

If we struggle to do this with those that we love, how will we do with those we don't even know? *"You have heard it said, love your neighbor and hate your enemy. But I tell you: Love your enemies and pray for those who persecute you, that you may be sons of your Father in heaven. He causes his sun to rise upon the evil and the good, and sends rain on the righteous and the unrighteous."* (Matthew 5:43-45)

This is what we are called to do. We are called to love and to forgive and to pray for those who persecute us. But if we struggle to do this in our own families, how will we be able to do this for the world? That is why we must be in a place of vulnerability and forgiveness even in our desire to be protected, for we are not the ones defending ourselves, but the Holy Angels are sent to do so for us.

As an example, perhaps a family member gets robbed. We have two basic choices – we can take action with love or do the opposite of love. If we choose love, we will spend our energy comforting the family member, making a police report, and thanking God that something worse had not happened. We also pray ask for Holy Angels to be sent to help the one(s) who committed the crime to give more opportunities for better choices, and we send forgiveness to them.

Why? Because if we leave this place of wounding exposed, it will become a large hole and much damage can occur there. Remember that even though the unHoly Angels look to break us, most of the time it will end up being only a bruising because we have been using The Divine Decrees and our prayers. This is why we can be thankful to God, for he sees the bigger picture, and much protection has already occurred for us that we probably won't even know about until later.

How deep is God's love? Remember that he asks us to love and forgive any who have harmed us. Would God ask us to do anything that he himself is not willing to do? No! God wants *all* to know that he holds love out to them, and wants all who are choosing darkness to turn from their ways and come back into a life of love. This includes the unHoly Angels themselves.

What do we need to do in all this? We align our will with God's Will, and this action of ours becomes a mighty battle call, for now we have trumpeted the horn for action and the swords that are used are not of our own, but carried and used by trained Warrior Angels, Holy of God!

As you continue to utilize The Divine Decrees, much expansion will happen with you. Your awareness, clarity, discernment, gifts and abilities will help you to receive more and more information from Love about what is going on, or about to go on, in your life, in your family's lives, and even the world. This is part of becoming the mystic as well. You will be able to hear more and more on your own. With this Divine intuition may come feelings or information about events or places, or of timing of things. For example, perhaps you always go to the store for grocery shopping on such-and-such day, at such-and-such time. One morning you just get a "bad feeling" about doing it. Something inside you just doesn't feel right about it, so you decide to heed that message, because you have developed more trust in yourself and the Love that made you, to listen to these whispers of intuition. Later, you find out that a major car accident occurred right when you were going to go, and you avoided a five-car pile-up of fire and destruction.

Now what if you had dismissed the feeling and gone ahead anyway? The Holy Angels would have a bit more work to do, and would continue trying to influence you to heed Love's call, to avoid the situation at all. But if you ended up being there, they would be battling fiercely for your protection. Yes, it is better to avoid a situation to begin with, but God does not give up on us and say, "well, we tried to tell her!" His love and protection goes much further than that. When we say the Protection Decree, we are asking for greater discernment to recognize any situations of harm, but we are also granting the Holy Angels free will interaction to step in and do whatever is needed for us. This includes sending protection backwards and forwards through time as well!

Teacher, review chapter 3 for more information about Angels, and chapter 8 about the Protection Act. Remember that the Angels that have chosen to be true to Love, 2/3 of all of them are helping God's Will to come to fruition.

The 1/3 of the Angels that fell (interesting how this corresponds to the 1/3 of mankind who are manipulated away from discerning love) are seeking to cause as much destruction and damage as they can to God and what he loves, because they know the court case is closed, they lost, and the time is short. The unHoly Angels are still Angels, and still have the gifts they were originally created with. The reason they are not as powerful as the Holy Angels that still serve God is not because there are fewer of them, but because love is stronger than fear. When each Angel decided to unplug from God and go their own way, they also unplugged from Love, and no more growth occurred for them. Remember that God continues to expand, Love continues to grow. So because of their choices, they have been left alongside the road, as the rest of the parade continues to move on.

This is one of the reasons why, when the unHoly Angels take Love up on his gracious offer of coming back into the Angelic brotherhood again, that they start at a place of lesser responsibility. One of the reasons is because they have to catch up.

They are now limited to the earth, because the original issues were raised here, and had to be solved here. *"And there was war in heaven. Michael and his angels fought against the dragon, and the dragon and his angels fought back. But he was not strong enough, and they lost their place in heaven. The great dragon was hurled down - that ancient serpent called the devil, or Satan, who leads the whole world astray. He was hurled to the earth, and his angels with him...Therefore rejoice, you heavens and you who reside in them! But woe to the earth and the sea, because the devil has gone down to you! He is filled with fury, because he knows his time is short."* (Revelation 12:7-9, 12)

The unHoly Angels know that the time is short. The marketing and advertising program of brainwashing people against the belief that a personal God *exists,* let alone loves and cares about them, is fully underway. Since they cut themselves off from love, a gang-mentality reigns among them, so they war against and manipulate one another too. They fight over areas of the world and they fight among themselves like ravenous dogs.

162

Because they cannot die, the pain they feel and make for one another makes for a tortuous existence of their own making. All along the way, the unHoly Angels have been warned to not cross certain lines. And all along there have been those who don't really think any consequences will come from their behavior. Because of this attitude of audacity, many have been removed from the scene all throughout time. Those who cross line have their Holy brothers to contend with. Love sends his True Sons to take these fallen ones out of commission. God sends the Holy Angels by his own request, *and he sends them in request to human prayer as well.* This is why our prayers and The Divine Decrees are so important, and to do them consistently in the times suggested.

The unHoly Angels do not go willingly, and the Angels that Love calls to do this work have the rank and responsibility of Warrior Angels. The unHoly Angels are placed in a confinement where they can do no harm to themselves or others; it is like a large sheet of glass that they can see out of, but cannot move. They have no further interaction with other unHoly Angels, the line of communication is completely broken; and they have no power to manipulate anyone or anything, or to be manipulated by each other. From this immobile position, they can clearly continue to see the outworking of God's love upon mankind and the earth. They are not tortured. A God of love would not do that. And even in this state, we are still in the period of time that all they have to do is say the word, and God will welcome them back.

But when all is said and done, there is a time when all decisions are final, and there is no place for anything not of Love. Energy cannot be destroyed, only changed. So there comes a moment when the energy that the unHoly Angels were given in wave form is now turned into particle, and they will then simply become a part of the ground the earth is made of.

The deliverance prayer: *"Lord, any unHoly Angels in, on, near or around (my brother...or my sister ...), I nail, hold them fast and silence them. I decommission, bind and encapsulate them through the power of the Shed Blood of the Lamb and bring them up to your Presence immediately Lord to deal with as you see fit. May you fill any empty place or lonely space within ... with your love and your light. Thank you Father, In Jesus' name, Amen."*

The Sixth Class

Healing the Environment

Focus: On information about storms, what they really are, how to manifest change in weather conditions worldwide. Healing for the air, water and soil.

<u>Outline</u>
I.   Opening Prayer
II.   What is our environment?
III.   Nature, the natural, and the unnatural
        Comments/Break
IV.   Today's topic, healing the environment
         Why nature?
        The Divine Decrees
                The Purification Act
        Teacher shares about Decree
        Comments/Break
V.   How we share in earth re-creation
VI.   What happens with faith
        Comments/Break
VII.   Review
VIII.   Questions and Answers, students share
IX.   Holy Angels, 4 in the Earth, 1 in the center
X.   Next class info…Homework: transforming and erasing clouds
XI.   Closing Prayer

Our focus in this class is about the earth and our relation to the earth, and also about connection and the interconnection of all things. Exploring the ripple effects of the things that are happening in the world, the increase in awareness of the impact upon the environment and what can be done to fix it. We are to remind all those in the class that God doesn't cause harm to teach a lesson. Love doesn't bring on disaster to teach us and he does not teach through fear and intimidation.

Just about everyone is aware of the interconnectedness of life. We can understand how cutting down more and more trees has an impact on the amount of oxygen in the air, which in turn affects the ratio of oxygen and carbon dioxide and nitrogen. We know the oxygen gases have an effect upon the temperature of the air and on the ozone layer itself. We have seen the impact of global warming; the polar icecaps melting; the increasing temperatures of the ocean drastically affecting the sea life and all that is dependant upon it; the patterns of streams of water and storms and the increase in pollutants in the air, water and the land.

What most have difficulty realizing is that these environmental problems are about much more than just the interaction of mankind and the environment, they are also about the impact of the unHoly Angels upon both man and the environment. *Whenever nature is perverted and becomes unnatural, the unHoly Angels are twisting it. Whenever there is loss of life due to the effects of weather or "mother nature" the unHoly Angels are distorting it. Whenever there is destruction and desolation the unHoly Angels are behind it.* Remember that the unHoly Angels are seeking to not only harm us but to harm even more of God's creation, namely, the earth. Many times God has stepped in to put a stop to their plans to cause massive destruction and death. Many times God has sent his Holy Angels to protect and defend us, his little ones.

People think of natural disasters as God's way of cleansing the earth. Not true. God decreed one flood upon the earth for a specific purpose and God even stated that he would never do that again: *"Never again will I curse the ground because of man…never again will I destroy all living creatures as I have done." (Genesis 8:21)* Love seeks to protect us and assist us.

God gives us the opportunity to learn from what is happening in the world. Many throughout time have bought into the manipulated idea that we have to be stimulated by fear to seek out love. This is not correct.

166

People can be intimidated easily by weather and the environment. We only need read the news to see how somewhere in the world there is damage due to an earthquake, a volcano, a tsunami, storms, floods, droughts, fires, and much more. We are all asked to recognize that these are not of God. Would it make any sense for God to give us a beautiful place to live and co-exist with the animals and nature only to rip it apart and destroy it? Certainly not.

In recognizing that the unHoly Angels are behind the manipulation of our environment, we must examine both the direct and indirect methods they use to harm this gift of the earth. They seek to create problems with manipulation of things that have no free will of their own, such as storms and winds. But they also seek to manipulate mankind into making bad choices in respect to the environment, and then they magnify that by perverting what is natural and twisting it that it cause even more harm.

We were shown that the earth could cleanse itself of the pollutants that mankind dumps into the air, water and land if it was left without manipulation. The unHoly Angels take advantage of what man has produced whether it is from fossil fuel emissions or other sources and they twist it to make it worse. They seek to manipulate the molecules to make it even more dangerous to mankind. We can see this through the example of acid rain. Without the direct manipulation of the pollutants in the environment the air and water by the unHoly Angels, the water would cleanse itself and it would be purified. But the natural process is twisted so that it is unable to return to its former state and causes great harm instead.

In first recognizing that God is not to blame for the "natural" disasters we can address the bigger issue of *what can we do to transform our environment?* This is where it becomes even more exciting. We have seen that we cannot manipulate free will, that we cannot force another to see the ways of love. Even God has not violated free will and allows for all of his children to come to him on their own. The fun part about things within the environment such as storms is that *they have no free will of their own.* When you pray for a storm to be transformed the effect is immediately felt, *there is no delay or rejection due to free will.* We can have an immediate and powerful impact upon our environment just from our prayers. This is fantastic!

167

We are given the ability to calm the storms, just as Jesus did: *"Then he got into the boat and his disciples followed him. Without warning, a furious storm came up on the lake, so that the waves swept over the boat. But Jesus was sleeping. The disciples went and woke him, saying 'Lord, save us! We are going to drown!' He replied 'You of little faith, why are you so afraid?' Then he got up and rebuked the winds and the waves, and it was completely calm. The men were amazed and asked 'what kind of man is this? Even the winds and the waves obey him!'" (Matthew 8:23-27)* How beautiful that we were given an outline of this long ago that through our words and faith, we can effect such great change!

It is suggested to take a break here, let the class have this resonate with them during their down time. Upon returning to class, right away we follow up with the scripture when Jesus was speaking to the Apostles, *"The words I say to you are not just my own. Rather, it is the Father, living in me, who is doing his work. Believe me when I say that I am in the Father and the Father is in me; or at least believe on the evidence of the miracles themselves. I tell you the truth, anyone who has faith in me will do what I have been doing. He will do even greater things than these, because I am going to the Father. And I will do whatever you ask in my name, so that the Son may bring glory to the Father. You may ask me for anything in my name, and I will do it." (John 14:11-14)*

This is the hope and faith we can have. This is one of the reasons why when we end our prayers including the phrase, "In Jesus' name," there is additional power given, which will be addressed in the next class. Faith is the recognition of knowing that changes really occur when we ask for them, that they have happened before, and will happen again. *"Now faith is being sure of what we hope for and certain of what we do not see." (Hebrews 11:1)* Faith will enable a person to be able to do what Christ himself did while here on earth, miracles! This is what is given to us, the ability to ask God to transform, to purify, to heal, to be free, to love and be loved. Demonstrate your love through your prayers to transform, heal and purify our earth.

168

Remind everyone that it is not about completely erasing the energy, for we know that energy cannot be erased but it can be *transformed*. Physicists have shown for years that matter can be altered and changed. This comes into play when we ask an enormous rainstorm be transformed to a drizzle that lasts over a couple of days, instead of being an overwhelming downpour that the ground cannot absorb. It is about transformation, not stopping it; it is about bringing it back to the natural. This is also a place of recognizing we can transform severe weather and tragedies of the past. Right up to the point of death itself, everything can be changed!

There are specific Holy Angels that we are asked to keep in prayer daily, they are asked to bear a great responsibility, and much is placed upon their strong shoulders. These Holy Angels are in charge of protecting and defending the earth. We are asked to keep them in prayer and support them with blessings, and this is a wording for this prayer: "*We pray specifically for blessings upon the 4 Angels of the earth and a double portion for the Angel in the center of the earth that they too may be faithful and true to their commission.*" By keeping them in prayer daily, we show our love and support for these that step in frequently through the love of God, to keep this earth from being destroyed. There is much more that is happening beyond what we can see. Remember, this is not an easy time for The Holy Angels either. They do not like to see the darkness upon what Love has created. This is hard work and all of us can use support and love, even the mighty Holy Angels. Love is plentiful and can always be shared. We will not run out of it! *We can also pray for the 1 Holy Angel assigned to the moon and for All Holy Angels that assist Love every day.* Remember, we are all in this work together. Both Angels and humans are part of God's creation. When we align our will with God's Will we are in the place of unity and support with all those who love and serve together.

Homework assignment # 1.

*It is suggested that all in the class pick someone they know and ask them about an event dealing with the weather/environment that has happened to them. *Get the information about what it was, a storm, a flood, etc. and listen to the person's story detailing the event. *Next, when you are apart from the

169

person, pray about it. See it being transformed, asking that less damage be done, that more people are aware of it ahead of time, that more people have the opportunity to get to safety, that there is less peripheral damage. *Use as many senses as you are able to integrate, putting a fan in front of you while asking the wind to die down, running the water at the sink while looking for it to lessen, whatever will help you to visualize and be a touchstone to transformation. *Lastly, go back and ask the same person about the incident again. See what has changed in their story, and they may not even know it. God will allow you to keep the memory so that you can see the transformative power of prayer but their memory of the incident will be shifted just like the incident itself!

This is a fantastic way Father grants us a demonstration of not only the power of our prayer but the opportunity to receive the feedback and see how truly powerful we are in changing past events. We have the opportunity to transform not only the present storms and past, but future ones as well!

Homework assignment #2.

*It is suggested that all those in class take the opportunity to pick a small cloud. *Once they have the small cloud in mind, ask God to erase the cloud with them. *Use any technique that is simple and easy to visualize, whether it is a pencil eraser or chalkboard eraser or even a breathe blowing through and dispersing the cloud, there are no limits with your creativity and joining with God to do this. *Look again at the cloud, is it still there? Does it need more erasing? Can you find it?

Love will show you his power through you. God started the entirety of creation by first sharing with another who came to be known as Christ. *"Through him all things were made; without him, nothing was made that has been made." (John1:3)* Since Love made everything with Christ, using the name of Christ for something to be remade or transformed also demonstrates a unity with God, the realization that all things were made by God, even the things that the unHoly Angels seek to pervert. Recognizing this fact and stating it in our prayers to transform strengthens the prayers. We are so loved that we are asked to be part of the re-creation of the world.

The Seventh Class

Christ, the Apostles, Holy Spirit, Saints and Mystics

Focus: On being a mystic. The mirror reflection of these greater things, the unveiling of Love beyond religion, who is Christ, gifts of Holy Spirit, attaining personal and experiential knowledge of God first hand.

<u>Outline</u>

I.   Opening Prayer
II.   Beyond great teachers
III.   Foundations and redemptive Grace, completion
        Comments/Break
IV.   Today's topic, Christ, Holy Spirit, saints
        Who Christ is, teaching the way of Love
        The Divine Decrees
                The Salvation Act
        Teacher shares about Decree
        Comments/Break
V.   Walking the way of hope
VI.   Love beyond religion
        Comments/Break
VII.   Review
VIII.   Questions and Answers, students share
IX.   Incorporation and fullness
X.   Next class info…Closing Prayer

Review homework from class 6 first. Today: Love beyond religion. There are many who have had empirical experiences with Love; whether by visions, Holy Angel appearances, near-death experiences, or numerous other ways of God making connection with mankind. Love has always wanted to answer our questions, and let us know he not only exists, but that he wants to fully interact with us, and to encourage us and help us remember who we are and what is going on.

When a person has an empirical experience with God, knowledge beyond what they were taught by others, they are often called a mystic. Since God wants all of us to hear him and build a personal connection with him, we are all called to become a mystic. The brighter we become, the more God can experience life through us, and the easier it is to hear him with clarity. There are many examples throughout history of clear thinking, for we can see people reflecting God's love throughout thousands of voices, to recognize love and treat one another with love. Love will always be the message of the mystic, for love is the message of God.

Love wishes to share with us continually, so we have answers for one of the basic questions humans have. "Where do we come from?" We come from God, as sparks off his Divine Flame; we are made by perfect Love. Humanity started with one couple, Adam and Eve, who were made of the earth and made perfectly as well. They had free will just as the Angels did. When Adam disobeyed God, humanity's light was dimmed from that one choice. God is of perfect Light and Love. Light and darkness cannot be in the same place together. So from that moment on, there was a separation between us, we could not be in the perfect Presence of Light, it was not possible for us, for we were now imperfect, and in darkness. There was now a dent in the mold of humanity. A parent can only pass on what they themselves have. No matter how much we tried, no matter how many lives we lived, we could not overcome the sin that lay upon us from our forefathers; it was like a generational bondage upon us. We could never polish even the basic facets of love. It would have been an existence of never ending struggle without brightening. But God had another idea in mind.

There is a perfect exchange in Love. That is why in perfect balance, "an eye for an eye" rings true. God had warned our original parents that sin (missing the mark of perfection) brings death. Yet, they unplugged from Light. *"The wages of sin is death." (Romans 6:23)* So to balance this for humanity, another man who is perfect must pay the penalty for sin, and die. This would then break the bonds of death, for a perfect man did not deserve it, and perfect law meant he would have to live again. This perfect man could not be found among Adam's kids. We could however have a Savior, one who could do this for us. It had to be another perfect son of God.

172

*"This is love: not that we loved God, but that he loved us and sent his son as an atoning sacrifice for our sins."(1 John 4:10)*Jesus Christ was the first-born creation of all that God created, he was the first born, the perfect one, he is also the one formerly known as Michael the Archangel. This is why all the Angels know him, and why the mention of his name, especially now since his fulfillment of redeeming mankind, carries great weight and authority. This is why we use discernment and ask all Angels or spirits that visit us, "Do you love Jesus now?" Because at one time they all did, but the only the Holy Angels and those that God sends are able to continue to say "Yes!"

"In the beginning was the Word, and the Word was with God, and the Word was God. He was with God at the beginning. Through him all things were made; without him nothing was made that has been made."(John 1:1-3)

One of the more beautiful things that we have learned through the Holy Stigmata is that it was Christ who approached God and asked if he could be the one to go down and break the barrier of death. *"This is how we know what love is, Jesus Christ laid down his life for us. And we ought to lay down our lives for our brothers."* *(1John 3:16)* For God it was an act of love in sending his first-born son, and an act of love in Christ's desire to go, continuing his perfect existence here on earth, including faithfulness through death. He could have made other choices. Being perfect, if he had chosen to have a family, and because of his genetic superiority his children would have lived forever. There would be another race of humanity on earth. But this would not have saved original mankind, and it was not according to the purpose and Will of God. So Christ was obedient, even to death. He was not thinking of himself, but of others.

"For God so loved the world that he gave his gave his one and only son that whoever believes in him shall not die but have eternal life." (John3:16) Prior to Jesus' surrender of his life for all our lives, all those that died with sin upon them would be reborn over and over again, to polish the basic facets of love to be able to complete their mission on earth, but none could ever do it.

Christ was the karmic redemption, he brought us all back before the Light, he broke the generational bondage upon us passed down through the poor choices of Adam and Eve. This is what is meant by the shattering the shackles of death. Christ freed the slaves from bondage. Since his death, all those who have polished the basic facets of love now can come before the face of God, we are light again that can be near the Light. In this place of Light, we are given choices, which include whether to come back to life on earth again or not, for there are many freedoms as children of Love. Yet many have come back to earth, even though they did not need to for they have polished the basic facets of love. They are here to help with this specific time of shift we are living in. And it was their free will choice of love that compelled them to, and in doing so they are following Christ's example of love. *"Love one another. As I have loved you so must you love one another." (John 13:34)*

Does it make more sense how Christ is greater than any one religion? This is not just for those who are of a specific faith, for God existed before religion and will exist long after religion. This is for all humanity. All the sins that were upon humanity were nailed to the cross and hung on the one who never sinned, Jesus Christ. This is also why people of all religions are getting Holy Stigmata, because Christ opened the door for all mankind, not just one religion. The Big Guy wants all his kids up on his lap.

The examples of who Christ is and what Christ did are all throughout scripture. These are the deeper things shared that you may understand what has been given to us, what we have been blessed with already! All of us are redeemed through Christ. He is the one who opened the door for us to come before Light again. We see this in Hebrews 4:14-16, *"Therefore, since we have a great high priest who has gone through the heavens, Jesus the Son of God, let us hold firmly to the faith we profess. For we do not have a high priest who is unable to sympathize with our weaknesses, but we have one who has been tempted in every way, just as we are - yet was without sin. Let us then approach the throne of Grace with confidence, so that we may receive mercy and find Grace to help us in our time of need."*

"Let us make man in our image." (Genesis, 1:26) Christ is the *"us"* and the *"our."* Christ was there for the beginning of creation. Knowing this helps us to understand how all this comes together. The Holy Stigmata, the deliverance prayer, the prayer for breaking generational bondage, the recognition of asking "in Jesus' name" these are all the places where we see the Glory of the Lord. This is where we gain understanding. *"Father, I want those you have given me to be with me where I am, and to see my glory, the glory you have given me because you loved me before the creation of the world." (John 17:24)*

"It is not to angels that he has subjected the world to come, about which we are speaking. But there is a place where someone has testified: "What is man that you are mindful of him, the son of man that you care for him? You made him a little lower than the angels; you crowned him with glory and honor and put everything under his feet. In putting everything under him, God left nothing that is not subject to him. Yet at present we do not see everything subject to him. But we see Jesus, who was made a little lower than the angels, now crowned with glory and honor because he suffered death, so that by the Grace of God he might taste death for everyone."(Hebrews 2:5-9)

Here we see the Glory of God bestowed upon Christ, once an Angel, the first creation, Michael and was made a little lower than the Angels, made into man. Christ fulfilled God's Will for him here on earth *"and was crowned with glory and honor and everything was put under his feet."(Hebrews 2:8)*

Christ is the one who opened the door for us back to God. Now you see why the unHoly Angels can do nothing to besmirch the love that Christ fulfilled by being true to God's Will for him. No matter how much blood the unHoly Angels seek to shed upon the earth, it will never wash away the blood of Christ that was surrendered, not taken from him. Can you see why the Holy Stigmata is being shared with so many world-wide, so all may know where Love comes from. The Holy Stigmata always comes with other corresponding gifts of the spirit as well, that is how we can see it is from God and not from men.

This is a good place to ask questions and take a break. Upon returning from break, checking in with everyone. Ask how they are doing with the information. We have found that many people find it much easier to understand the message of who Christ really is after having this information added. Now many will understand better the reading of The Salvation Act.

So, now armed with the information of who Christ truly is: we can have a greater understanding and acknowledgement of the love of God, the power of the name of Christ, why we call on the Shed Blood of Christ to break generational bondage, curses, hexes, spells, incantations, negative prayer and evil intent. We can also grasp the power of why it is through the act of salvation, through Christ choosing to lay down his life for us by surrendering his blood for all of humanity. Jesus followed through on his commission, on what God's Will was for him. We have the power of choice to also align with the Will of God and follow through. Christ's example can inspire us follow through on our commission, to do what we agreed to do before even coming into a body. It is exciting and awe-inspiring how we are not only redeemed by Christ but that Christ serves as an example of how to live in vulnerability and love.

We were shown in the Holy Stigmata just how loving and compassionate Christ is. We were shown Christ's great desire to fulfill God's Will and to do it so well that no questions could ever be raised about the mission. *"An angel from heaven appeared to him and strengthened him. And being in anguish, he prayed more earnestly, and his sweat was like drops of blood falling to the ground." (Luke 22: 43,44))* This is how passionate, this is how honorable, this is how perfect, faithful and loving Christ is as our Savior and Redeemer. He had so much power to stop the situation and save his own life, but he was more dedicated to doing the mission and doing it well. Much was at stake on heaven and on earth.

This is truly good news, a message of love and hope, a call to look beyond the darkness and know there are wonderful things going on and we are part of it. The Apostles were called by Christ to *"Go into all the world and preach the good news to all the nations."(Mark 16:15)*. The Apostles were not the first to preach the good news, nor were they the last.

176

Prophets like Isaiah were asked as well *"The Spirit of the Sovereign LORD is on me, because the LORD has anointed me to preach good news to the poor. He has sent me to bind up the brokenhearted, to proclaim freedom for the captives and release from darkness for the prisoners, to proclaim the year of the LORD's favor, and the day of vengeance of our God, to comfort all who mourn."(Isaiah 61:1-2)* In this message from Isaiah we can see that the good news is the salvation of mankind to be brought through Christ, to help those who are in despair to have hope for what is to come. As well, Isaiah speaks about freeing the captives, releasing the prisoners from darkness. Can you now see what deliverance work is? It is freeing the captives, delivering them from the evil one. And Isaiah goes further and speaks of God's day of cleansing, to rid the "world" ("cosmos" Greek. Means "surface arrangement") of all the unHoly things in it that it may be able to attain the original purpose that God intended for the earth and all of humanity in it.

People are still being asked to share God's love and be the place of love for one another. We are still helped and encouraged by God to do so. God still sends his Holy Spirit upon us to do his Will and to follow through on our purpose of love. There are those who receive the Holy Stigmata that they may have the deeper information directly through God about what is happening at this specific time. Many are those who have the courage to live out a life of love rather than fear. Many are those who are not afraid of what people in the world think of them because they know that it is more important to please God. We all have gifts, and there are many kinds of gifts and ways to use them. *Psychic Gifts in the Christian Life – Tools to Connect* by Tiffany Snow (Blessed Tiffany) shares many games to access your sensitivities, and how they might be utilized. If you look, there are stories everywhere about God's blessings of upon people. Many of us have more than one gift as well. But it does no good unless we share the fruitage of the gifts with one another!

This work of sharing Love continues on. All those who have lived Holy lives have stood up in the face of adversity, have stood out from what the world thought of them and have courageously faced down darkness. All of us are asked to do this work until the shift is complete. All of us are asked to point to the open door, and be fearless in our work, for even death is not what it used to be. We are free to go to Love. Once more, Love Wins!

The Eighth Class

Everyday Life and Abundance

Focus: What moves us to greater compassion, what touches the heart of man and how pray for it. How and why we can pray for abundance in all things!

Outline
I.   Opening Prayer
II.   What is abundance? For whom? Why?
III.   How to attain and maintain
        Comments/Break
IV.   Today's topic, everyday life and abundance
        Why compassion in business is essential
        The Divine Decrees
                The Abundance Act
                Teacher shares about Decree
        Comments/Break
V.   How to share abundance
VI.   Abundance of gifts, examples
        Comments/Break
VII.   Review
VIII.   Questions and Answers, students share
IX.   The news, whose news, the noose and good news
X.   Next class info…Homework: news as a prayer list. Closing Prayer

This class is about love and the overflowing of love. Start out asking everyone this question: What is abundance? The answers will help you to see where people have been focused on abundance for not only this class but for ages. Remember, the unHoly Angels target finances as one of the big three places to attack, health, finances and family/relationships.

After hearing from several people on how they view abundance, we can bring them into the broader perspective of love.

Many people think of abundance and immediately go to the thought of money, though abundance is about more than finances. Look at what God is sharing with us now: the abundance of love that is always present for us, signs and wonders such as miracle healing, our body and the spirit within this body, this earth and all the natural things in it. We have the gift of connection with God to further our experience of love and to be able to share love. There is much!

But abundance *also* includes money, and money is not evil. Many people have confused the *phrase* of "money is the root of all evil" with the *scripture "for the love of money is the root of all kinds of evil." (1 Timothy 6:10)*. There is a difference here in the wording. Money is a place of trade, and is a very useful tool necessary to provide things that we need such as shelter, food, and clothing. The idea of money has been manipulated all throughout time. The unHoly Angels have used it to prod humanity into committing many grievous sins, by perverting the balance of it, by either too much or too little. Money is *not* the root of all evil but the *love of money* can lead to many problems.

The scripture goes on to say more about money and balance: *"But godliness with contentment is great gain. For we brought nothing into the world, and we can take nothing out of it. But if we have food and clothing, we will be content with that. People who want to get rich fall into temptation and a trap and into many foolish and harmful desires that plunge men into ruin and destruction. For the love of money is a root of all kinds of evil. Some people, eager for money, have wandered from the faith and pierced themselves with many griefs. But you, man of God, flee from all this, and pursue righteousness, godliness, faith, love, endurance and gentleness. Fight the good fight of the faith…Command those who are rich in this present world not to be arrogant nor to put their hope in wealth, which is so uncertain, but to put their hope in God, who richly provides us with everything for our enjoyment. Command them to do good, to be rich in good deeds, and to be generous and willing to share. In this way they will lay up treasure for themselves as a firm foundation for the coming age, so that they may take hold of the life that is truly life" (1 Timothy 6:6-19)*

This is an encouragement to place our hope in God, not in money. This letter speaks of richness in good deeds, generosity and sharing. This is how God intended for us to be with one another, sharing. This love in sharing is the theme we have seen throughout these classes.

We have seen how those that are easily manipulated by the unHoly Angels, those of the 1/3 view money. They view it as a never being enough and that they must fight to get their share. This is contrary to what God tells us and what God shows us. Love is all about abundance, *God never puts just one wildflower upon a hill!* And we were created to have lives of abundance in all things.

Because of this, we are encouraged to go to the source of all good things and ask for help when we need it, and not to take the things that belong to another. God gave us the Ten Commandments that we may be reminded of the basic knowledge of what to do and what not to do. *"Thou shall not steal."(Exodus 20:15)* Stealing is spoken of many times: murder is stealing the life of another, coveting what belongs to another, whether it is property or whether it is their spouse (adultery). When we take from another, we demonstrate that we do not believe in a God that provides for us all but we instead think that we must take from another to get what we need or what we want. This is not what God tells us, we are asked to come to him, and the things that are good for us will be provided. What areas in your life are in lack? In prayer be *specific* with your needs and requests, and then look for the Divine opportunities placed in front of you. Give *God something to bless,* and you will see the power of Love in abundance! Remember that God answers our prayers in 3 ways: "yes," "not just yet" and "I have a better idea than that." This means it is also alright to ask God what you need to do his Will. Love will give you all that is needed, including his strength to follow through on the purpose and plan that both of you agreed to for this life before you were even born.

In addressing anything to do with money, it is important to do it with peace and Grace. Again, humanity has been worked over again and again by the unHoly Angels in all places of finances.

181

We do not have to look far to see the gap that continues to grow between those who "have" and those who "have not." This is a place that the unHoly continue to create problems seeking to further divide humanity to create division and separation, to make people think that they have to take from one another rather than just receiving freely from God. Thankfully, Love has a built in plan that is sure to ease this suffering, it is called *compassion*.

When we have compassion it is easier to see what is happening and step in through love to help. So what can we do with all we have learned to help those whose abundance is being manipulated? This is what we are called to do: let our hearts be moved! When we have found treasure, we are asked to share it and let others know where to attain it themselves. Many are the treasures that have been given to us, and with whatever we have, it is still enough to share. This is not just about material gifts, but our spiritual gifts as well. Here is a beautiful example of this: *"One day Peter and John were going up to the temple at the time of prayer at three in the afternoon. Now a man crippled from birth was being carried to the temple gate...when he saw Peter and John about to enter, he asked them for money. Peter looked straight at him, as did John. Then Peter said, "Look at us!" So the man gave them his attention, expecting to get something from them. Then Peter said, "Silver or gold I do not have, but what I have I give you. In the name of Jesus Christ of Nazareth, walk." Taking him by the right hand, he helped him up, and instantly the man's feet and ankles became strong. He jumped to his feet and began to walk. Then he went with them into the temple courts, walking and jumping, and praising God. When all the people saw him walking and praising God, they recognized him as the same man who used to sit begging at the temple gate called Beautiful, and they were filled with wonder and amazement at what had happened to him...When Peter saw this, he said to them: "Men of Israel, why does this surprise you? Why do you stare at us as if by our own power or godliness we had made this man walk?...It is Jesus' name and the faith that comes through him that has given this complete healing to him, as you can all see. (Acts 3:1-16)*

We all have gifts, share them! Encourage others to see their gifts as well, and of the good news and hope you have learned.

Many feel hopeless and helpless about their lives and the world, and see no way out of being oppressed physically, emotionally or spiritually. You have much treasure now that has been given to you. Are you going to make others decisions for them by pre-judging what you think they will say or how they will react to your words? Are you going to recognize the one who is in need, yet pretend they don't exist, and walk on by because of your own fear? We are activists. Love asks us to be active in our faith. This is what *"loving our neighbor as ourselves"* means.

The news. The news is your prayer list. It couldn't be any clearer that the dark is getting darker than when simply watching or reading the news. We are called to use the places that touch our hearts the most, so that we may be able to pray for them and all may be transformed through love. For as much as the media focuses on what is wrong in the world and all the darkness that goes on, there is much love in the world that is not shown. There are many of us Love has been using for change in the world. Remember the fullness of the message: the dark is getting darker and the light is getting lighter, Love wins and to have hope for the things to come!

God has told us *"see, I have carved you on the palm of my hand." (Isaiah 49:16)* This means that God never sets us down, we are always held by God. How reassuring! So even if all around you seems in darkness, *you are held by God.* Even if all that surrounds you seeks to intimidate and bully you, *you are held by God.* Even if you see suffering all around you, *you are held by God.*

We are not called to simply ignore the darkness and pretend it doesn't exist. This is what the unHoly Angels are looking to manipulate us to do. We cannot be shut down by what is happening in the world, we are called to be moved by the things of the world, *not overwhelmed by them. Do not let the news be a noose around your neck.* We have to be able to respond to what is happening out of love, no matter what is happening. So read some of the news, allow it to be a touch-stone for you to do the greater work of transformation. Let your compassion be moved. Ask God to send the Holy Angels to the place you see or to the tragedy you have just witnessed. God has the power, you have the opportunity to ask that it be done, that love be applied like a healing salve.

Do not allow yourself to be shut down by the darkness in the world, do not let yourself be intimidated or take yourself out of the active role of recognizing an indent to help facilitate your power of prayer. All God is asking is for you to recognize what is of love, and what is not, and allowing healing to take place.

You can always ask for these 5 things to be shared in any place of darkness and it will be helpful: Hope, Trust, Faith, Discernment and Love. All will be needed. It is important for people to know to have hope for what is to come. We are never to be in a place of hopelessness for this is where the unHoly Angels seek to place us that we may take ourselves of the ability to be utilized by God to transform. We are to ask that trust be there as well, that people may not be smacked around on the trust in relationships from person to person and in their ability to trust in their relationship with God. Faith is extremely important to be an added component wherever there is darkness that all may know that God did not cause harm or teach through fear. God always teaches and offers opportunity through love. We must continue to have faith and to put our faith into action transforming fear to love and darkness to light. Discernment, a very important ingredient. We are all called to discern what is of God, what is of love and what is not. Discernment is a vital key to avoid the traps of manipulation that the unHoly Angels seek to lay for us. We must have discernment and be able to recognize the manipulation sent against us to do our prayers, ask God for help and clarity, to know what to do and then to do it!

Lastly, and as emphasized in the previous four steps, we are to ask that love be where we have seen the harm and the fear. Let love cover and coat these places and these people involved, their families, the survivors, loved ones and all those impacted by the ripple effects that the darkness has perpetrated upon us. We are all in this together and when we ask that love be sent to a place damaged by the unHoly Angels, we help the people there and offer an opportunity to the unHoly Angels themselves who pushed and manipulated people to see that love wins, no matter what! We teach through love. Be the love we wish to see in the world, we send love, pray and connect through love, be the place of love, transform through love and heal through love. This is the good news! And it is all about Love!

The Ninth Class

Politics, Religion, Commerce & Prophecy – Things to Come!

Focus: This class is focused on those in power in 3 major areas: religion, politics and commerce. We will also be sharing information about what is to come, Prophecy!

Outline
I.   Opening Prayer
II.   Religion
III.   Politics
        Comments/Break
IV.   Today's topic, politics, religion
                The Divine Decrees
                The Representation Act
                The Hierarchy Act
        Teacher shares about Decrees
        Comments/Break
V.   Global responsibility, prophecy
VI.   *The Rainbow Act*
        Teacher shares about Decree
        Comments/Break
VII.   Review
VIII.   Questions and Answers, students share
IX.   Transforming the world
X.   Last class…info on Called and Commissioned, Closing Prayer

This is the final class of the 9 classes and it will focus on the areas of religion, politics and commerce. What we have learn from the previous 8 classes is the power of free will, what we are called to do, how we can transform all things through prayer during this time of shift into timelessness.

Note: It is very important to remember that this work is not about stopping the shift, it is not about having perfection right now, that will come.

185

This is about damage control! We are looking to ease the suffering that we know will be occurring. We have already been told about the shift that is coming and many are already aware of the Second Coming of Christ. This work is not about a doomsday mentality or to prevent Armageddon from happening or to bring it on through the hand of humanity. This is about how to make it through and working side by side as participants of change with God and the Holy Angels.

The focus for this class is on those who are in positions of power in politics, religion and commerce. The unHoly Angels seek to cause great destruction and try to prove that fear is the way to rule, not Love. The unHoly Angels seek to cause the largest negative ripple effect possible to harm the greatest amount of people. So they look to manipulate those who are in charge of making decisions to enact policies that are detrimental to our wellbeing. If they can manipulate people to control the laws, rules and ways that we live then they can manipulate and cause more damage to a greater number of people and the environment. The negative ripple effect is much more than just one on one, it can be huge!

Can you see why those in power are under the greatest attack? Those in power are prized territory for the unHoly Angels to try to manipulate. These that are in positions of power have no idea of the onslaught that comes against them daily. Ever wonder why those that go into politics have things that they say they will do prior to coming into the position *and then* they do something different once they are in the position of power? Ever wonder why so many renege on their promises of change and growth, peace and prosperity? This is why those in positions of power and authority need our prayers. It is never about tearing down but always about building up!

Think about the general consensus of how people talk about those in power. Yes, there is a recognition that those in power are not making good choices but it goes beyond that. People start to attack those in power, they ridicule and slander those in power. Generally, the public is upset about why people in power make choices that don't benefit the greatest good but only a select few. In fact, in any social gathering people will tell you that the two topics that most people do not like to discuss are religion and politics.

186

Why? These are charged topics and people get very emotional in talking about them. Politics and religion are hot topics and always have been throughout history. These have always been places where the unHoly Angels have sought to manipulate with fear.

Now you know the inside scoop about what is happening and what has been happening: *manipulation.* Now, picture that the number of unHoly Angels that come against those in power. Those in positions of power need our prayers for support of the Holy Angels to assist them in the ongoing battle.

Picture an even larger scale of destruction. If one person who is in charge of a country can be manipulated to instigate an attack or a war against another country there is a ferocious chess match going on behind the scenes. Remember that the unHoly Angels are looking to spill as much blood as they can, that the unHoly Angels are seeking to keep those that work for God out of the equation through fear and intimidation. We do not have to look far in this world to see poverty, repression, isolation and despair. Many countries have people in power that make choices that only benefit those in power and harm those that they have sworn to protect, the masses. This is an awakening for many. For others, it is easy to understand. Just look at how a person in power ages during their reign. Look at how they are visibly worn out when they are done. And what about all the scandals that rock the world of those in power, politics, religion or commerce? Understand now why it all happens?

All those in designations of power and authority over people will come under attack. Our prayers have a specific purpose. Our prayers are to help all these in positions of power that they may not fall prey to manipulation, that all these in positions of power may be able to act for the betterment of mankind and not to its demise. We are called to transform the darkness into light through our prayers. Let your light shine on those who come under attack by the unHoly Angels. Pray for those in positions and designations of authority.

Now, see the ripple effect when politics, religion and commerce are attacked. If the unHoly Angels can manipulate those in power over our laws and justice systems, over our religious communities, over our means and methods of transactions for money then it will affect us all.

187

This is what is referred to as the number of the beast. *"He also forced everyone, small and great, rich and poor, free and slave, to receive a mark on his right hand or on his forehead, so that no one could buy or sell unless he had the mark, which is the name of the beast or the number of his name. This calls for wisdom. If anyone has insight, let him calculate the number of the beast, for it is man's number. His number is 666."(Revelations 13:16-18)*

This is the furtherance of the information shared with us through scripture and the Holy Stigmata of Blessed Tiffany. The number 6 is used here as a place of imperfection, 7 being the perfection. This is the combination of the imperfection of politics 6, the imperfection of religion 6 and the imperfection of commerce 6 coming together forming the 666.

There will be a movement to unite the religions of the world under the guise of unity and tolerance. It will be set up by the evil one himself, the first fallen Angel. Many people will be fooled into joining the religion, thinking that it represents unity and the way of serving God but it does not. It is a trap! This false religion can be recognized by being based upon having to earn God's Love. The truth is that we never have to earn the Love of God, for it is a gift freely given to us! Pay attention so that when you see these things coming you will understand. This is the final thrust of the unHoly Angels, to try and deceive as many as possible into thinking that they have to earn God's Love. The unHoly Angels will try to ignore the redemption of mankind through Christ and deceive people into thinking that it is only through constantly working and doing deeds that we can attain salvation. We already know that salvation has been given! We are already granted the salvation of Grace through Christ! Pay attention that you may see and recognize the signs, that you may shine your light brightly!

As well, there will be a movement seeking to unite this new religion with politics under the guise of peace, and together they will try to manipulate all commerce and exchange, to unleash the most damage possible to humanity and the earth. The unHoly Angels are gearing up for one last fight that they will not win.

188

This is about sharing the information with you that when you see these things happening, you can stand firm in faith, no matter what comes against.

How we transform is through prayer. We pray that those in designations and positions of authority will have greater opportunity of love and be able to recognize the things of love! We know that they will be under greater attack, pray that the Holy Angels have free will access to protect them and assist them during the difficult times.

What we are sharing is information about what is to come that you may have hope! It is about the new things coming upon the earth that will occur after the shift into timelessness. It will be a place of such peace and love. All will know of God and God's Love. All will be in the place of sharing and learning, hearing about the experiences and interaction of God and the Holy Angels. We will be bright enough when all is done with this shift to see the Holy Angels. We will be able to share with all the spirit creatures from all throughout creation.

"A shoot will come up from the stump of Jesse;
from his roots a Branch will bear fruit.

The Spirit of the LORD will rest on him—
the Spirit of wisdom and of understanding,
the Spirit of counsel and of power,
the Spirit of knowledge and of the fear of the LORD -

and he will delight in the fear of the LORD.
He will not judge by what he sees with his eyes,
or decide by what he hears with his ears;

but with righteousness he will judge the needy,
with justice he will give decisions for the poor of the earth.
He will strike the earth with the rod of his mouth;
with the breath of his lips he will slay the wicked.

Righteousness will be his belt
and faithfulness the sash around his waist.

189

The wolf will live with the lamb,
the leopard will lie down with the goat,
the calf and the lion and the yearling together;
and a little child will lead them.

The cow will feed with the bear,
their young will lie down together,
and the lion will eat straw like the ox.

The infant will play near the hole of the cobra,
and the young child put his hand into the viper's nest.

They will neither harm nor destroy
on all my Holy mountain,
for the earth will be full of the knowledge of the LORD
as the waters cover the sea.

In that day the Root of Jesse will stand as a banner for the peoples; the nations will rally to him, and his place of rest will be glorious."(Isaiah 11:1-10)

This scripture from Isaiah lets you know that Jesus Christ has already taken care of us, it is a preview of what is coming that you may be at ease and do what God asks for you to do, transform through prayer. Give more opportunity for love to shine in the darkness. We know that beauty and perfection will follow. Keep strengthening your faith in love.

This is all being shared with you that you may have greater hope, faith, trust, discernment and love. You are already a bright place of love for God to share his Love with others in the world, now you will shine even brighter.

Closing prayer and thanks for participating and being a place of love and light in the world. For those that are further moved and wish to know more, info on Called and Commissioned. Love always gives opportunity. For once we demonstrate faithfulness in smaller things, God can give us the greater!

Called and Commissioned
A Minister's Manual for Specific Blessings

"Praise be to the name of God for ever and ever…He gives wisdom to the wise and knowledge to the discerning. He reveals deep and hidden things; he knows what lies in darkness, and light dwells with him…There is a God in Heaven Who Reveals Mysteries." (Daniel 2:20-22, 28)

Divine Decrees for the Called and Commissioned

(1). I Decree as a Spirit of God, born as a child of man this soul's free will Holy Intention to remain steadfast and unshakable in faith and true to my commission and designation of sacred office and Holy orders by vows freely given before God.

(2). I Decree full authority and free will interaction of All Holy Angels assigned and Guides assigned to aid this soul with the fulfillment and dispersement of the duties of ordination this day and every day through the end of and fulfillment of time and into the never-ending expansion of timelessness until the Word of God is seated and the rightful sovereignty of the Kingdom of God reigns victorious.

(3). I Decree this soul's free will agreement and alignment of All Holy Prayers and Holy Intentions with Holy Prayers and Holy Intentions of the Called and Commissioned Brotherhood of The Divine Decrees to aid ministry to teach, guide, defend and protect in full submission, humility and unification with All Holy Angels assigned and Guides assigned to ease the manipulations and unHoly intentions against the children of mankind and all living creation in relationship to man and the earth.

(4). I Decree full protection of this soul, spirit, body and mind by giving full authority and free will interaction to All Holy Angels assigned to render harmless any and all unHoly intentions, traps, attacks and false illusions manifested by the one-third or any and all manipulated ghosts sent toward me, and to clearly make known these individuals, methods or devices at the appropriate time for it as it is seen fit by the Will of God.

(5). I Decree this soul's free will agreement to stand aligned in battle formation beside my brothers of The Divine Decrees and to heed only the Clarion Call of the One True Voice and not that of my own. I acknowledge the danger and limited protection available when choosing my own battles and the disruption of purpose and timing and the manipulations this may create upon my faithful brothers to protect and realign me, thus breaking formation and endangering themselves. By free will I ask for and accept All God-Given opportunities and realizations to recognize additional opportunities for love and to resist and turn from evil and to reinforce and encourage the remembrance of convictions.

(6). I Decree this soul's free will desire to receive continual and consistent ability to react to all wrongdoing with the love, power, and forgiveness as reflected by Christ in the Passion of his Suffering and the Patience and Temperance of the Love of God, and for the free will interaction of All Holy Angels assigned and Guides assigned as a remembrance to do so.

(7). I Decree this soul's free will choice to fully expand into light and stand as a representative and deliverer of the message of love rather than the statement of fear, and to boldly shine this light even when darkness surrounds or threatens.

(8). I Decree full authority and free will interaction of All Holy Angels assigned and Guides assigned to aid this soul to a fuller understanding of the hidden and known hopes of the children of man and to nurture the seed of faith where it may be found by words and actions of inspiration, compassion and remembrance of our birthright, redemption and acceptance in the love of God.

(9). I Decree this soul's understanding and agreement of alignment of my Holy Prayers and Holy Intentions while fulfilling all duties of ordination, and the effect of this soul's actions and reactions of the choice of love or fear upon the Brotherhood of The Divine Decrees. I acknowledge and accept the commission of us unified by Grace and service to the Will of God. I give full authority and free will interaction to All Holy Angels assigned and Guides assigned to aid this soul in awareness of any and all areas of potential events of slights or misunderstandings or inappropriate actions of reactions so that this soul may act in accordance with wisdom and love.

(10). I Decree this soul's free will ability to receive full protection of this soul, spirit, body and mind and any and all souls who ask of me by All Holy Angels assigned while exposing and encapsulating the unHoly whether named or unnamed, in whatever level of hierarchy involved and any and all evil machinations and unHoly manipulations devised or yet to be devised. This includes blessings upon the land and houses of prayer and fellowship, I acknowledge my ordination and power as a child of man aligned with the Grace and Power of God to complete the promises of The Word and carry them to fruition with The Holy Spirit and All Holy Angels assigned, that which is bound on earth being bound in Heaven.

(11). I Decree this soul's free will ability to recognize and transform any unnatural manifestation and any and all unnatural movements of elements beyond normal measures and cleanse and purify and bring back to clear recognition what is Holy and of God and what is unHoly and separated from God through granting full authority and free will interaction of All Holy Angels assigned to render harmless, bind and encapsulate, deliver and exorcise as given by rightful law of the Sovereignty of the Love of God and the Warrior Son of the Kingdom of God and his Holy Armies.

(12). I Decree this as binding on earth as it is in Heaven by the alignment of the will of God and man within the expanded commission and vow of sacred office, bridging all past, present or future events until the Anointed High Priest of the Kingdom of God assumes full authority by order of the Hierarchy Act as ordained by the Blood of the Covenant as witnessed and given through the Holy Spirit by the Love of God. Amen.

Visualization: Succession of shepherd's staff being given from one to the other from God, through mankind and mankind giving it back to God, rows of hundreds of people. The color silver.
Duration: 10 days but can be repeated as often as needed for strengthening and suggested to be used as such, by those ordained for the greater work.

What is Called and Commissioned?

Called and Commissioned is a response to the greater calling that Love has placed within our hearts help even more. To be Called and Commissioned is to choose to become ordained by God, which enables you to have more Angelic help and guidance to do the greater responsibilities. There is much to do in the greater work: the blessings upon the houses of prayer and fellowship, the blessings of anointing, the blessings for teaching the Becoming The Mystic/Divine Decree classes, the blessings to teach the Called and Commissioned Classes, the blessings to ordain others, the blessings upon the land, the blessings upon the air, the blessings upon the water, the blessings for the deliverance work, the blessings for calling in the Holy Angel in the center of the earth and those who work with this Angel and the blessings of the breath of the Holy Spirit. Some will feel a desire to specialize in one or two of these, others will do a little of everything, as called. When you step up to this greater work, God also gives you the tools of deeper knowledge and all the tools to help you accomplish it well, including greater discernment and confidence in Love and yourself.

Is Ordination Necessary for the Deeper Work?

There are many things any of us can do. As children of God, we all have different gifts, and with each of those gifts come additional blessings and additional responsibilities. Ordination is another gift that we can receive to help us help one another. Receiving an ordination is a physical, emotional and spiritual free will act showing our heart's motivation to step forward in the work and expand. The act of ordination is both a gift given from God to mankind, and a gift that mankind gives back to God by receiving the gift graciously and with full trust. This opportunity also gives us a different arrangement with the Holy Angels. Basically when we step up for the deeper work, we get more Angelic heavy-hitters helping us. This is necessary for most deliverances, all exorcisms, and many of the different kinds of blessings, such as land blessings.

God has always presented opportunities for his children to become closer to him, to know him better, to recognize love and choose love for in doing so, they choose God. This is an opportunity to step up to the challenge and make your statement for the glorification of God's name. You have choices all the way through your life. All of these choices, both conscious and unconscious have an impact upon yourself, the world and all those in it.

There is a ripple effect of your choices. Becoming ordained is a choice that gives God greater opportunity to brighten you and all those impacted by the ripple effect of your choices of love over fear. You already are Love's mobile sacred space, right now, just as you are. You are a bright flame that shines the Light of Love, the light of God. Becoming ordained transforms that bright flame into a bonfire! You become even more useful to God for you have chosen not only to align your will with God's Will but have asked for more responsibility. God grants this responsibility freely with his Holy Spirit.

What does this mean? We will be asked to be more Christ-like, to make all our choices out of love and not fear, no matter what may be going on around us. We will be asked to bear the blessing of this responsibility by balancing our great desire with humility and submission to Love's Will for us.

195

"But you are a chosen people, a royal priesthood, a Holy nation, a people belonging to God, that you may declare the praises of him who called you out of darkness into his wonderful light."(1Peter 2:9)

This bonfire will brighten many and provide light for many who are in the dark. Becoming ordained brings you into the hierarchy, under the Apostles who are under Christ, under God. If it has already been placed upon your heart to do the greater work, then you will need the additional guidance and protection that God provides through the ordination. The God of Love is the one who is in charge and is the one we all follow. In his perfect wisdom, he asks that those who are called to the greater work will be required to be ordained to receive the opportunity for greater responsibilities. Through the gift of ordination, God grants us the corresponding tools for the fulfillment of these responsibilities. Love sets us up for success, all we are asked to do is to receive and follow through!

What Happens During an Ordination?

The ordination is not from man but from God. It is God's Holy Spirit poured out upon you. The previously ordained person who now shares the ordination with you is given instruction of what to say, questions to ask and statements to make. When the candidate is able to answer affirming their choice of God and their desire to serve him in accepting the greater responsibility that is offered to them, the person ordaining you is called to lay hands upon you. This is the ceremony of love that has been passed down from the Apostles through all these many years. With this affirmation of us before God and man, we are gifted with God receiving us into the greater work. As a recognized commemoration of this by man, a certificate of this ordination is given as well.

What is Required to Become Ordained?

A person must have already been baptized in a religion that loves God. This is a personal statement affirming your choice of God. This is a necessary step in the process. It doesn't matter which religion, for God is accepting of all the religions who love him.

It is about the personal interaction, standing up for yourself and proclaiming your choice of God, your choice of Love. As well, a person must be of legal age in their state, province or country. A person must have their own authority and autonomy to make their choices. For example, a child may be considered a minor in their state until they reach the age of 18, then they are considered an adult by the law of that land. When they are legally recognized as an adult and are able to choose for themselves without having to ask permission of another, then they can seek to become ordained. They must not be legally under the authority of another; for the act of ordination requires our ability and desire to place our full authority under God.

What Do I Need to Do After the Ordination?

Rest and play! Make sure that you have set enough time aside to recuperate. God is not shy about coming through during the ordination with a great amount of power and love, and it will feel similar to a great healing. It is important to be well hydrated, well fed and well rested afterwards. Take the time to let God's love expand you. Sleep, eat, pray, and rejoice…for the real work is just beginning!

Is This for Everyone?

No. But many will be called. There are many who are born now just because of their desire to do the greater work of shifting the world into light, and their hearts will lead them to do all they can. Those who are led to ordination have sought out the deeper things, have digested and assimilated both the milk and the meat, are consistent with aligning their will with God's Will through The Divine Decrees, and are prayerful and consistent in their God connection. They have great compassion for those being troubled upon the earth and the environment, and they want to be part of the change. They have taken the Becoming the Mystic/Divine Decree Classes and have their own spiritual experiences and are expanding upon their gifts as well. They also have personal traits that are kind, loving, gentle, honest and peaceful. We remember we do not have to be perfect, but we seek to be loving in all our relationships. *We must be temperate, loving, kind, considerate, self-controlled, hospitable, not violent but gentle. (1 Tim.3:1-3)*

197

We will always be called to perform these works in the way that they are meant to be done, through love. All this work is about love, we must be the love to do the work of love. This work is for those who are capable of being moved by love, have the desire to do the greater work, know that they are loved and act out of this love. It is a blessing for us to be Called and Commissioned, it is also a blessing and testament to the Love of God, and to our desire to help and love our neighbor, we become a blessing to them as well.

How Do I Know If This is for Me?

God is the one who places these intentions in our heart to begin with. God is leading many to see that this is something he is calling them to do. Asking God, searching your heart and listening for God in the quiet, gentle, soft whispers in your heart. This has been outlines throughout this book and the Becoming the Mystic/Divine Decree Classes as well. Taking the time to listen in an important and essential step in doing this work. If we struggle with taking the time to listen to God, how will we be able to do the greater work? Practicing love, living a life of: love, non-judgment, compassion, righteousness, patience, understanding, kindness, and service to God is the beginning. Love has much more for us, always. It is a question that only you will be able to answer. Remember that *"God knows the secrets of your heart." (Psalm 44:21)* Being Called and Commissioned is not about being perfect. It is about seeking out the greater things, seeking to do the greatest good for the greatest amount of people, seeking to ease the suffering of all of mankind assisting in this transition to God's perfection of us all.

Ask yourself these questions:
1. Have I been moved by the things of this world to greater compassion and love?
2. Have I taken the Becoming The Mystic/Divine Decree Classes to learn the basics in order to be ready to do the greater work?
3. Am I doing the specialty prayers and The Divine Decrees as instructed?
4. Is this something God wants me to do?

198

If you can answer yes to all four questions, you will know. If you cannot, consider what you are asking in regards to being Called and Commissioned. God doesn't set us up for failure, God sets us up for success! It is his Holy Spirit that makes all these things of love possible. These are the requirements for going on to do the greater work. Showing faithfulness in smaller things that we may be called to do the greater things is an important recognition of how God asks for things to be done. God is in charge and will place within our hearts the desire to do more, to be made more useful to him and to be Called and Commissioned.

Do I have to be Called and Commission to be Useful to God?

No. God works through those who love him and whose hearts are true to him. This is an opportunity that God presents to those who hunger and thirst. This is for those whose most fervent desire is to serve God.

This is not something forced upon you. You always have a choice. God will always love you. This is not a way to prove yourself, this is not to be done to prove worthiness or acceptance for we are already deemed worthy, already loved and accepted as demonstrated through the redemption of mankind through Christ. This ordination is not to be used to prove to yourself or another that you are worthy, for we all already are through the love of God. This is to be entered into with respect, solemness, humility, a burning passion for Love and to do God's Will, love for all mankind and all of creation, honor for the One who bestows the ordination (God), patience, obedience, and kindness. If these aspects are *not* already in place, reconsidering the choice to become ordained at this time is suggested. We are called to be the perfect reflection of the love of God. Many will be watching, those of the flesh and others who are not. Once ordained we have a responsibility that is unmatched prior to this ordination. We will be called upon to do great works, greater than mankind will be able to see or to recognize. We are asked to be God's tool, easily moved by his Spirit as a feather moves easily upon the breezes.

Does it Cost Money?

The ordination does not, the 2 day class that accompanies it does cost money. You are not paying for the ordination; you are paying for the class time and information. The ordination is a free gift from God to those Called and Commissioned. The exchange of energy is for the one(s) teaching the class and their expenses, just as with the Divine Decree/Becoming the Mystic classes.

What Does it Entail?

The Called and Commissioned Class is a 2 day class. The first day and most of the 2nd day will be sharing the information needed to do this work, explaining the blessings more fully, sharing the meaning behind each blessing and preparing everyone that they feel comfortable in doing these blessings. This will be an added instruction that must follow The Divine Decrees/Becoming the Mystic Classes. The Called and Commissioned Classes will not be offered to those who have not completed the Becoming the Mystic/Divine Decree Classes. This work builds from simple to the more complex. We are asked to learn and digest, demonstrate that we can do well with the deeper things and then, if you are ready and if you feel called to do this greater work, then the Called and Commissioned class is your next step.

For those teaching the Called and Commission classes, hearing God's Word about those who are coming to you for these classes will be essential as well. Does it make sense that in order to do the greater you must first show proficiency in doing the lesser? We are all demonstrating our choices, love or fear in all our intentions and our actions. *"No good tree bears bad fruit, nor does a bad tree bear good fruit."* *(Luke 6:43)*

Can a Woman be Ordained?

Yes, of course. This specialty work is for those who are called to it, male or female. This work is blessed by God and given to us to spread love and help in this time of transition.

This is not done through a church or through a religion but directly through God. This is not about conforming to what religion has set up but doing this in accordance with how God wants it to be done, by his Holy Will.

Ordination

The ordination is to come from either Fr. Billy Clark or those that have been ordained by Fr. Billy Clark, which continues to grow by leaps and bounds. This is specialty work, this is not for those seeking to have a parish or congregation. This is not about starting a religion or a church. This work is about love. This is what has been asked of us through the Holy Stigmata of Blessed Tiffany, to share these things of love that there may be less suffering in the world during this time of shift and transition into timelessness.

Those that have been ordained by Fr. Billy Clark will have successfully completed the requirements asked of them and the work that our Heavenly Father has asked of them. These that have been approved and ordained are listed on our website, www.thefourthhealing.com under the tab of "Ordained." There will be a reading of information, an answering of questions and the hands-on in which God's Holy Spirit comes through the lineage that began with Christ and the apostles.

The first step is recognizing that the ordination happens by God's Will. God allows mankind to participate in his Holy priesthood. The ordination happens through man but by God. Once someone is ordained, they are always ordained, *it cannot be taken away.* This is a weighty responsibility. When we commit ourselves to God and his service, we accept great responsibility for our actions, our intentions, opportunities presented and opportunity missed. God will use us for much greater work. We become brighter with an ordination and closer to God. God loves us all and there is no greater or no lesser. We are given the opportunity to share in his Glory and in his interaction with his children.

The ordination is to be entered into respectfully.

After the proper preparation has been made: baptism, education (Becoming The Mystic Classes/Divine Decrees completed), there will be a meeting of both parties (those seeking the ordination and those performing the ordination) and the special two day Called and Commissioned class and then ordination can occur. You will be taught how to do these blessings through the hands-on example of the one(s) who have ordained you. This work will grow and grow. It is important that the time be taken to teach how to do these blessings as we have been instructed, for it is better to do this work well than it is for it to be done fast. This is sacred and Holy work. It is an honor to be in this place of doing God's Will and following through on what has been asked. To do this work in love and through love is a statement of recognition of the one who asked us all to share in the story of God's Love. *"Be joyful always, pray continuously and be thankful in all things, for this is God's Will for you in Christ Jesus." (1 Thes. 16-18)*

What about Baptism?

Baptism is a central step in the process of ordination. It will be <u>required</u> of every one who wishes to be ordained. One of the reasons why it is required is that it shows the intention and follow-through of the individual seeking to be ordained. Becoming baptized shows the free will acceptance of the person in stepping forward in faith with God. This scripture from Ephesians about unity in Christ explains it further: *"As a prisoner for the Lord, then, I urge you to live a life worthy of the calling you have received. Be completely humble and gentle; be patient, bearing with one another in love. Make every effort to keep the unity of the Spirit through the bond of peace. There is one body and one Spirit -just as you were called to one hope when you were called - one Lord, one faith, one baptism; one God and Father of all, who is over all and through all and in all." (Ephesians 4:1-6)*

For those who are already baptized, it will not be necessary to be baptized again. It doesn't matter which denomination you were baptized under for all the denominations are under Christ, under God. *"And this water symbolizes baptism that now saves you also - not the removal of dirt from the body but the pledge of a good conscience toward God.*

202

It saves you by the resurrection of Jesus Christ, who has gone into heaven and is at God's right hand - with angels, authorities and powers in submission to him."(1Peter 3:21)

For those who wish to do the greater work, for those who are Called and Commissioned, baptism will be required before ordination. Baptism is a rinsing clean, a repentance of sins signified through Holy Water. It can be sprinkled, poured over an individual or even through full immersion. Baptism is for the repentance of sins. It is a demonstration of our free will to be brighter in order to be the place of love that our Heavenly Father may use for the greater work. It is a preparation for us so that after we are baptized with the Holy Water, God may baptize us with The Holy Spirit during the laying on of hands that comes through the ordination.

"There are different kinds of gifts, but the same Spirit. There are different kinds of service, but the same Lord. There are different kinds of working, but the same God works all of them in all men. Now to each one the manifestation of the Spirit is given for the common good. To one there is given through the Spirit the message of wisdom, to another the message of knowledge by means of the same Spirit, to another faith by the same Spirit, to another gifts of healing by that one Spirit, to another miraculous powers, to another prophecy, to another distinguishing between spirits, to another speaking in different kinds of tongues, and to still another the interpretation of tongues. All these are the work of one and the same Spirit, and he gives them to each one, just as he determines. The body is a unit, though it is made up of many parts; and though all its parts are many, they form one body. So it is with Christ. For we were all baptized by one Spirit into one body— whether Jews or Greeks, slave or free—and we were all given the one Spirit to drink. Now the body is not made up of one part but of many. If the foot should say, "Because I am not a hand, I do not belong to the body," it would not for that reason cease to be part of the body. And if the ear should say, "Because I am not an eye, I do not belong to the body," it would not for that reason cease to be part of the body. If the whole body were an eye, where would the sense of hearing be? If the whole body were an ear, where would the sense of smell be?

203

But in fact God has arranged the parts in the body, every one of them, just as he wanted them to be. If they were all one part, where would the body be? As it is, there are many parts, but one body. The eye cannot say to the hand, "I don't need you!" And the head cannot say to the feet, "I don't need you!" On the contrary, those parts of the body that seem to be weaker are indispensable, and the parts that we think are less honorable we treat with special honor. And the parts that are unpresentable are treated with special modesty, while our presentable parts need no special treatment. But God has combined the members of the body and has given greater honor to the parts that lacked it, so that there should be no division in the body, but that its parts should have equal concern for each other. If one part suffers, every part suffers with it; if one part is honored, every part rejoices with it. Now you are the body of Christ, and each one of you is a part of it." (1 Corinthians 12:4-27)

Many of us have different gifts to share in service to God, some will be called into the deliverance ministry, some to healing, some to blessings of houses of prayer and fellowship, some to land blessings, some to teaching and more! We are all parts of the same body, The Body of Christ. Baptism is a recognition of this unity and a place of willing participation to turn away from fear and turn towards love, to be unified under Christ, under God.

How Do We Perform a Baptism?

Baptism can be done simply. It will require 3 things, one who is ordained, one who is to be baptized and Holy Water. It can be as simple or elaborate as you wish. The vital step in the process is the acknowledgement of the one who wishes to be baptized that they do, in fact, desire to be rinsed clean, to repent from past transgressions and to willingly choose to be closer to God. This is about the desire to be turning from the things in the past, things of darkness and fear to the things of the future, things of light and love. It can be as few witnesses as the one who is ordaining and the one who is receiving.

The water is to be placed upon the individual desiring baptism (in whatever way chosen: sprinkled, poured or immersion) and the words added "I now baptize you in the name of The Father, The Son and The Holy Spirit" and the sign of the Cross + made over the person. They are now baptized.

How Do We Pray?

Prayer is a time of connection for hearing the voice of Love, brightening, aligning our will with God's Will for us and giving thanks. We take the time to spend with him, Holy and humbly. We remember that we are sharing with God who loves us and calls to us to hear him and feel the love that he has for us. God is the one who made us, we are the spark off of his Divine Flame. We remember that he is always looking to remind us of his love and share with us. We are his children and we are loved. There is to be no fear with prayer, you are encouraged to share as you would with a friend, being that open and honest, that caring and desiring to share. Yes, it is true that *"God knows what you need before you ask," (Matthew 6:8)* but how much more precious does prayer become when we understand that God is looking to share with us, that we are so loved that God seeks us out, calling to us, constantly pursuing our heart and our love.

God doesn't do this as a need, but as a loving Father truly would, because he cares. God wants us to recognize him, to see him as what he is: *"God is Love" (1John 4:8).* God asks that we recognize all the things of love, for they are of him. That we have discernment to see what is of love and what is not. We are called upon to recognize the way of love, choose the way of love and be the way of love for ourselves, our brothers and sisters throughout the world and all creation.

When God see us, he only sees the things of love that we have done and are working on. God doesn't see anything else. God could see those things that is certain but out of his love for his children and the salvation of Grace that came through his son, God sees us through the eyes of love and encourages us to do the same with ourselves and one another; gentle and loving, caring and open to love.

We can remember to pray with an open heart and a *"listening tongue."* *(Isaiah 50:4)* We were given an example of how to pray, a prayer often called The Our Father, by Christ himself: *"Our Father, who art in Heaven, hallowed be Thy Name. Thy Kingdom come, Thy Will be done, on earth as it is in Heaven. Give us this day our daily bread and forgive us our trespasses as we forgive those who trespass against us. Lead us not into temptation but deliver us from the evil one." (Matthew 6:9-13)*

Such a simple short prayer is quite powerful. The Lord's prayer, as it is often referred to as, gives not only the milk and meat of what a prayer can be but also a how to guide our own prayers. The prayer starts out addressing the most important recognition of all, the name of God and all that stands for. With the recognition of his Glory comes our desire that his Kingdom comes and his Will be accomplished on earth and in heaven. This is important to remember as it focuses on what we have been told, specifically that God's Will goes out from him, comes to be and returns to him completed. The Holy Spirit makes this happen. God's word never fails to come to fruition. This is the hope we can rely on, knowing that love always wins the war! This is a place of great comfort for those who are fearful, knowing that man will have the Glory of God made manifest in the original intention of mankind's purpose upon the earth. This also shows our statement of recognition of Love's right to rule, his sovereignty. God is the one who has all the wisdom and the love. We are blessed that he shares it with his children.

After we give recognition, we ask for assistance. We ask the giver of all good things to share with us our daily bread, giving to us what we need for the day. The daily bread is not only our sustenance for this day, our food and needs for the day but is also about sharing his son, Christ with us each day. Christ has often been referred to as the Bread of Life. Christ states this himself as well: *"I am the Bread of Life." (John 6:32, 35, 48, 58)* We recognize the Salvation Act of the Love of God, Christ's birth, death and resurrection in asking for our daily bread.

We continue on in the prayer asking for forgiveness of those we have wronged and offer through our free will forgiveness for all those who have wronged us. This is an important awareness, we offer forgiveness while asking for it as well. An extremely humbling act. Here we also can see that we acknowledge that people can be manipulated and thereby make poor choices. We know that darkness is upon the earth and that the unHoly Angels seek to harm us and God as well. Asking for forgiveness allows for healings to take place.

One of the most beautiful things in regards to forgiveness what shown to us in Stigmata experienced by Blessed Tiffany. When Christ asked God, *"Father, forgive them for they know not what they do" (Luke 23:24),* the unHoly Angels that had entered into those that were torturing, cursing, spitting and harming Christ could no longer be in these people. The unHoly Angels left those doing these horrible things to Christ, and the Holy Angels immediately came and supported these people. Christ asked God to forgive these who were harming him. The unHoly Angels couldn't be in these people any longer after Christ had shone his perfect love upon them. His Love scattered the darkness, his forgiveness made it possible for these people to heal and be in that light once more.

So when we pray, we give thanks to God for all that he has given and continues to give. Then we pray for ourselves, speaking what is in our heart and on our mind. We ask to be forgiven for when we have wronged another (remembering when possible to ask for forgiveness from those we have wronged before coming to pray to God). We ask for ourselves first before asking on behalf of another for we cannot give what we have not received. He asks us to fill our cup before passing it to others. We are told to be the place of strength for our brothers and sisters in this world and to do so; we must receive his Love for ourselves. In this way, we can give from him and his unending source of love. We don't end up being depleted, unable to give, out of balance, agitated, upset or anxious. We learn to constantly fill from the Source.

After we are strengthened, we pray for others, asking for what we see a need for, without judgment, with love, compassion, forgiveness. We include all Love's light-workers, all those doing his will. We pray for those he has shared with (the Sharing through Holy Stigmata), for all the heads of divisions of government that they may have the freedom to choose without manipulation by the unHoly Angels, to enact policy that benefits all and harms none and that they have greater opportunity to experience his love, that they may recognize love and choose the way of love.

We pray for the houses of prayer and fellowship: that *all* houses of prayer and fellowship come together in peace, love and harmony, united under Love. We pray for all those coming and going from these places that they may be protected from manipulation as well. We pray for all the vulnerable children of man, and for all the children who were born after the spring of 2003. These children are all Holy Ones who did not have to come back into the body in this life. We pray that they may all be true to their commissions, that they may have their veil lifted for a longer period of time and that they may communicate freely with the Holy Angels. We pray for all those in our hearts and minds, all those indented to us in anyway, throughout time, that his Holy Angels may protect and defend us all against the evil one and strengthen us to do God's Will. We add our intentions; whatever he has placed upon us, what is in our hearts God desires to hear.

Remember that our prayers are our love song to God, open our hearts and pray as if we were talking to our best friend, the one who fully loves us unconditionally. We pray for change to manifest wherever darkness is that there may be light instead. We pray that brother and sister throughout the world be a reflection of God's love for one another.

We pray that wherever there is darkness being spread that love ripple forth instead, being specific when possible and stating that there be "love, peace, hope, trust and discernment in these areas and a transformation of darkness into Light." We pray as well for the Holy Angels, for the 4 Holy Angels that protect and defend the earth and a double portion for the 1 Holy Angel in the center of the earth, for the 1 Holy Angel on the moon and for all the Holy Angels that he sends to work with all his servants here on earth.

208

We pray as well for the unHoly Angels that they may turn from their wicked ways and repent and return, that they may remember the love they were created in, created to be, knowing that God extends his hand even now for them, out of his mercy that they may return to him, that they may turn away from their ways. For their unHoly ways hold no wisdom and there will never be wisdom found in their ways, for their ways are not of God. We pray that they call out to him and return to God, ask for forgiveness and receive a new name.

We state our response for the original issues: that we come to God not for what he can give us but to serve him, that we cannot do it on our own, that God is the Sovereign one and we seek to do his will, that we give God these bodies, these spirits to use however he wishes, trusting in him always. We pray for his Kingdom to come and that it may come now. Recognizing that it is important to see the wisdom in his timing and trust in that. We remember to do all these things in remembrance of Christ, his obedient and faithful son.

And we remember that God answers our prayers in any of these 3 ways; "yes," "not just yet," or "I have a better idea than that!" We pray specifically so that God has something to bless, and so we recognize his intervention upon us when as we see many of the specifics occur with his Divine interaction. We pray for our alignment of our will with his Will, and his Will to be done on earth as it is in heaven. We pray to thank him for all we hold dear. We can also pray the prayers that have been used throughout the centuries, such as the Our Father, (Matthew 6:9-13) Hail Mary and the Gloria. These prayers are blessed by God from all the Holy who have said them and all those who have shown reverence from their use. They carry a blessing upon them for all those who recite them:

"Hail Mary, full of Grace, the Lord is with thee. Blessed are thou amongst women and blessed is the fruit of thy womb, Jesus. Holy Mary, Mother of God, pray for all sinners, now and at the hour of our death, Amen."

"Glory be to the Father, to the Son and to the Holy Spirit. As it was in the beginning, is now, and ever shall be, world without end. Amen."

We pray as well that all of creation remember to invite God in to their day. Remember that this time in prayer is essential, this is your time to spend sharing and listening as well for his words for you. Take some quiet time without talking and relax into his Presence. Let him guide you and offer you assistance. Speak with him from the heart, as a trusted and respected friend.

And finally, we can end with the two best prayers to God: "Thank you!" and "I love you!"

Hearing Answers from God with the Confirmation Prayer

How do you know what are your own emotions or what is your Divine intuition? Until you know the voice inside you is the whisper of God, this is a prayer for confirmation of what is God's Will. This is asking for a physical sign, something that has been done for thousands of years. But instead of seeing just any sign and trying to interpret it, this is a precise and accurate way to ask Father to connect with us in a way we are looking for. Putting it in a specific period of time helps us get by the analytical brain which may say: "Oh, I would have seen that eventually, how do I know that is from God?" Instead of seeing a physical sign, you may also ask for a song or sound within the period of time. Remember that God takes every opportunity to connect with us and let us know he cares about us and wants to interact with us. It builds our relationship, like a trusting child with a wonderful and loving dad.
This prayer is extremely important to keep simple. The confirmation prayer has 5 steps as follows:

(1). *"Lord, if it is your Will for me to:…"* (state intention/question here)

(2). *"Show me this sign:…"* (stated specifically and separate from the will of another, for example, show me an eagle, NOT-have John stop by with a coffee for me)

(3). Set the time parameter *"within 3 hours"* (or any time you wish, remembering that if it is something you need an answer to quickly to ask for it quickly. It is also important to remember that if it happens outside the chosen time parameter it is a "no")

(4). Have gratitude. *"thank you Father"*

(5). State the authority to receive it. *"in Jesus' name, Amen"*

This is simple and is to be kept as such so as not to cause difficulty. When we first start to hear or see or learn more about God's Will, we may need confirmation. It is okay to ask God for what you think would be helpful for you. In addition, it is a blessed prayer since you are looking to know God's Will for you. This makes it a protected channel between you and God.

Remembering that if you see the sign in the allotted time, it is a yes; it is his Will for you and if you see **no** sign in the allotted time it is a **no**, it is not his will for you.

Do not let this be a stumbling since it is intended as a useful tool to help us to hear God better and demonstrate our obedience by following through on Love's will for us. Remember as well, when we ask for a specific sign like a dove, we may be shown the sign as a dove stamp, picture, hat or an actual dove. The more specific you get in asking the more God can show you specifically. This helps to expand our faith, as we get clarity on discerning what is best for us, and that we are always successfully guided when we ask to be. God knows best. Be patient and let Love show you how it all works. Remember if you are not sure, you can verify by asking again: using another sign, and using another period of time.

How Do We Ground and Balance the Physical Body?

The body is the combination of the spirit and the flesh. There are two components to what is referred to as the soul, the spirit and the body. The body and the spirit interact throughout the day. There is a balance of work and rest for each in a full day. The day begins with the body being awake and the spirit active, both are alert and ready for work. Towards the slower part of the day, the early evening, the body starts to slow down. This is the time for the balancing of the spirit.

The body will still be awake and can do many things for the relaxation part of the day. Playing, having the body do some simple repetitive task allows for the spirit to relax. Now we have reached the last part of the day, the body's turn to rest while the spirit goes to work with Father, night time. Our spirit can be used for great work while we sleep, we can also be given information that will be helpful for what is coming up. Father can use our spirit in what we see as dreams to help our brothers and sisters. God uses scenarios that elicit great compassion from us to have us assist and grant greater opportunity for those involved to recognize love. The spirit works hard at night.

It will be easy to recognize when we are out of balance for we will feel worn down and tired, we will feel overworked. This indicates we need more play time, more time for the spirit to rest and relax. This is an essential component. We have been aware of letting the body recuperate and now we know the importance of letting the spirit recuperate as well. It is better to work a little and play a little than overwork, be overwhelmed and unable to work the next day. There will always be more work to accomplish until it is all finished through God and his Holy Son, Jesus Christ and his Holy Armies.

Do not allow yourself to be overwhelmed, take the time to play, it is essential for balancing the body and the spirit. We come into the work, not because it is easy but because we recognize the importance of it and know that it needs to be done. We know that it will greatly ease the suffering of our brothers and we are allowed to share in this work. Be gentle upon yourself; remember that Father has many workers! And we can always pray for more: *"Ask the Lord of the harvest, therefore, to send out workers into his harvest field." (Matthew 9:38)*

The physical needs of the body are essential for keeping it well balanced, food, exercise, water, rest, and play. These are all required for doing this work well. The body is a gift as is the blood within it. Remember to take good care of the gift, do what is essential for keeping it healthy that you may be better able to be used by Father.

For those who are in physically challenged bodies, never fear for God will use you to do amazing things. Remember we are told: *"Brothers, think of what you were when you were called. Not many of you were wise by human standards; not many were influential; not many were of noble birth. But God chose the foolish things of the world to shame the wise; God chose the weak things of the world to shame the strong. He chose the lowly things of this world and the despised things—and the things that are not—to nullify the things that are, so that no one may boast before him. It is because of him that you are in Christ Jesus, who has become for us wisdom from God—that is, our righteousness, holiness and redemption. Therefore, as it is written: "Let him who boasts boast in the Lord." (1Cor.1:26-31)*

We are to pay attention to what the body needs and making the time to do it. We are not to pour out for it is better to obey than to sacrifice. *"And this is love: that we walk in obedience to his commands. As you have heard from the beginning, his command is that you walk in love." (2 John 1:6)*

Getting in nature, shoes off, standing on the ground is one way. Laying on the ground, again in nature. Exercise, eating well, drinking plenty of water and good upkeep on the vitamins. Paying attention to balance time for the body, taking time to let the spirit rest, play time! Sexual relations in a healthy relationship. Good sleep habits as well. Balance with all things, physical, emotional and spiritual.

Why? Picture that we are like a 3 legged stool, one leg is the physical, one leg is the emotional and one leg is the spiritual. We are to keep all three growing together, strengthening and not ignoring one leg and giving too much attention to the other leg. This stool is who we are. God has mighty work for us to do and we must be able to support and balance the weight of that. If we are out of balance, if one leg has grown without the support of the other two, when pressure is applied it will tip over. This is what we have seen in the world with many who have chosen to be celibate. They have chosen this way to serve and that is well if they are able to balance their lives. For those who haven't been in balance, when the physical desires are overwhelming, they can easily be manipulated by the unHoly Angels and go against their vows to God.

This is not to say that it is not acceptable to be celibate, many of our Holy brothers and sisters have done this well. This is to state that we must pay attention to all aspects of our lives that we not fall over like the unbalanced stool when our adversary comes to strike. We must have a good balance in our lives. We must also have a place to relax, refresh and renew. We are not to live in a place of strife within our own homes. God never wants us to be in turmoil but in peace and love with him. So, pay attention to your home life and make sure that you are doing the same that you preach, forgive, love, heal, comfort, guide and care for those in your home. And know that God wishes this to be there for you as well. God never wants us in a scenario where we are being abused in any way. He wants us to recognize love and see that Love is of him.

How Do We Encourage Others?

We are to encourage others with the humility and forthrightness of the knowledge that we are used tools of God himself, his words, his mind, his heart. Remember we are not to judge. We listen with kindness, patience and compassion. We allow them to feel as if they have been heard, without judgment. Then we share with them what we know of God's love and how it applies to the situation. We have one ear to heaven listening for God's guidance and another ear towards our brother or sister to hear them as well. We let them know that we all have responsibility for our own actions and that it is important to put God back in the equation. Inviting them to remember who they are as his children, loved unconditionally and fully. We bring them to the awareness of the power of their free will, and how it is respected by God and how God will not violate their free will but awaits their invitation to come in and assist. We remind how the unHoly Angels seek to bully, to manipulate, to tear down, attacking the 3 major areas, health, finances and family/relationships. We remind them why, that if the unHoly Angels can manipulate us into making our choices out of fear, doubting who we are, doubting that we are heard by God, then they will try to push us even further attempting to make us feel separate us from God. Reminding them that God does not ask that we sit idle and let ourselves be bullied but to call upon him to deliver, to defend and protect, to send his Holy Angels to assist us in our situation.

214

We are active in our faith. *But not because we are trying to earn love,* for God's love is not earned, it is a free gift from a loving Dad. We already have it, by Grace.

How Do We Recognize and Do a Deliverance Prayer?

We recognize the need for a deliverance if any of the three major areas are showing signs of attack, signs of manipulation or weakness. We freely give the deliverance prayer with their free will agreement demonstrated by their stating "Amen" at the end of the prayer. The deliverance prayer:

"Lord, any unHoly Angels in, on, near or around (my brother...or my sister ...), I nail, hold them fast and silence them. I decommission, bind and encapsulate them through the power of the Shed Blood of the Lamb and bring them up to your Presence immediately Lord to deal with as you see fit. May you fill any empty place or lonely space within ... with your love and your light. Thank you Father, In Jesus' name, Amen."

We offer as well the prayer for breaking generational bondage, asking them to recognize something in their family line, physical, emotional, mental or spiritual where they see a repeated pattern that is unhealthy. This allows us to call out all that is unknown as well in the prayer. This too requires their free will unity with an "Amen" at the end of the prayer.

The Deliverance Prayer Explained

This prayer encompasses several factors:

#1. The unHoly Angels can be in, on, near or around a person... This helps to cut any connection. It is important to see that if a person is on blessed ground where the unHoly Angels are not allowed that the unHoly Angels would re-attach or attack immediately after this person moves to unblessed ground. This is why it is important for people to say the prayer, to cut the ties or bonds to the unHoly so they are not immediately attacked again after leaving blessed ground.

#2. Nailing, holding fast and silencing... This is the essential first component to the prayer since it will keep many problems from surfacing. When the unHoly Angels are nailed, they cannot move away from the Holy Angels coming to take them away. Holding them fast keeps them in place and silencing them keeps us consciously or unconsciously from having to listen to any blasphemy or filth.

*#3. Decommission and binding...*Angels have rank, similar to the military. Even the unHoly Angels share the gifts Father blessed them with in the beginning. Decommissioning them removes them from the place of power that they held, knocking them down in rank so they cannot put up as much of a fight against their Holy Brothers. Binding them. The scriptures tell us, *"You cannot enter the strong man's house until first you bind him." (Matthew 12:29)* This refers to asking that the unHoly Angels be held that they may not cause damage to any. It is like putting a straight jacket upon them. This also makes it easier for the Holy Angels to do Father's work. Remember that Father is the one who does the deliverance.

*#4. Encapsulating them...*This is where we can see even more of the love of God. Not only does God wish for his children to be free of the captivity of the unHoly Angels but in his love and mercy, God places the unHoly Angels in a glass-like container where they can now watch but not interfere with the sons of mankind. From here they can see the interaction of God and man without manipulating and without hearing the manipulations of the rest of the unHoly Angels as well. This is how loving God is, he allows these who tormented his children to learn about love as well. This is the preferred method obviously over simply driving them out to parched places where they would have opportunity to harm another. Remember as well, what is bound on earth is bound in heaven.

*#5. Sending them to Father, immediately...*This is huge. We are never just to send them out of the person but to give a direction, a destination that is the most appropriate. We are not to send them to the desert or the moon or anywhere but back to God to let him take care of them as he sees fit.

"Immediately" also prevents any problems and shows the free will desire of the one doing the deliverance prayer that it be taken care of now!

*#6. Filling any empty place or lonely space…*This prevents what we have seen mentioned in scripture, filling the void with the love and light of God. For if the house is left empty, 'seven more demons, worse than the first' will take their place. This is symbolic and not an actual number, for it can be much more, even 'Legion' as Christ delivered.

After a deliverance it is still up to the person to make their choices according to love and not fear, shoring up their free will with good choices. But this cleansing gets them started on the right path to doing so. Again, seeing the love of God made manifest. We can share the Holy Eucharist with the freed captive, the one who just was delivered by God, this is an excellent strengthening.

The deliverance prayer can be done more than once and as often as the need arises. It is important to note that the deliverance prayer is the cleansing off of the unHoly. It is still up to the individual to close up the holes in the free will that led to the problems to begin with; willful sin, unforgiveness of self or others, sexual abuse, emotional abuse, physical abuse, negative patterns of behavior, addictions, failure to make choices out of love and not fear. Holes can be punched in the free will by external and internal forces. Have them examine their choices, their treatment of themselves and others and their love for themselves, others and God. It is about strengthening them and teaching them, that they not fall prey to manipulation again but rather they strengthen in their interaction with Love, growing in trust, faith, hope, discernment and love!

Lastly, since these deliverances and blessings hinge on the free will of those in need, it is imperative that they state "Amen" at the end of it. This demonstrates their free will. If they fail to say "Amen" the prayer does not take for them. There are times that Father takes care of this in the instances where someone is unable to speak, in a coma or physically or mentally challenged but all are encouraged to participate and state "Amen" since all are blessed with the gift of free will.

217

The Prayer for Breaking Generational Bondage

This is a specific prayer that Father has given us to combat the problems that most attribute to genetics or familial history. Generational bondage is a problem that comes down through the family line and can be of any nature, physical, mental, emotional or spiritual. It is a problem that can be remedied quite simply with the following prayer.

It is important to ask the receiver to examine their family to see if they can spot anything that is a problem, whether it is physical, emotional or spiritual. This is what Father blesses us with, for if we can recognize one known problem and call it out, God calls frees us from all the unknown generational bondage as well. It is like we are sailing through the Artic, and God asks us if we see anything up ahead. We say "yes, I see an iceberg." God then says, "what you see is only the tip of the iceberg, and much more of it is below the water. Now that you have recognized the tip of it, I will scoop all of it out for you and make your path clear." How beautiful!

Another beautiful aspect to this prayer is the fact *that it goes back and forth throughout time,* to all the relatives previous to them in their blood line and all those who will come after them, such as their children, as well. For instance, a man recognizes in his family that heart attacks near middle age are common in his family. By seeing this and calling it out, this man can heal and take care of all those who have come before him and any and all that will come after him. We are given the ability to share in the healing for all of our family through our blood line.

Here is the prayer: *"Lord, if there is any generational bondage, such as that which is known (state known problem here) and all that is unknown as well, going backward and forward throughout time, I null and void it all through the power of the Shed Blood of the Lamb and send back love in return. Thank you Father, in Jesus' name, Amen."*

There is a glorious ripple effect with this prayer, as we become a healer for our family, even without them knowing it, by breaking generational bondage.

218

Breaking Curses, Hexes, Spells, Incantations, Negative Prayers or Evil Intent

As for curses, hexes, spells, incantations, negative prayer and evil intent it is necessary to have the person who is afflicted available to state "Amen" at the end of the prayer. To break these types of problems, it is necessary to have either the one who started the curse or the one whom it is upon. Either the giver or the receiver is needed to break these. And, again, their free will participation is essential for it to take effect.

Here is the prayer (it can be added to the Breaking Generational Bondage Prayer as well):

"Lord, I ask that any curse, hex, spell, incantation, negative prayer or evil intent sent against my brother (or sister) here be null and void through the power of the Shed Blood of the Lamb and we send back love in return. Thank you Father, In Jesus' name, Amen."

It is broken and rendered harmless through the power of the Shed Blood of Jesus Christ. This is crucial to understand, just as in the deliverance prayer and the generational bondage prayer; it is recognizing the Salvation Act of the Love of God, the surrendered Blood of Christ, shed for all mankind. This is how it works, through redemption and by the Grace of God.

In addition, we send love back in return. This is the remembrance of loving thy enemy, healing the past hurt and allowing for the one who caused it to have an opportunity to learn more about the love of God.

Other Deliverance Essentials

It is suggested that, when possible, two people be there to do the prayer with the one being delivered by God. It is acceptable to do it one on one if the faith of the one doing the prayer is very strong. The prayer is as it is stated above and for the above reasons. It is not to be changed. Every word has meaning and is essential.

219

As an illustration: Demons or unHoly Angels are like the contaminated substance. We are brought in to disarm safely that no harm may come to any. We must have the safe area ready, sealed and prepared before taking care of the contaminated, unHoly Angels. The prayers are the protective suit we wear, the gloves and suit. The Holy Angels are the tools used to do this, to touch the contaminated and bind them. They are the direct connection to bring them to Father, where they cannot injure.

Steps for a deliverance or exorcism:

1. *Building must be secured.* Blessed land and Holy Eucharist in the ground. Manipulated ones held.

2. *Protection put in place.* Asking Father to have the Holy Angels sent to us. Give them free will access to protect and defend and be specific, how long a period of time, how many people, or from first to last person of the day, etc. Must give the Holy Angels the invitation! Recognizing the importance of interacting with the Holy Angels, the hand tools of Father. Must also have partaken of the Holy Eucharist prior to the deliverance!

3. *The Deliverance prayer is said...* "*Lord, any unHoly Angels in, on, near or around (my brother... or my sister...), I nail, hold them fast and silence them. I decommission, bind and encapsulate them through the power of the Shed Blood of the Lamb and bring them up to your Presence immediately Lord to deal with as you see fit. May you fill any empty place or lonely space within...with your love and your light. Thank you Father, in Jesus' name, Amen.*"

4. *Cleansing and strengthening...* Take the Holy Eucharist, do a deliverance upon those involved and participating, invite the Holy Angels to clear and cut any remaining ties to the unHoly Angels and purify ourselves.

5. *Repetition* of these things frequently so they become second nature.

6. *Blessing upon the land,* recognize frequency needed.

7. *Thank Father!*

8. Remind those there about brightening themselves, choosing love and the importance and significance of what has occurred here. Now it is up to them to brighten, reading scripture, their prayer life, their inclusion of The Divine Decrees in their prayer life and being the bright place for God to share.

Remind the one just delivered to copy off and carry the deliverance prayer with them always so that they can say it for themselves whenever they feel pressure or darkness upon them. Help them recognize they have many tools at their disposal to help them continue to be free.

Another illustration...Father knows the house is in need. First he sends in the plumber, next he teaches us how to use the tool placed in our hands, then he gives us a tool box with many tools. Further, he teaches us specific information on specialty tools, and then gives us the jobs that require the specialized tools and training!

Deliverance is about the weakening and cutting of ties. How to weaken the ties:
(1).   Priesthood
(2).   Touching - the touch of one who is approved (ordained) is a powerful tool for Father, allowing the brightness of one to affect the other.
(3).   A Holy Oil Anointing
(4).   The Crucifix
(5).   The touching of the Stole upon the place where the spirit lays within - the body from the head down the spine.
(6).   Holy Water
(7).   Scripture reading
(8).   Singing God's praises, psalms, songs of love. These raise the vibration of the area and allow for a greater brightening to occur.
(9).   The name of God spoken aloud, since we are indented to Father
(10). The stating of the positive answers to the 3 Original Issues
(11). The stating of the Salvation Act of the Blood of Christ
(12). The stating of the lives and choices of the Saints, those approved by Father for they have had blessed lives, Holy Mary, the times of faith carry a blessing and anointing upon them.

God is the One who will give the unHoly Angels the opportunities again and again to come home. It is emphasized here that *we do not talk with the unHoly Angels*. Work on your self confidence and God-confidence. Know that God uses you well already as his mobile sacred space, work on trusting in your communication with God. Know that you are highly protected and loved, and have all the Warrior Angels needed to get the job done.

How and When Do We Cleanse After a Deliverance?

After a deliverance, we do a deliverance prayer for ourselves and all those who assisted in helping at the deliverance. We add at the end "Lord, may your Holy Angels cut any tie or bind to the unHoly Angels that we may be pure for you." We then take communion. We do this every time to rinse clean any indent from working with the unHoly Angels. What is the frequency of cleansing? As often as needed, whenever an attack against health, finances or family/relationships is felt. At least once a day. It is also recommended to do a daily cleansing prayer for deliverance for breaking any curse, hex, spell, negative prayer or evil intent sent toward us.

This will help to brighten and strengthen you considerably for this work. Trusting God, spending time in personal prayer is essential. You are to spend time with just you and God filling up your cup, that you may have something to share with others. It is absolutely essential for this work, conversation with you and God together. It is how this work is done, through him.

How Do We Do Exorcisms?

Exorcism is about God further demonstrating his love for his children and setting the captives free. If you are given the names of the unHoly Angels, you can keep them to yourself, saying them without the afflicted person hearing the name. Fallen Angels are very proud of their name and the destruction they have done is attached to who they are. Sometimes a name will be identified after what they specialize in, such as "the spirit of mockery," or "the spirit of lust."

222

Many of them will give a name that is ancient and not in a common language, for it is the personal name they have used for thousands of years. The reason it is not necessary to state any name of the unHoly Angels out loud is because this tends to cause fear for those being delivered, although when the afflicted individual already sees and knows the name, it is recommended to use it, to call out "the spirit of (state the name)."

A deliverance is different than an exorcism because of the amount of attack on a person and their inability to gain control. A deliverance is for a person who still has control over their free will, though he is under attack through holes in the shield. An exorcism is necessary when the afflicted individual has lost most or all control of their free will and is being fully manipulated. It is encouraged and suggested that more than one person be present to assist. The assistants can be reading scripture, singing hymns, praying common prayers, reciting The Divine Decrees, calling in the Holy Angels for assistance and being a bright beacon of love and trust.

It is also suggested that to whatever extend the afflicted individual can participate that they are encouraged to do so, even if they can only say one word, have them participate. Remember that this is about brightening. The deliverance prayer will be said here as well.

"Lord, I ask that any unHoly Angels in, on, near or around my brother (or sister) here be nailed, held fast and silenced. I decommission, bind and encapsulate (state the spirit if given it by God or the person) any unHoly Angels here through the power of the Shed Blood of the Lamb and bring them up to your Presence immediately to deal with as you see fit. Father, may you fill any empty place or lonely space here with your love and your light. In Jesus' name, Amen."

If the individual has spiritual gifts such as the ability to see the other side, seeing the unHoly Angels especially or hearing the other side, *they must say the entire prayer with you when possible.* This teaches them the prayer and helps to give them confidence for the unHoly Angels know they have the gift(s) and will try to manipulate them away from trusting God and using them.

223

They are to be encouraged and reminded to make their choices out of love and not fear. It is also important to educate those who assisted the afflicted one and give them the prayer as well. All who assist can say a deliverance prayer when it is finished adding *"Lord, may your Holy Angels cut any tie or bind to the unHoly Angels that we may be pure for you. In Jesus' name, Amen."* This removes the indent of the unHoly Angels in doing this work.

A special thing to pay attention to: The unHoly Angels operate like a gang, they know what each have done to torment and individual and when you call out one, another may take the exact same form of the one who just left to create confusion and cause doubt. Let this not deter you for the unHoly Angels who were delivered have been brought up to God. Keep at it until all are removed and there are no remaining unHoly Angels. This is where it is necessary to have the one who is afflicted repeat the prayer as well. The unHoly Angels seek to intimidate and create problems to frustrate those doing the work, trust in God, he will set his children free for you ask through the name of his Holy Son. *"For what you ask for in my name will be granted so that the Son may bring Glory to the Father."* (John 14:13)

This is about teaching them as well. Teaching them how to use the deliverance prayer for protection, teaching them about The Divine Decrees for greater protection and teaching them how to identify any places of weakness so the holes can remain closed in the free will.

How Do We Protect and Cleanse After an Exorcism?

Follow with the cleansing as after a deliverance, and suggest and emphasize all to follow The Divine Decrees as recommended. Repeating them before they need to be repeated keeps everyone protected, leaving no room for error. It is similar to knowing that the thief will come at night and constantly having the door locked. *"But understand this: If the owner of the house had known at what time of night the thief was coming, he would have kept watch and would not have let his house be broken into."* (Matthew 24:43)

There is no need to leave the door of the spirit open for even an instant, why take the chance of a problem?

224

Say them within the stated parameters given and you will be well protected.

"Finally, be strong in the Lord and in his mighty power. Put on the full armor of God so that you can take your stand against the devil's schemes. For our struggle is not against flesh and blood, but against the rulers, against the authorities, against the powers of this dark world and against the spiritual forces of evil in the heavenly realms. Therefore put on the full armor of God, so that when the day of evil comes, you may be able to stand your ground, and after you have done everything, to stand. Stand firm then, with the belt of truth buckled around your waist, with the breastplate of righteousness in place, and with your feet fitted with the readiness that comes from the gospel of peace. In addition to all this, take up the shield of faith, with which you can extinguish all the flaming arrows of the evil one. Take the helmet of salvation and the sword of the Spirit, which is the word of God. And pray in the Spirit on all occasions with all kinds of prayers and requests. With this in mind, be alert and always keep on praying for all the saints." (Ephesians 6:10-18)

Why is Confession Part of Cleansing?

Confession is a spiritual cleansing and an opportunity to be vulnerable in front of another - not only a human, but all the Angels looking on, both Holy and unHoly. The reason I like to establish this fact is so that you can understand the difference between you *asking God* for forgiveness and you asking *one that God has blessed* for forgiveness. We are given the opportunity continually to ask God for forgiveness and as well to ask that forgiveness be granted through those in the hierarchy ordained by God. There is a difference.

As such, we are encouraged to ask God for cleansing of any of our transgressions, where we have gone against Love's Will for us. We are showing our humility and recognizing openly that we are not perfect, knowing that we can ask openly and it is freely given. This is a great witness to all onlookers in the Spirit world.

Because we humans are asking in our imperfection to come into better alignment with God, knowing that he will forgive us, already has, and is joyous for our desire to come closer to him. The unHoly Angels were once in perfect alignment with him, and will be forgiven freely if only they ask for it. If imperfect humans know the need and can ask for this, how much more precious is it to show our vulnerability and God's forgiveness to the unHoly Angels? God desires them back as well, and they too, will be forgiven if they only ask.

We are always encouraged to see God as you would a best friend, one who loves us and seeks to let us know that we are loved. As any relationship that we are interested in pursuing, it takes time, sharing, love and opening to love. God is that place where we can open to love, know that we are loved, know that we are forgiven, and know that this is something that is a free gift from a loving Father! God's love has been shared with us and continues to be shared with us. *"For God loves us so much that he gave us his only Son, Jesus Christ for us." (John 3:16)* We already are forgiven and redeemed through Christ, our sins have already been forgiven.

What confession does is recognize the fact that when we do something separate from love, we do something separate from God. We err, miss the mark, sin. In stating this out loud we accomplish several things:

#1. We demonstrate our vulnerability in sharing what is personal in front of another.

#2. We state what we know to be wrong, things not of love, both the things we are aware of and things we are not aware of.

#3. We show that we know that we are loved and state for all those watching (those in body, in Spirit, and **All** Angels) that we know we have done wrong and ask God to forgive us publicly.

There are ripple effects from each of these 3 points. Being vulnerable to love and seeking out love no matter what, seeking to make it right when we have done wrong. Acknowledging what is of love and knowing that even when we did not choose it that we know better and know that when we do choose love, we are choosing God!

226

And, perhaps the least known is that we teach all those watching that if we can get it, that they too can choose love and be forgiven. For if God forgives us who are imperfect, how much more can God forgive the unHoly Angels who were made perfectly when they turn back to God and ask for forgiveness?

We become a teacher when we realize that we are not perfect, that we do not have to be perfect at this time for that future time will come and that we love God and look to please God and we take the steps needed to act on these beliefs showing all that we know that it matters not what man has to say about us for we belong to God. This is powerful.

A beautiful gift that was shared through the Holy Stigmata of Blessed Tiffany is that when we go to confession and declare what we know to have done wrong, the unHoly Angels cannot use this as ammunition against us. Confession serves as a protection where God steps in and says that the unHoly Angels cannot manipulate this or that for the person has the awareness of their sin and asked God for forgiveness. This demonstrates even greater trust and confidence in God's power and strength and in our ability to receive Love through being humble, knowing we cannot do it on our own, asking for God's strength and being vulnerable.

God detests the proud and gives Grace to the humble. It is pretty humbling stating where we have erred in front of another imperfect, though ordained, person. This is the deeper meaning to the scripture that God sees when we acknowledge that we struggle and cannot do it on our own and when we recognize that we need God. It is again, all about building our relationship with Love, knowing that we truly do nothing alone, God is always with us. *God shows himself strong to those whose hearts are true to him.* As to how often you can go to confession, it is up to you. Ask God to show you how often is best for you. The more you are called to do the greater work, the more important it is to have the awareness of what is happening for you along your path. Confession helps you to have more clarity, humility, helps all spiritual onlookers, cleanses our own spirit, and gives us a renewed sense of peace.

227

Who Are the Manipulated Ghosts?

Ghosts are humans who have died and not yet gone back to Father. *Manipulated ghosts* have fallen prey to the manipulations of the unHoly Angels and become manipulated thinking that they are demons too. The unHoly Angels twist the manipulated ghosts and use them against God's children. Remember these manipulated ghosts are at their core children of God, and they still have the chance to go back to Father, to learn more about love and have more opportunity to share in his love. We use the prayer for manipulated ones with respect since these are our brothers and sisters, God's children, who are being manipulated and kept from God.

We were given a specific prayer that to assist us in this battle. Since the manipulated ghosts are like pawns to the unHoly Angels, they are sent against to cause difficulty and attempt to weaken us so that we may make bad choices, choices separate from Love. Watching over our tongue and keeping in a place of peace even while doing this work is helpful.

This is the prayer: *"Lord, I ask that any manipulated ones here in this perimeter be nailed, held fast and silenced. I ask that their Angel show them their true name. As the homing Angel departs they too are allowed to leave and I say to them, Wake up O' Sleeper and rise from the dead and Christ will shine upon you. Wake up O' Sleeper and rise from the dead and Christ will shine upon you. Wake up O' Sleeper and rise from the dead and Christ will shine upon you. (Ephesians 5:14) Thank you Father that these may come home to you. In Jesus' name, Amen."* This prayer is set up specifically to assist with the returning of the manipulated ones. It is not a forcing back home but an awakening to who they are as children of God. When we hold them and silence them, they cannot cause any damage. The unHoly Angels typically give some power to these manipulated ghosts to cause disruption and damage, attempting to convince them into thinking they were never human at all, and were truly part of the brotherhood of unHoly Angels from the very beginning.

The homing Angel (or the Angel of Death as some refer to him) is a beautiful and very maternal and comforting Angel, this is the one assigned to bring us back to Father. This is a task of love. When our bodies are dying, the Homing Angel brings our friends and family members who have already transitioned to help us know that what we are seeing is real and not a hallucination. This helps to assist in dispelling fear and go touch the hand of the Angel and go home to the Light and Love we are created from.

How does a ghost state happen? Because even at this time, the one who died still has free will choices. These include whether to return to God or not. Free will is respected when the person is dead just as it is when the person is alive. Some people may still not believe they are dead, or feel that they have unfinished business, or fear going to God because of belief in traditions that make them afraid of what might happen to them. If they don't go with the Homing Angel, this creates a ghost state. One who goes to Love is at a higher vibration, a spirit and not in a ghost situation. As you can see, being in a ghost situation makes oneself open to attack and coercion, not all ghosts are manipulated, but many are, and the ones that aren't are under constant pressure to become manipulated. So it is an act of love for us to do the prayer for manipulated ghosts as often as it comes to mind.

It is important to know the Homing Angel will never force someone to go, but offers the way. The part of our prayer asking that "their Angel show them their true name" is referring to their Guardian Angel, the one that has been with them the whole time since before their birth. This Angel shows them their true name, not as we may know a name to be, like Henry or Steve but all that they truly are, including the aspects of love that they have polished over all their lifetimes and the ones worked on the last life.

This awareness given to the manipulated ghosts of who they truly are as a child of God, frees them from the control of the unHoly Angels and allows for communication to start up again between them and their Guardian Angel. Now add the prayer (which also works for any ghost) *"Wake up O' Sleeper and rise from the dead and Christ will shine upon you. Wake up O' Sleeper and rise from the dead and Christ will shine upon you. Wake up O' Sleeper and rise from the dead and Christ will shine upon you."*

This allows the Homing Angel to return and provides opportunity for them to return to God. It is still up to the ghost, so adding our own blessing asking that they return to God is powerful as well. Our intention combined with prayer and God's power in a specific direction! The Homing Angel will now come again awaiting their decision.

This prayer can also be separated into 2 parts, the part about holding them fast and silencing them and the part about them returning home to Father. This can be used to clear a whole area (up to a 100' perimeter) holding all manipulated ones there for a period of 24 hrs. After the 24 hrs, they will be free to go, whether you release them or not. Remember, since they were once here in the flesh just like us and Father has much more work for them to do, we are to show them respect as children of God and remember to finish out the prayer, giving them more opportunity to return to Father. This is very powerful and quite a beneficial prayer to use not only for yourself but for setting a perimeter in a common place such as a frequently visited coffee house, or a bank or a school can help many people and keep them from attack. Remember, we are covered in The Divine Decrees from the damage that the unHoly Angels may attempt to inflict but those who are not saying The Divine Decrees can always use this help. In addition while The Divine Decrees afford protection they are not used for helping the manipulated ones to return to Father. This prayer for the manipulated ones is used for that purpose, to ease the suffering of our brothers and sisters, even those who have passed. How much more beautiful to see that our brothers and sisters again have the opportunity to return to Father!

Who are the One-Third?

We talk about the 1/3 right after we talk about the manipulated ghosts, because the 1/3 are humans that are still alive and yet easily manipulated. These are the 1/3 of humanity who have consistently not polished facets of love throughout all their many lifetimes. They are referred to as those who are "lazy in spirit." Life after life, they have had the same choices as everyone else to choose love or choose fear, and they chose fear time almost every time. So life after life, they learned very little about love.

Love has many facets to it; forgiveness, how to receive and give love, patience, endurance, self-sacrifice, etc. We build from the things we know, the foundation that we have secured. The 1/3 have not laid a foundation, so there is inherent weakness at many levels.

This information is shared with you **not** so that you can be prejudiced against or hate the 1/3. This information is shared that you may recognize and know what is of love and what is of fear. Those that have not polished the needed facets of love from lifetime to lifetime are easily manipulated by the unHoly Angels, because they lack discernment about what is of God, what is good for them and what is the best cause and effect of their conscious and unconscious choices.

This is the meaning within this scripture: *"Awake, O sword, against my shepherd, against the man who is close to me!" declares the LORD Almighty. "Strike the shepherd, and the sheep will be scattered, and I will turn my hand against the little ones. In the whole land, " declares the LORD, "two-thirds will be struck down and perish; yet one-third will be left in it. This third I will bring into the fire; I will refine them like silver and test them like gold. They will call on my name and I will answer them; I will say, 'They are my people,' and they will say, 'The LORD is our God.'"(Zechariah 13:7-13:9)*

The first part of this scripture speaks of what happens to Jesus Christ, for Christ is the shepherd of all mankind. The sheep will be scattered, as what happened to the Apostles, running from those who came to take Christ away to torture and crucify him. The next part speaks of what happens: the 2/3 will be struck down and perish. This is not death as we think of it but death to the things of this world, for we are told to be in the world, but not of it. For as Christ said: *"I have told you these things, so that in me you may have peace. In this world you will have trouble. But take heart! I have overcome the world."(John 16:33)*

The last part of the scripture refers to a time to come, the time of 1,000 years of humanity and the environment coming back into perfection, with a great teaching program underway. During this time, the unHoly Angels are locked away, and cannot manipulate anyone or anything.

It will be during this time that the 1/3 will be refined; they will be able to learn about the love of God without manipulation from negative outside, demonic influence. The 1/3 will be as tender and innocent as new children, able to have great opportunity to recognize God and thereby recognize love. *(Revelation 20)*

We are never to judge, that is not what we are called to do. A reminder from scriptures: *"What causes fights and quarrels among you? Don't they come from your desires that battle within you? You want something but don't get it. You kill and covet, but you cannot have what you want. You quarrel and fight. You do not have, because you do not ask God. When you ask, you do not receive, because you ask with wrong motives, that you may spend what you get on your pleasures. You adulterous people, don't you know that friendship with the world is hatred toward God? Anyone who chooses to be a friend of the world becomes an enemy of God. Or do you think Scripture says without reason that the spirit he caused to live in us envies intensely? But he gives us more Grace. That is why Scripture says: "God opposes the proud but gives Grace to the humble." Submit yourselves, then, to God. Resist the devil, and he will flee from you. Come near to God and he will come near to you. Wash your hands, you sinners, and purify your hearts, you double-minded. Grieve, mourn and wail. Change your laughter to mourning and your joy to gloom. Humble yourselves before the Lord, and he will lift you up. Brothers, do not slander one another. Anyone who speaks against his brother or judges him speaks against the law and judges it. When you judge the law, you are not keeping it, but sitting in judgment on it. There is only one Lawgiver and Judge, the one who is able to save and destroy. But you - who are you to judge your neighbor?" (James 4:1-12)*

We can see from this suggestion by James to submit ourselves to God that we are to be the place of love, paying attention to the love that God has for us, acting out of this love, living for God and not for the things of this world, for everything is transient but love. This is an encouragement by James for those that are sinning (missing the mark, going against God's Will) to pay attention and to choose the way of God.

In addition we are cautioned against judging one another. We are not the ones who will sit in judgment; we are the ones that the unHoly Angels seek to perpetrate their manipulations upon. For all are God's children. Do we get upset and curse the child who is slow in learning? No. We are all learning together, God is the ultimate teacher. We simply do not have the capacity nor the ability to teach those have not gotten it over thousands of years, to teach them in one life time. Only the teacher, God can lay the right foundation with them, and he has shown that this will happen during the time of the 1,000 years without the manipulation of the unHoly Angels.

We are asked to have discernment. Discernment is extremely important in all aspects of this work. Especially in who you are focused on teaching. You will not be able to teach those of the 1/3, it is like trying to fill up a sieve. No one on earth will be able to teach them at this time. Once Christ has come and the 1000 years has begun, then all will be able to learn without any problems! The 1/3 have demonstrated again and again that they cannot learn when the unHoly Angels are interfering. Even if you were to do a deliverance upon the 1/3, the holes in their free will are so plentiful that it is not hard for the other unHoly Angels to come and enter the person again and again. This is the meaning of the scripture, *"they will seek to enter into the house and if it is found empty, stay."*

How Do I Recognize Who is of the 1/3 and Who is Not?

There are easy ways to recognize the third. There are many problems with their attitude about life, and they have an adrenal response of "fight or flight" on everything, not just the normal stresses of life. Here are some aspects of the attitude they may show: a mind-set of kill or be killed; there is never enough and they must fight to get theirs; and that the world and other people owe them and are out to get them; that real truth is up to the eye of the beholder; that they will never have what they need so having others give and do for them is normal. It is simple to see how this attitude can create such huge holes in their free will that the unHoly Angels can cause so much harm through them.

233

This is being shared with you *not* so you can scorn and have ill-will towards the 1/3 but so that you can have understanding of why some people will just not be able to get it. Since the 1/3 have not taken the time to polish the facets of love, they cannot discern what is of God and what is not. The 1/3 are still God's children, just as we are, and are to be treated with respect. Soon they will have the opportunity to learn without being influenced negatively, and to build the facets of love. This too is another example of God's great love for all of mankind.

Recognizing those of the 1/3 is recognizing the difference between *an honest cry for help, and a transfer of responsibility.* An illustration to make this simple to understand: God provides a fire for us while we are outside in the cold and darkness. God tells us where to get more wood that we may be warmer and have more light. When we go and get the wood, even though we are afraid, we have more light. As it gets brighter we see that God has a shelter set up for us, a tent in which to sleep. We are encouraged to keep on brightening the fire, to keep adding wood. We do so. As we add even more wood we see that we have been camping in God's front yard. We see God's house, the door is open, our favorite food is inside and we are invited into God's warm house. But it took our participation to get this far, it took us following through on our responsibility of getting the wood and putting it on the fire. Yes, this requires having faith that even though we are scared that it will be okay, that we can do it. Once we take the step of faith and add the wood, we gain encouragement and continue on. Those who recognize the light will keep seeking it out.

The 1/3 are those who are too lazy in spirit to put the wood on the fire. These are those who say to God "can you put the wood on for me, for you have given me the fire, so can't you put the wood on for me as well? Or these other people around me, can't they do it for me? I might get hurt out there, I'm scared, I don't trust that I'll be all right if I put my own wood on." The 1/3 are those who every time their faith has been tested have failed and not demonstrated that they have faith. The 1/3 seek to have everything done for them, seeking to manipulate and never taking the opportunity to learn to do it themselves. This is where their transfer of responsibility to someone else occurs.

234

It is not our job to put the wood on anyone else's fire. We are all called to have the courage and faith to know that there is wood where God said there would be wood. Then when we follow through and take the step in getting the wood and placing it on the fire, we have been faithful in small things, and are then given bigger things. We cannot get wood for another and tend to their fire; we have our own fire, our own learning of God's love that is occurring. We are to pay attention to what God is asking of each one of us. Every one of us is asked to take the necessary steps themselves. This means not being lazy in spirit but having the courage to trust in God and know that we are loved no matter what the illusion the unHoly Angels seek to put upon us. Then the joy and self-confidence builds as well, for in the three aspects of 'Love God and your neighbor as yourself,' the 1/3 have not even the foundation of confidence and love in themselves, since they have not experienced the joy of accomplishment of what they can do.

Those that have not done this when the time was slower, without as much manipulation upon Love will definitely not be able to do this as the time is speeding up and the pressure increases, for Love is what strengthens us. If the 1/3 failed to get God's message of love over and over again prior to this time of massive manipulation how will they ever get it when the unHoly Angels are seeking to do even more destruction? They will not. The 1/3 will not be able to learn with the amount of darkness that is occurring at this moment and will not get it as it continues to speed up. Take heart though, for it is as God has stated through Zechariah earlier, *"This third I will bring into the fire; I will refine them like silver and test them like gold. They will call on my name and I will answer them; I will say, 'They are my people,' and they will say, 'The LORD is our God.'" (Zechariah 13:9)*

This refining for the 1/3 will come after Christ has been victorious and the unHoly Angels are all encapsulated to watch the story of God's love unfold. This time of the 1000 years will be the time for all to learn without any manipulation of the unHoly Angels. All will know the Glory of God. So have no fear, for God's love is great and God will take care of his children!

235

The reason this information is being shared with you for additional discernment of why some people may act the way they do, and is so you will not waste your time trying to fill the sieve up with life giving water, just to see it pour back out again.

Why Would Time be Wasted? Aren't I Still Teaching About Love?

Yes, you are teaching about God's Love and that is what it is all about. Unfortunately, when you spend your time teaching the 1/3 you are giving milk to those who spit it back up every time rather than those that are dying of thirst. You are to give the message of hope and love to those who are able to swallow and digest the milk, those that strengthen and seek out the meat after they have had the milk. The deeper things need to be taught and spread all throughout the world. The message of hope and love needs to be put in the hands of those that are able to transform the world. It is not about teaching people to have faith, it is about teaching those who already have faith *what to do with their faith!* Remember, we are not to put the wood on someone else's fire; each of us is responsible for our own spiritual growth toward Love. We are each here on our own journey. We just point to the source of the wood.

What if One of the 1/3 Tries to Become Ordained?

Since God is the one who is doing the ordination through man, God is in charge of whom his Holy Spirit rests upon and who it does not. Even if one who is of the 1/3 was to make it through the Becoming the Mystic/Divine Decree classes and actively sought out the ordination, made it through the 2 day class for the ordination and made it all the way up to the place where hands are placed upon for the ordination to pass through man from God, God is the one who is in charge and the Spirit would be withheld. The 1/3 have shown that they have not polished enough facets of love, that they have been lazy in spirit, asking others and God to take their steps for them. The 1/3 have chosen fear rather than love. They have struggled with the easier things of love, how much more difficult will it be for them with the more challenging aspects of love? Not only are they easily manipulated by the unHoly Angels but they cannot be given greater responsibility until they have demonstrated that they can be faithful and trusted on smaller responsibilities.

236

"Well done good and faithful servant. You have been faithful in a few things; I will put you in charge of many. Come and share in your Master's happiness." (Matthew 25:23) So if one of the 1/3 attempted to become ordained, God would not allow it. Even if the hands on were to take place, God's Holy Spirit wouldn't come through. God is in control and chooses whom he blesses.

How Do We Make Blessing Oil

The recipe for the oil that we use for blessings and anointing came through the Holy Stigmata of Blessed Tiffany, and was given the name the "Oil of Thanksgiving." It wasn't until several months afterward that she discovered the word *Eucharist* comes from the Greek word for *thanksgiving.* So the name given us for this oil is very appropriate, and it is with a heart of thanksgiving that we share it here with you. This oil will be used for many blessings you do. The blessings that require the use of the Oil of Thanksgiving are:

Deliverance Prayer
Generational Bondage Prayer
Breaking of curses, hexes, spells, incantations, negative prayer and evil intent.
House blessings (for the windows, doors and mirrors)
Blessings upon individuals
Blessings upon the Houses of Prayer and Worship
Vehicle blessings
Blessings of objects (key chains, medals, religious items)
Anointing
Daily blessings for self, after communion

There are two parts to making the Oil of Thanksgiving.
First, mix the ingredients in the correct ratio:
50% olive oil (pure virgin)
20% frankincense oil
20% myrrh oil
10% spikenard oil

The second part that is needed is a blessing on the oil, consecrating it to God. Here is the blessing you can use: *Heavenly Father, maker of all good things, thank you for this gift. I ask that you bless + (make the sign of the cross) this oil transforming it into the Oil of Thanksgiving. Thank you Lord, that it may be made Holy by you for all the blessings you set forth. I ask that all this Oil of Thanksgiving touch be brightened and made more useful to you. Thank you Heavenly Father, In Jesus' name, Amen.*

The Oil of Thanksgiving is to be applied to your finger tip first and then your finger will touch the object for blessings (person's forehead, picture for distant deliverances, objects, etc.) It is suggested to use a leak free container, something that seals up well. There are some very good small anointing oil receptacles available online, some with a keychain attached to carry and hold the vial easier. A good friend of mine uses old film containers (the small black ones with the grey lids) and places a small amount of oil on the bottom and then puts cotton balls on top of those, this keeps the oil in without any dripping out. Then all you have to do is to touch your finger tip to the cotton ball and viola! You are set!

How Do We Make Holy Water?

One of the most beautiful things about being ordained is the fact that God gives the blessing to you through the ordination to do blessings upon all God's creation!

The blessings themselves are wonderful gifts that aid tremendously in the work. One of the most frequently used gifts is the gift of Holy Water. Holy Water is used in the blessings of the land, the blessings on homes/businesses, blessings on bodies of water, blessings at communion, blessings of cleansing for people, places and things. Holy Water has been used for centuries for many blessings. The blessings listed above are just a few uses for this gift.

Holy Water can be used at anytime to rinse us clean from anything that we feel is not of God's light and love.

We can use Holy Water upon our heads and hands after doing a deliverance or exorcism. This is a great example for you know that you are already protected by Love and his Holy Angels in doing the work. Adding the fact of asking for an additional cleansing to rinse away anything that is not of God is a nice brightening to add to the work.

There have been many blessings through the years utilized to make Holy Water, many blessings that have been allowed by God. What we need to realize is that it is Love who sanctifies, Love who blesses and Love who makes things Holy. It is not done by what mankind dictates but what God allows. As such, God has accepted and allowed the blessings that have been used for centuries for blessing of the water and asking that it be made Holy Water. The most important part of the entire blessing comes in the sign of the Cross that is made over the water by one who has been ordained.

The one who has been ordained has chosen to carry additional responsibilities and is a strong conduit for God to use in the work. The blessing that comes through the hands of one who is ordained is through the channel that God has established through his son, Jesus Christ as the High Priest for all of mankind. This is why I, Father Billy, was asked to be ordained in the line of Apostolic Succession, to go under the blessing and protection that Christ began through his blessing and laying on of hands for the Apostles.

As you have been ordained and blessed by God to do this work, the sign of the Cross is of great significance and importance. This is how all our work is done, through Christ. As such the recognition and inclusion of the sign of the Cross is central to the blessings to be done. The blessing for the Holy Water must contain the sign of the Cross within the spoken blessing upon the water. The appropriate placement for the inclusion of the sign of the Cross will be shown through this symbol + in the blessings.

Here are several blessings you may use to make Holy Water. All three blessings have been shared already in the St. Joseph's Sunday Missal, Catholic Book Publishing 1999. Remember to have a container to place the water in as well to bring it wherever you travel.

Any container will do and it will be helpful to have a container that you use regularly for storage. You can make and use as much Holy Water as you wish. There is no expiration date on Holy Water! The following blessings are acceptable for the work God is calling you to do. You are free to add to the blessings knowing that you are well heard for you are bright and you are loved. Whatever is allowed with what you add will be allowed and whatever is not simply will not occur. God is in charge and God is the one who bestows all blessings. We are fortunate that God allows for the blessings here to take place through mankind.

God our Father, your gift of water brings life and freshness to the earth; it washes away our sins and brings us eternal life. We ask you now to bless + this water, and to give us your protection on this day which you have made your own. Renew the living spring of your life within us and protect us in spirit and body, that we may be free from sin and come into your Presence to receive your gift of salvation. We ask this through Christ our Lord, Amen.

Or:

Lord God almighty, creator of all life, of body and soul, we ask you to bless + this water: as we use it in faith forgive our sins and save us from all illness and the power of the evil one. Lord, in your mercy give us living water, always springing up as a fountain of salvation: free us, body and soul, from every danger, and admit us to your Presence in purity of heart. Grant this through Christ our Lord, Amen.

Or:

Lord God almighty, hear the prayers of your people: we celebrate our creation and redemption. Hear our prayers and bless + this water which gives fruitfulness to the fields, and refreshment and cleansing to man. You chose water to show your goodness when you led your people to freedom through the Red Sea and satisfied their thirst in the desert with water from the rock. Water was the symbol used by the prophets to foretell your new covenant with man. You made the water of baptism Holy by Christ's baptism in the Jordan: by it you give us a new birth and renew us in holiness. May this water remind us of our baptism, and let us share the joy of all who have been baptized at Easter. We ask this through Christ our Lord.

240

You are also asked to exorcise the water, that is to do a deliverance prayer upon the water. *Father, I ask that any unHoly Angels in, on, near or around this water be nailed, held fast and silenced. I decommission, bind and encapsulate them through the power of the Shed Blood of the Lamb and I bring them up to your Presence immediately Lord, to deal with as you see fit. May you fill any empty place here with your love and your light. Thank you Father, In Jesus' name, Amen.*

This ensures that the water is blessed and made Holy by God. This water will be used in driving out darkness. This is why it must contain no darkness in it. It serves as an example of how we are to be; clean and pure for God that we may be bright enough to do his work, and is a symbol and reminder of our baptism as well. It is a place of new creation, a place where everything is cleansed and made anew.

These blessings can be used for taking water and asking that it be transformed into Holy Water. It is always suggested to use clean fresh water to start out. It does not have to be distilled, whatever you would safely drink can be used as the base for making Holy Water. After the water is blessed and transformed into Holy Water it is now acceptable to use it for the blessings shared in this book. Remember that it is God who made this water, God who made you, and God who granted you the authority to share in these blessings through ordination. May we not forget to give thanks and praise to our God of love who allows these spiritual tools for all the amazing things for this shift from time into timelessness!

What is the True Spirit of Animals and Why They are Here?

Just as we are a spark off of the Divine Flame, domesticated animals are smaller sparks off of our own flames. We are given the choice before coming into these bodies of how many sparks we wish to let out to become our delegates. Delegates serve a specific purpose, they are here to teach us more about love, the giving and receiving of love, balance within these bodies and most certainly how to play! Delegates take these roles very seriously.

241

Delegates operate within our own free will, they are a part of us and are here to help us.

Our sparks drop into what people generally think of as pets or domesticated animals. Once we have taken ownership and while the pet takes its first nap, the spark or delegate comes into the pet and it becomes our delegate. It does not matter if they were owned by other people before us. Think of it this way: when we sleep, our body is on automatic, our breathing continues, our heat continues to beat, our body is still alive; but meanwhile we are not conscious of any of these things or even of having a body. This is because our spirit is out at night school and also doing other things that God calls us to do, but our spirit is not attached. That is why sleep is often likened to death. Except in death, the spirit does not re-enter the body. Now with delegates, when we have made a free will choice to bring one home, once that choice is made, the very first time the animal goes to sleep our delegate spirit ascends upon the animal. This is why you may see similar personalities of animals you have had, repeat time after time, while you work on those specific characteristics that you are expanding on.

I would like to expand upon something else here as well – *when death of a person or an animal is imminent, God lifts the spirit out.* This is a place of comfort for you to know, since any images that you have seen of the body going into spasm or destruction before death is not felt by the spirit, since it is not in the body at that time; the body is only reacting on automatic. Before the body hits the ground from a tall building, before the car bursts into flames, before the animal's throat is torn, before a murder takes place. This is how gracious and loving God is! Can you see how we never truly have anything to fear?

We can have more than one delegate at a time. It depends on how many we choose to let out from us when we were coming into this body, this life. These sparks wait around us as parts of us until we have taken ownership of a pet or animal. Wild animals and fish will never be our delegates. While a fish take may be calming to look at and watch, fish will always remain a food source. Our sparks will not drop into fish or wild animals.

242

Can you see why people love their pets so much? Can you see the attachment, and why the care and the longing for pets is so important? It is truly, the reuniting of a part of our spirit that has descended into our pet helping us to remember the place of love that we come from, the place of love that we are! Pets are so much more than pets, they are our delegates of love allowed for us at this time to experience even more about love. This is why people are so attached to their animals for they are a part of their very self! This is also why when you see animals being treated with abuse, you will see their owners being hurtful to themselves as well.

What about the non-domesticated animals or wild animals? These all belong to God. These are what we can think of as Father's delegates. These are the place of love and joy for Father to feel and experience. It is easy to see how people of all cultures have had respect for animals in some regard and how those that we think of as being more spiritual have picked up on the respectful treatment of animals. When we take care of the wild animals, when we show love and respect for them, we demonstrate love and respect for God.

Many people, after knowing this information, turn and ask "well what about eating meat, does that mean I am a bad person?" No! It does not. Blessed Tiffany specifically asked the question of why this information had not been written in the Bible about the role of animals, and about meat. God said it was because if mankind had known, they would not have eaten meat, and would have perished right after the flood, because there was not enough sustenance in the land itself through any other means. Before the flood, you will see that no animal meat was eaten, but afterward *"everything that lives and move will be food for you. Just as I gave you the green plants, I now give you everything."* (Genesis 9:1-4) When meat was given to mankind it was with the provision that the blood in it was poured out to God. As we have seen, even the blood circulating in our veins is not ours, but on loan by God, it is considered his.

God is so loving that he would allow for encroachment upon himself rather than have mankind suffer and perish by not having enough to eat. This is a precious insight into the tenderness of Love.

243

This is God's Love in action everyday, literally laying down one's life for another. *"Greater love has no one than this, that he lay down his life for his friends." (John 15:13)*

Be encouraged therefore to partake of the blessings that God has ordained for us. For God has allowed mankind to eat meat that mankind not suffer or be in lack. This is a blessing upon us. Yes, in all cultures throughout time we have seen the natural inclination that as spirituality increases, many have chosen to eat less meat or not to eat meat at all. But this is not required by God, this is a choice of man, and at this time of world imperfection, we are able to eat meat as needed or even desired.

We are told that if a person has faith that is strong, it will not matter what they eat. If their faith is weaker and they see a limitation upon themselves that they have imposed or bought into from an imposition of another and they think that they cause themselves harm by eating this food or that food, then they are not to be pushed to change. It is up to them. Accept their choices and allow their faith to grow with God. (1 Corinthians 8:1-13)

From this we can also better understand the sacrifice of animals all throughout scripture. In the Old Testament, we have many examples of an animal being offered as a sacrifice, to wash away sin. God asked that these animals be the first born, be pure and without defect and he asked that their blood be used as a cleansing. Does it make more sense now, knowing that it was God's blood, through the animal, that was being used as a cleansing? God himself was rinsing away sin through his own blood within the animal offered.

Let it be up to each individual whether or not they eat meat. That is between the individual and God. This knowledge is shared with you not for it to present a stumbling in faith but so that you may understand the deeper things of what is shared, to have the deeper knowledge of life and understand even the bigger picture of why things are the way they are, and now these glimpses are being offered to us to help us strengthen, understand and grow.

244

Does it make much more sense now looking at why there are many organizations that look out for the welfare of pets and animals? All animals, whether they are our pets/delegates or they belong to God are a gift for all to learn about love. Those that understand love and seek to protect love have also sought to protect the aspects of love and righteousness, specifically in this case, the delegates of our animals.

What if there is only one domestic animal in a family? Our delegates related specifically to an individual. If you are in a family and there is only one pet in the family, that pet is a delegate of only one person. Now this in no way limits the giving and receiving of love. Many know and understand the value of having a pet and although there is work and maintenance that goes along with it, the love that is there is immeasurable. When there is a pet within a family, there is love that is shared with all, and when that delegate is loved by others in the family, the person it is attached to is also loved.

Again it is important to look at how we treat our pets, since it is a reflection of how we do with love. Are we too hard on ourselves? Do we expect perfect behavior? Do we seek to have constant attention? Do we want to control everything around us? These are things that we can see reflected in the ways that we interact with our pets, and opportunities to change behaviors. As such, when we are kind and loving to our pets, we are learning more about love as well as showing love to the person whose delegate is the pet!

This is another reason why those who have pets may feel rejection when someone doesn't care for their pet or when someone is mean to their pet. If the pet is neglected or ignored it is as if that person is neglected or ignored as well. When we show kindness and love to the pet of someone else, we are showing kindness and love to that person. This is a pretty neat way to experience the giving and receiving of love! To those that have pets or desire to have pets, this will make perfect sense. To those who don't desire to have pets at all, know that you made this choice before coming into this life, and are not forced now to have them, since there are no delegate sparks there from you waiting to come in. They are only an additional opportunity Love gives us, and we can choose freely as we like for each life to have none, one, a few or many. It is, and has been, up to you all along.

245

And each life you get to choose again what to decide for that time.

Like us, pets are in a physical body and these physical bodies have to be taken care, and their bodies need balance and care to survive just as ours do. Remember this when you are questioning why your dog is eating rather than coming over to play with you. It is not that the dog doesn't want to play, it is simply that they must eat to survive in the body. With all this information, we are not to take personally what our pets do or how they react or respond. We are to look at it all as an opportunity!

Have you ever been pestered by your pet to talk to them or pet them when you are having a really tough time? Ever feel annoyed because your pet wants you to take them out for a walk or play when you are frustrated? Ever feel the last thing you want to do is stop your work, yet that is the very thing that your pet is asking you to do? Can you see and understand now why all this is happening? It is precisely when you are frustrated or upset that your pet knows and feels this as well. As your delegate, they are intimately connected with your spirit. If you are in a bad place, they feel it. Their job is helping you to balance, to choose love, to lighten and to play! Your delegate is happy when you are happy and your delegate is sad when you are sad. Knowing that they are a part of you makes this easier to understand. This is all about love. We are given these gifts, these pets, these delegates that we may better understand love and be expanded in love. This is how loving God is, that God allows for these opportunities of love.

Now, when the body of a pet is worn out, when it is time for a pet to die, it is extremely important to understand that it is only the body that dies. The spirit of the delegate lifts out and awaits the next new body that you accept into your life as your pet. The delegate doesn't die; it just awaits the next interaction.

Depending on how many delegates you have waiting to come in, how many you agreed to let out before you came into the flesh, the delegate that was in the body that just passed may come right back or may wait as another delegate or spark off of your flame, drops in.

246

Either way, it is about God's Love being shown to you and you having the opportunity to experience more about love.

So as the pet is dying, it is important to let them know how great a job they have done, and that they have taught you a lot and helped you so much. Letting the pet know that it is okay to die and let go and when you are ready, you will choose a new body for them to drop in and share more love with you. It is important that you give your pet permission to die and it is a relief knowing that the spirit of the pet, your delegate never dies. Have faith knowing that love never dies!

When you decide to buy or receive a pet, once you accept the pet as your own and take ownership of the pet, it is then that your delegate spark drops into the pet the first time it goes to sleep. It is up to you to choose what kind of body you will be giving your delegate to share love. It is not necessary to choose a body that has been already beaten up. Many people gravitate to the animals that are sickly and in need of love. That is okay, but it is important to understand that the healthier the body of the animal, the longer the delegate can be around. It is just as important to understand that the delegate doesn't die when the body of your pet does. You are in charge of your choices, the type of body for your delegate or if you want one at all. God doesn't love us any less because we don't have pets. Pets are an opportunity as our delegates for us to know more about love and therefore know more about God! You have the choice. Continuing to do blessing upon your pets will help them, as well as helping you.

How About Blessings for Animals and or Delegates?

Our animal delegates are covered in much of the protection offered in The Divine Decrees. We can use this prayer to cover our delegates and any other animals in the vicinity (up to 100 foot perimeter from the place of blessing)

Here is the prayer to use:
"Lord, I ask that your Holy Angels protect and defend all the little ones in this perimeter and our delegates as well that they not fall prey to any manipulation by the unHoly. Thank you Father, In Jesus' name, Amen."

247

This will last for 24 hours and can be repeated before the end of the 24hr period to ensure that no gap takes place. It is important to understand that animals can be easily manipulated by the unHoly Angels. The unHoly Angels can use them as fear tactics or to attack. An animal will not take a human life unless darkness has entered into it, the same as a person cannot take a human life unless darkness has entered into it as well.

Remember that The Divine Decrees offer you much protection already from the manipulated ones and from the unHoly Angels, this prayer will afford your even greater protection. Remember as well, wild animals are sparks off of God and our domesticated animals are sparks off of us as we are off of God. All these beautiful creatures are to be respected and loved. This prayer will help you to see this love as well.

How Do We Bless a Vehicle?

Using the Blessed Oil, making the sign of the Cross upon it and state *"Lord, may there be no opportunity for any exterior physical manipulation, manipulation of mechanical devices or electrical devices and may a safe perimeter be established around this vehicle keeping it safe from any incident or accident all through the power of the Shed Blood of the Lamb. May your Holy Angels protect and defend my brother (sister) here and keep them and all those who ride with them free from harm. May this be a place of brightness such that all those who come against must either transform and become brighter or move away. For this vehicle carries my brother (sister) and they carry you. Thank you Father, In Jesus' name, Amen."*

Let the owner of the care know that this is a prayer for protection and they must still pay attention and remember that they are responsible for their own actions, and cause and effect of these actions as well.

How Do We Bless the Air?

We are given the opportunity to use our bodies as a purification for the air around us without harming our bodies at all.

248

This is done by the following prayer, breathing in the surrounding air and exchanging it with our Holy breathe, cleansing and purifying, expanding many fold through God's power. This is to cleanse the areas we can sense that are struggling with pollutions or toxins, to help all that is carried over by this air as well, people, plants, animals, etc. This is a powerful prayer that is greatly magnified by God's power. We are to do this when we know that it is needed.

This is the prayer: *"Lord, I ask that the air here be cleansed and purified, brought back to its former state without the manipulation of the sons of man or the unHoly. In the name of the Father (inhale and exhale the Holy breathe), in the name of the Son (inhale and exhale the Holy breathe) and in the name of the Holy Spirit (inhale and exhale the Holy breathe). Thank you Father, In Jesus' name, Amen."* To close the prayer, make the sign of the cross upon yourself.

This can be done anywhere at anytime. Inside places, enclosed spaces it is very powerful. Outside, the air is expanded and a very toxic place may require repeating this prayer at 3 different places within the area. It is extremely important to remember that this is a Holy gift and to be treated with respect. It is also suggested to not overdo this specific prayer, to take a break when needed. Pay attention to lightheadedness, which is demonstrating that you are reaching your limit for this prayer and may have to wait for a bit. This is a powerful prayer!

How Do We Bless the Water?

We start out by taking Holy Water and as we sprinkle it upon the water we are asking to be cleansed we say: *"Lord, I ask that this water here be blessed, I ask that this water be cleansed and purified, that it be brought back to its former state without the manipulation of the sons of man or the unHoly. In the name of the Father (sprinkle water), in the name of the Son (sprinkle water), and in the name of the Holy Spirit (sprinkle water). Thank you Father, In Jesus' name. Amen."*

The same rule applies here for an area that is clearly polluted or toxic: Bless it 3 times in 3 different places. Father is the one who again makes this stronger, amplifying your prayer and intention with his power and strength. This means that a single, enclosed body of water, blessed in 3 times within 3 different areas at one separate instance can purify the entire water system. The blessing can be repeated as needed keeping in mind that the more polluted an area, the more work it will need.

You can bless it more than the 3 times, blessing in more than one instance. For example, Monday: you bless Lake So-and-so, cleansing it by blessing it 3 times (repeated the prayer 3 times while sprinkling the Holy Water) in 3 different sections of the Lake. The blessings do not have to be far from one another, just not while standing in one place for all 3 blessings. You know that Lake So-and-so is a dumping ground for chemical waste. You can go back to the Lake the next day, several days later, several months later or not at all to repeat the blessing. The blessing works on the concentration of pollution, the more an area is polluted, the more blessings it will need. If the pollution is stopped, the Lake will not need as many blessings.

How Do We Do a House Blessing? Or Sacred Ground?

Blessing a house is best done with at least two ordained people, during the daylight. The Holy Eucharist, Holy Water and Blessed Oil will be needed. It is important that the owner or renter of the property be present. This demonstrates the free will permission to have their place cleansed and blessed. There are 10 steps to blessing a house:

(1). Start out with a *blessing on the land.* (see Land Blessings).

(2). Then a prayer to hold any manipulated ghosts: *"Lord, I ask, any manipulated ones here in this perimeter, that they be nailed, held fast and silenced."* The remainder of this prayer is to be said at the conclusion of the blessing of the house.

(3). The next step involves making the entire area *Sacred Ground:* the perimeter extends for a 33 ft. circumference.

We take the Eucharist, place in the ground (after lifting the dirt) then pour the Blessed Wine over it, replace the dirt, pray: *"that this now be made into Sacred Ground and that it remain so until the end of days, and that the Holy Angels may have free will access to protect all those in this perimeter in Jesus' name, Amen."*

This consecrates the ground and changes it into Scared Ground. This blessing grants free will access to the Holy Angels to protect all those in the perimeter without having to be called in! You can use this blessing wherever and whenever you feel darkness, not just for blessing houses (such as where covens meet, etc). Remember, the consecrated Eucharist can never be sullied, it brightens everything it touches. God gave us this blessing to add to our protection, giving the Holy Angels ever greater ability to help us. It is suggested to bring plenty of Eucharist and Blessed Wine with you (already blessed). The Sacred Ground blessing lasts until the end of days, even after any buildings are gone, helping even those passing by or through the area.

(4). Next, a room by room blessing, anointing of the windows, mirrors, doorways and entrances with the Blessing Oil in the sign of a Cross. One person does the blessing with the Blessed Oil while the other takes the Holy Water and sprinkles it throughout the house, liberally. It is important to pay attention to the more well-used areas of the dwelling, assuring the resident that it is about brightening, inviting in God's Holy Angels to protect and defend, teaching them as you go so they have less fear and can see that this is an act of love, not fear. If called, singing hymns or songs of praise to raise the vibration is appropriate.

(5). Paying attention to problem areas, wherever you or the homeowners feel something of darkness, blessing the specific area with Blessing Oil and Holy Water and placing your hand on it, sending love forth, sealing the area in light and love. Next, having them place something of a remembrance of the Love of God there, whether it is a Crucifix (a stronger reminder than a Cross of the gift of salvation), pictures of those who have led Holy lives or articles of faith, even pictures of what gives them joy, family, friends. Scripture verses, Bibles all carry an anointing upon them as well.

(6). Next, teaching them this: our house is like an extension of our free will, what we invite into our house is important. Teaching them about bringing in love and having it be a place of love and light. Ridding of anything that has negative or uncomfortable energy with it. Remembering that many people have heirlooms, items from garage sales, hand-me-downs, etc that can have energy patterns of all those who have owned them before. Blessing these things and asking for a removal of any negative energy, anything not of God and sprinkling again with Holy Water.

(7). If something doesn't feel clean even after the Holy Water, it is to be removed, burned, sprinkled again with Holy Water and buried with a prayer asking God *"to cleanse it and return it to its former state without the manipulation of man or the unHoly, in Jesus' name, Amen."* These are things that have been consecrated to unHoly Angels, used in unHoly rites, or unclean in other ways.

(8). This is a good place to teach them about The Divine Decrees, how they are here for us to use for protection and aligning our will with God's Will for us. This is a tremendous way for them to brighten and purify their house! Giving them appropriate contact info so they know they are not alone and to alleviate any fear.

Letting them know as well about counseling and brightening their own personal house, their bodies, free will, original issues, cause and effect and most importantly the Love of God! Reminding them that as children of God, they have the authority to state what is welcome in their home and what is not!

(9). Have them walk you out and offer to bless their vehicles as well.

(10). Before leaving, close the prayer for the manipulated ones held in that perimeter saying *"Lord, I ask that any manipulated ones held here, that their Angels show them their true name, and as the Homing Angel departs, they too are allowed to leave and I say to them: Wake up O' Sleeper and rise from the dead and Christ will shine upon you.*

252

Wake up O' Sleeper and rise from the dead and Christ will shine upon you. Wake up O' Sleeper and rise from the dead and Christ will shine upon you. Thank you Father, that they may return to you. In Jesus' name, Amen."

This prayer will also help ghosts that are not manipulated. The prayer allows for the Homing Angel to come down and give additional opportunities for their spirits to return to God.

Blessings of Items, and Discernment of Energies Already on Items

It is also very important in doing this Holy work to understand that God allows for great things for us at this time. While we can be in a house and do a blessing upon it, or bless a car, God also allows for us to be able to bless the keychain that carries the keys to these places (and work, office, Post Office box, etc). We can do a blessing upon all these places just by blessing the keychain that holds all the keys to all these places! How beautiful is that! We are allowed touch-stones to help us in our expansion of faith, trust, hope, discernment and love.

Here is a blessing that you can use on the keychain that will cover all that all the keys that are or will be placed upon the keychain: *"Heavenly Father, thank you for your love. Thank you for this allowance of your overflowing of love. May your Holy Angels have free will access to protect my brothers and sisters in these places. May these be places of brightness such that all that comes against must either transform and become brighter or move away. I pray the Anointing of the Shed Blood of the Lamb over these places that my brothers and sisters may be protected here and have the peace needed to do your will, without the manipulations of the evil one. Thank you Lord, in Jesus' name, Amen."*

We are allowed touch-stones to strengthen our faith. There are also objects that already carry blessings upon them: The Divine Decrees, objects from sacred and Holy places (even rocks), photographs of those who have lived Holy lives (such as those who have been blessed with the Holy Stigmata), objects of devotion to Mother Mary and all the Saints, Holy Books such as Bibles.

253

And especially those things that recall the salvation given through Christ, such as Crucifixes. Crucifixes differ from Crosses. Crosses depict the wooden cross that Christ was nailed to and died upon. Crucifixes go even further into the remembrance and have Love surrendered and vulnerable to God upon the cross. These can carry a wide range of wonderful blessings and is a furtherance of the information of why a Crucifix is to be above your bed (and in the houses that you bless).

For the examples of touch-stones, we recall how Father had blessed the Apostle Paul's handkerchiefs so that when they were left or sent to a person, that person received a blessing as well. *"God did extraordinary miracles through Paul, so that even handkerchiefs and aprons that had touched him were taken to the sick, and their illnesses were cured and the evil spirits left them." (Acts 19:11-12)* God had not stopped giving signs and wonders in the 1st century, and he hasn't now. Love has continued all throughout time to show himself to mankind and encourage humanity on their path towards him, and he has littered that path with miracles and blessings.

Even now, in the modern age, many things can carry a blessing, books, websites, MP3 recordings, music, paintings, etc. Use your discernment to know what things are of love and softness, or even carry a Holy blessing upon them. There are many differences. Energy tracings are like a dusting of energy on an item that has been around strong energy, and can either be various stages of good or bad. Just when you go into a room where there has been an argument, you can feel the thickness of the air, the heaviness of it can be like cutting with a knife. Good feelings have a lightness about them and have an energy tracing of love that they were immersed in; but it is different for items that are blessed, for this is a gift of energy added by God – and it is a pure, Holy and exciting energy, almost like a portal connecting you directly to the Love of giving and receiving of the life experiences of that person, and helps greatly the energy and connection of the person who brings this into their home and surroundings, for it adds a blessing, and often a healing, to that as well.

Likewise, there are things that can also carry curses, hexes, spells, incantations, negative prayer or evil intent upon them.

This is why you are given the opportunity to do blessings to create an atmosphere of light and love around you whenever you discern there is a problem.

If you go to a garage sale and pick up an item that has negative intent or was used to harm a person or even used in a profane ritual to the unHoly Angels and you purchase this item and bring it into your home you have just given darkness a touch stone to you in your own home. It is essential that we understand that discernment is a big part of this work and is to be included in our own property that we not make it more challenging for us to hear the voice of God by having things of darkness around us. We are asked to have a clean and bright place especially where we live; that we may be unencumbered by anything that is not of Love, that we may be in a place of brightness without manipulation and connection to things that are of a lower vibration, things that are unHoly.

The Arrival Act helps to rinse away harm from items that have been given to you by the 1/3, things that are harmful to you. It is also important for you to have discernment of things so that you may be able to surround yourself in God's Love and have things that are bright and uplifting around you, things that help you in your path of love not things that disrupt or can harm you. *Bless the items in your house,* especially items from garages sales, estate sales, even gifts from friends or relatives that can carry high emotion upon them. Strengthen your discernment so that the place you live in can be a place of light and love, a sanctuary for you to be able to do God's Work.

How Do We Do Land Blessings?

When doing the blessings it is essential to understand that you have not only asked that God bless the land or that God bless the house of prayer/fellowship but that you leave an indent upon the area as well. As such, you are asked to be cognizant of the emotional state you are in when doing the blessings. A place of high negative emotion, being upset or frustrated leaves the indent of a negative emotion upon the area blessed. A place of love and gratitude leaves a blessing of brightness upon the area. We are called to do all this work through love. The message we share is love.

How we share the message is through love. Therefore, be bright and joyous when doing this work and always do every blessing in love.

For land blessings it is a deliverance upon the land itself. This will require 3 commissioned people. The blessing is not permanent and depends on the free will choices of all the people who live or move through the area. The more these choose love, the longer the blessing will last. The less they do, the quicker the blessing drops. It is best to do this from the highest point attainable while still on the ground itself.

Each commissioned person will then each look all the way around themselves in a full circle stating: *"As far as the eyes can see, I nail, hold fast and silence any unHoly Angels here. I decommission, bind and encapsulate them through the power of the Shed Blood of the Lamb, and bring them immediately up to you Lord, to deal with as you see fit."*

One of the three will be given the gift of hearing the names of the unHoly Angels or their hierarchy, you are to call them out individually adding: *"I decommission, bind and encapsulate the spirit of ... through the power of the Shed Blood of the Lamb and bring them immediately up to you Lord to deal with as you see fit."* When the naming is complete, asking that *"only love and light be allowed to enter here, we return this land to you Father, purified and sanctified that every knee shall bow to you O' Lord, in Jesus' name. Amen."*

Holy Water in the shape of a Cross with a circle around it is then made upon the ground. Then proceed to take communion and say a deliverance prayer for the three involved in the blessing itself. Remember that in this prayer by calling out the named ones, these unHoly Angels as well as those that are unnamed, the lesser ones are all brought out, decommissioned, bound and encapsulated and brought back to Father for him to deal with as he sees fit. We are never to pass judgment even on these who torment the sons of man, that is not for us to do. Judgment belongs not to us. Treat this respectfully and remember, *"I have given you authority to trample on snakes and scorpions and to overcome all the power of the enemy; nothing will harm you. However, do not rejoice that the spirits submit to you, but rejoice that your names are written in heaven."* (Luke 10:19-20)

Many will be helped by this land blessing. It will remain blessed for a short period of time, depending on the free will choices of those on the land and upon the attack of the unHoly Angels upon the land. The unHoly Angels vie for property and available, freshly cleared land and people who do not fill themselves with the love of God after a deliverance.

Remember it is not about permanently clearing the land, it is about easing the suffering of our brothers and sisters for what ever time it lasts. There will always be fires to put unto until the Warrior Son and his Holy Army are victorious. So be patient and see that we will be fighting and cleansing, battling and healing, providing opportunity and blessing until this time. Do not be discouraged, you will also not see all the fruits of your labor or realize the full impact of your choices of love but they are vast! Remain faithful and trusting in Our Lord and Savior, Jesus Christ.

For the land blessings, 3 people will be needed. If one of these is gifted with the Holy Stigmata only 2 people will be needed since the third that will be there will be Christ himself, placing his hand upon theirs. One of these 3 people will need to be blessed with the gift of hearing. It will be necessary for them to be able to hear Father clearly to be given the names of the unHoly Angels to call out for the blessing.

This person will not be required to speak out-loud the name of the unHoly Angel, and since their names are unusual, only the beginning is needed, spoken in our mind. Father knows who these unHoly Angels are and will send his Holy Angels to bring these unHoly Angels back to him.

The unHoly Angels have the opportunity to leave the area that will be blessed right up until the actual blessing itself. God grants this to them that they may yet use their free will choice to come back to him on their own. The unHoly Angels may call out to Father and immediately they will be brought back to him. They will have the opportunity to call out to God anytime and return.

This work is not about vengeance or attacking the darkness. This work is about brightening the light.

We are given this blessing to ease the suffering that is upon mankind. This is not done out of aggression, out of anger, or out of vengeance upon those who have chosen to separate from God. We are not judging, we are bringing the love and light of God. All this is done out of love. We are given this blessing as an opportunity to rinse the land clean from the manipulation of the unHoly Angels. Mankind will have a period of time to make their choices without manipulation upon them. According to their choices, so goes the duration of the blessing. The more people are choosing love the longer the blessing lasts. The more people are choosing fear and seeking darkness, the shorter the duration of the blessing.

The unHoly Angels have choices; they can leave the area about to be blessed and have further opportunity to come to God on their own or they can choose to stay and the Holy Angels will place them in encapsulation.

You will notice that this prayer for the land is similar to the deliverance prayer. The same place of nailing, holding fast and silencing begins the prayer. Again, this is that the unHoly Angels may not move about. They are nailed and held fast just as Christ was nailed to the cross. The silencing keeps all from having to hear the blasphemy and cursing that they will do. The next part is calling out the name of the unHoly Angels: *"I decommission, bind and encapsulate the spirit of ...(name the unHoly Angel or unHoly Angels here) and through the power of the Shed Blood of the Lamb, I bring them up to your Presence immediately to deal with as you see fit. Father may your Holy Angels assist my brothers and sisters here at this time that they may have the opportunity to brighten without manipulation upon them."*

The encapsulation that occurs in this land blessing as well as the deliverance and exorcism work is not a place of torture or pain and suffering. This is a place, a container where the unHoly Angels are placed that they may see the interaction of God with all his children and do so without hearing the manipulation of their fallen brothers, the unHoly Angels. They will not have further communication with any of the unHoly Angels. They are given the opportunity to watch the story of God's love but no longer to interfere. They will no longer be able to cause harm for God has not asked this of them. This means that they will not be able to manipulate mankind during this time.

258

When someone does a deliverance, exorcism or land blessing according to the wording shared here in this book, these unHoly Angels will not be able to manipulate mankind again! There will be others that seek to come into the territory, to foul the freshly cleansed land, to attempt to claim it as theirs. A land blessing brightens an area for a short period of time. This is up to the choices of those in the land, love or fear. What do the sons of mankind do with the opportunity of choice presented to them without being manipulated by the unHoly Angels? This work will continue on, the land will need to be cleansed again and again. It is not about the land being entirely clean, that time will come through God. It is about helping mankind to have more opportunity to choose without manipulation upon them.

This encapsulation is not a punishment for the unHoly Angels, it is simply a placement of non-interference. They will not be allowed to manipulate mankind or each other through the encapsulation. The unHoly Angels will now see the story of God's love without manipulation, they may watch God in action, see their Holy brothers doing his Will and watch his perfect timing and his wisdom at work.

We are told that those unHoly Angels who choose to call out to Father, to come home to him, are given the opportunity to ask for forgiveness and given a new name. They will also start out with a lower responsibility but are still shown the mercy and love of God. Love wants all of his children upon his Holy lap, even those that have sinned against him. This is between Father and that Angel. Father's love is immeasurable. It is up to Father to judge. That is not our place, *"...who are you to judge another's servant? That is the job of the Master." (Romans 14:4)*

When Christ and his Holy army prevail, all unHoly Angels who have not come to Father will be held and will watch the story of God's Love unfold for the 1,000 years. During this time mankind will have the ability to learn without manipulation. Mankind will be able to see and hear Christ speaking and teaching. This will be a great time of brightening. At the end of the 1,000 years we will be bright enough to visibly see our fellow servants of God, the Holy Angels. We will reach our original purpose, we will be as God intended us to be, in physical, emotional and spiritual perfection.

This is a time when all those who have demonstrated difficulty in learning about love while manipulation is upon them will have opportunity to learn without interference.

At the end of the 1,000 years of learning and brightening, the unHoly Angels will be freed. All will have one final opportunity to choose love or fear. For us humans, it will be like each of us is given personally the same choices of Adam and Eve in the Garden of Eden. If a person chooses against love, they will be separate from God by choice, and their energy reduced to particle form and placed within the earth, the same as any unHoly Angels who choose to remain separate from Love. They will be forever a part of the earth, part of the ground, helping things to grow. We were shown through Holy Stigmata that the earth would have eventually gone the way of all planets, but because of the original issues raised and settled here for all the cosmos, the earth now will stand forever, as an everlasting memorial to the Sovereignty of Love.

This work is Holy work. We are always to treat it with love and respect. Remember that Love and Light are even more active, that God has placed all kinds of signs and wonders here upon the earth and that many of these signs are through the hands of people. These have been chosen not by merit, worthiness or perfection but because of their willingness to be used as a tool for heaven. More and more signs and wonders are to come! This is the most exciting time humanity has ever known!

All of these gifts are for the betterment of humanity. We are to use the gifts that God has given us out of love and service to him, respect and love for one another and all creation without judgment. God alone is the judge of all, including any of those who still do not choose the way of love even after the 1,000 years. Our job is simply to bless and love.

Ten Minute Land Blessing

We are given the ability to ask that the Holy Angel in the center of the earth come up to an area of struggle and cleanse it of any of the unHoly Angels there so that our brothers and sisters may not be manipulated. This is for areas of conflict only.

The Holy Angel in the center of the earth is very powerful and has many Angels working with him. We are to respect this power and use it when we can. This blessing lasts but a short time, 10 minutes and can be repeated at the end of the 10 minutes. It may not sound like much time, but 10 minutes of no shelling in the middle of a war, or 10 minutes of peace in a city undergoing mob violence, can save a lot of people by giving clarity of thought and new choices in the midst of chaos and destruction.

Here is the prayer: *"Lord, I ask that your Holy Angel in the center of the earth be given free will to come up to the area of (state the place of conflict, city not country) and rinse it clean of any of the unHoly Angels that my brothers and sisters here may have the freedom to choose without manipulation. Thank you Father, In Jesus' name. Amen."*

How Do We Bless a Place of Worship?

This is a blessing and strengthening for a house of prayer or place of fellowship to worship. This includes any church, temple, mosque or other sacred place of gathering in recognition of Love. This is a prayer used for the buildings already built and established. This is for unity of all houses of worship, together under Christ under God. Remembering here that they do not have to be Christian, remembering that God is beyond religion as was the redemption of man through Christ, and the unity we are blessing is in recognition of that, as brothers and sisters we are all together under Love. But for ease in reference, we will simply call this a church blessing.

This blessing is not to be confused with the individual church blessings often done for the first celebration offered in that particular place. Each individual church will have their own blessing and rite done for them by those who run that house of prayer, this is different than that. This is not a calling to do that.

We understand that all of us who seek Love are under attack by the darkness, and we are a part of the Love and not separated from his Light anymore. We are redeemed by the peace that was made by the main minister who encourages worship and fellowship, Jesus Christ.

261

Thus, we bless all churches as such: we seek out a place that will remain on the site, such as a place of wood, the most preferable being the entry door. If there is no such place of wood on the building, a tree upon the property will do. Wood is a more natural state, not as altered by the sons of man, and God was specific when he asked for wood, rather than metal, to be the place to receive his blessing.

Next we take the oil of thanksgiving upon our finger and anoint the church to be blessed in this shape:

X   X

X

This is the unity of the Father and Son in heaven and the One church here on earth. This is the symbol that will be used for every church blessing.

After anointing and while still having your hand pressed upon the wood, state the following prayer: *"Lord, I ask for a blessing upon this church that together with all your churches, in love, peace, trust, hope and discernment they may unite under your son, under you. May all these here protect one another, take care of one another, help one another, feed one another and never feed off of one another. May this be a place of brightness open to all who reach out for you. May all these here recognize your sovereignty and act in unity with your Will. Thank you Father, In Jesus' name. Amen"*

After the prayer is completed, you will write the name of the church in a book that will be used only for blessings of churches. This book will contain the name of the church, and the basic location (city, state and country). That is all that is needed to keep in the book. The book itself will be prayed over each morning and each night, repeating the prayer used for the church blessing itself: *"Lord, I ask for a blessing upon this church (or house of prayer and worship) that together with all your churches, in love, peace, trust, hope and discernment they may unite under your son, under you.*

May all these here protect one another, take care of one another, help one another, feed one another and never feed off of one another. May this be a place of brightness open to all who reach out for you. May all these here recognize your sovereignty and act in unity with your Will. Thank you Father, In Jesus' name, Amen."

Those who are called to bless the churches can do it as stated above. This heals and helps the unity of all houses of worship under one God of Love.

<u>How to Bless the Host and the Wine</u>

The Host is referred to as the Eucharist, the unleavened bread of communion. The Host and the Wine are the central focus of communion. Communion, which is literally coming together in union, is a place for you to receive strengthening from Christ. *"I can do all things through Christ who strengthens me." (Philippians 4:13)*

Communion is a precious time of sharing. Many find that they can hear God very clearly during this time, and find it is a place of peace and love like no other. This is a personal time between you and Love. It is a place for you to share your trust in God's purpose for you and for all mankind. It is a time of recognizing what Christ did in redeeming us from the darkness. Jesus never asked us to remember or celebrate his birth, though we gladly do it anyway, but what he did ask was to remember his death. He said: *"Keep doing this in remembrance of me."(Luke 22:19)* It is the only thing he asked us to celebrate, the reason why he came to earth and the meaning of his death to release mankind, the remembrance of Love.

Before him, none of us could break the bondage of sin - the bad choices of our original parents and our own accumulated bad choices. None of us, no matter how many lifetimes we lived, could ever polish enough facets of love to come before God, to be bright enough on our own. It was a never ending cycle of darkness, we could not plug ourselves back in again, since we ourselves could not shake the generational bondage upon us. This is where the notion of karma came into being.

263

People inherently realized that they had trouble overcoming what they had done before and what was done before them and passed down to them. This is why Christ is known as the karmic redemption of mankind. God is light, and light and dark cannot be in the same place together, so on our own, we could never be bright enough to be near God. The wages of sin is death. Jesus did not sin, yet was put to death as a sinner. That broke the chains. So only since the death of Jesus, when a human spirit has polished the basics of love and become bright from that polishing, we can come before God, and we can stay, or we can decide to come back, or even other things such as going off-world for a time. The point is, if Jesus hadn't balanced the scale, we would be in a place of accumulated darkness. Christ not only shattered the bonds of death, but brought us back before God in brightness.

In symbol, the bread is Christ's body, and the wine is his blood. (Matthew 26:26-29) At their last meal together, Jesus knowing what was coming upon him and why, said: *"The Son of Man will go just as it is written about him...While they were eating, Jesus took bread, gave thanks and broke it, and gave it to his disciples, saying, "Take it, this is my body." Then he took the cup, gave thanks and offered it to them, and they all drank from it. "This is my blood of the covenant, which is poured out for many...(Mark 14:20-24)* Blood belongs to God, it is on loan to us while in the body.

This blessing will allow for you to be able to ask that this simple gift of bread and wine be transformed to the Body and Blood *of Christ*. You are given this gift through your ordination from God through man. God is the one who blessed you and made you are brighter vessel for his Holy Love. This blessing will enable you to take communion wherever you go for the work, for those in need and for yourself. It is an honor to be able to ask that this simple gift be transformed. It is always to be respected. During Holy Stigmata, it was shown that Christ takes the offering of our communion and brings it up to Father. The offering of communion is the recognition of the redemption of mankind through the salvation of Christ. It is a special time and a precious gift, and healing and revelations of all kinds can happen at communion.

You can purchase the Eucharist from any church book store or church supply store.

It does not matter which type you buy for it is the blessing that is bestowed upon it that's of the greatest importance. You can purchase as much at a time as you like, for once you do a blessing upon them it never wears off. After the blessing, it will always remain the Body of Christ.

You can use any wine you would like. Many people have preferences as to the wine they use, most prefer a red wine to more accurately symbolize the meaning of blood, but feel free to use whatever wine you wish, for again, it is the blessing that God bestows upon the wine, through your ordination, that makes the difference.

On the altar or communion table you have set up, you can place the bread and the wine. You are also to have a small plate for the communion, a cup or chalice for the wine and a cloth to wipe the chalice after the blessings of communion are completed. You will need to have a container of Holy Water present on your altar as well. The chalice, plate and cloth are to remain together until the blessing is said, and to be placed back together immediately after the blessing is done. This reverence for the Body and Blood of Christ is central to the understanding that all this Holy work that God has for us is a sharing that God allows for us. It is not that God needs us to do this work, it's that he is so loving he desires to share it with us, to actually participate with him even now. When we take Communion, we recognize and acknowledge the love that has already been shared with us through the gift of his son, and we demonstrate our acceptance of redemptive Grace and our longing to share ourselves with God by taking Christ into our bodies, an act of Oneness. Communion is a strengthening to be done whenever we feel we need help. God is present for us always. Taking communion is recognition of this truth and an invitation to build us up and help us through our struggles.

The blessing: Again, the central focus is the sign of the Cross + that is made over the bread and wine. Once you have been ordained, you are given this precious ability to transform these simple items made by the hands of man into something so much more. Remember that whatever words you use, when you bless the bread and the wine, you are asking that they be transformed into the Body and Blood of Jesus Christ.

265

Use these words: *Heavenly Father, thank you for this opportunity to come before you and ask for your strengthening, your assistance. May you help me to be more like your son, Jesus Christ, in all ways. Lord, I ask that this simple gift of bread and wine be made acceptable to you. It was your son who sat with the Apostles and ate. After sharing a meal together and satisfying their bodily hunger, your son went on to satisfy their spiritual hunger. Christ took bread and wine, broke the bread, gave it to the disciples and said: "This is my body which will be given up for you, take it and eat it. Do this in remembrance of me. This is my blood which is poured out for many for the forgiveness of sin. Take it and drink of it. Do this in remembrance of me."(Mt. 26:26-28) Father, in remembrance of your son, I ask that this gift of bread and wine be transformed into the body + and the blood + of your son, Jesus Christ + Thank you Father, In Jesus' name, Amen."*

Once the blessing is done for the transformation you may hold the Body and Blood of Christ up in the air and pray: *"Lord we invite you in, Lord Jesus, The Holy Spirit, The Holy Angels, Mother Mary, The Holy Ones, all those you see fit to share this communion with and our Guides as well. Thank you Lord that we may all be more like your Son."* Offer the Body and Blood of Christ up and ask *"Lord Jesus, may you bring this gift up to Father."* (Take the Body and Blood of Christ here - you can take the bread in your mouth and then drink all the wine from the cup swallowing both the Body and Blood of Christ together)

Next, pour some of the Holy Water into the cup, swirling the water around to rinse any remainder of the Blood of Christ from the cup and say this prayer: *"Heavenly Father, as the Blood of your Son is rinsed from this cup, I ask that the area of (pause, listen for guidance and then state the country, city, or region) be rinsed clean, as well that anything there that is not of your light and love be rinsed away, that only your light and love remain. Thank you Father, In Jesus' name, Amen."*

Take a clean cloth and wipe the cup dry. Place the plate that held the Eucharist on top of the cloth and then place both upon the cup/chalice.

266

We were shown to do this as a recognition that the Body and Blood of Christ are always to be placed together. It is done as God has asked us to do it.

As for the prayer mentioned above, they too are what God has asked us to include. The prayer asking Christ to take up this gift to Father was a truth unveiled to us through the Holy Stigmata. We were shown that Christ is the only one that brings the communion up to Father whenever it is offered. Tradition within many houses of prayer and worship have recognized that it was brought up to God, but many have asked that God's Holy Angels bring the gift up to Father. This is not what we were shown. We were shown that it is Christ himself that comes down to bring the gift up to Father. It was Christ who came down to be made into man and Christ who died for all of us and it is Christ who brings the gift back up to Father in recognition of our acceptance of his sacrifice and the completion of the work that he faithfully was sent to do and fulfilled.

The prayer following communion, rinsing the cup clean and asking for an area of the world to be rinsed clean is another blessing we were shown. Holy Mary, who comes to Blessed Tiffany as Mother of All Nations, wishes to add a blessing over any city or nation that we ask to be cleansed. Now this blessing doesn't rinse all darkness from an area but it does add light and love to the area. The more an area is prayed over the brighter it becomes. We are asked to spend time listening for which areas need more prayer. This will help you to strengthen your hearing and add a blessing for the areas that need it. All the nations need blessings, all the cities need blessings. Let yourself be guided to listen where the blessing can be given now. This may change from communion to communion.

Holy Mary has been given many names by God, and one is the Mother of All Nations. She is one that God allows the blessings to flow from going to these places that are in need. Allow yourself some time without being rushed to listen to the areas that need help now. Then add the city or nation and continue with the prayer. It is also important to remember that you may be guided to an area that goes by an old name or older area to be blessed. Know that Holy Mary has also been the Mother of All Nations that already existed in the past. Let yourself be open to stating whatever you are given.

267

Each blessing that is done for an area in the world adds love and light to the area. It doesn't mean that any bad things will ever happen in the area. It does mean that less darkness will be there because you have asked for God's love and light to be there to brighten the area and the people in it. You may not know the effect of your blessings but they are powerful! Have the faith and confidence in your ability to hear and the faith and confidence of God's power to bring his transformation to the area, blessing it.

This information shared with you about communion is for your brightening and for your strengthening in your relationship with God. Know that each time you take communion, you brighten. Use communion any time you feel the need. You are in charge of when and where you take it, it is a loving gift from a loving Father. Use it often and enjoy the precious time of being "kissed by God." May the peace and love of God be with you!

How Do We Take Communion?

This information is given as if the wine and host have been consecrated already. The Holy Eucharist or communion is the sharing of ourselves with God as well as the sharing of God with us. We have both the wine and the bread blessed by one who has been called to make a sacred vow before God to the designation of sacred office and has received Holy Orders. We make an altar for spending time with God. We have a chalice or a cup to pour the wine into and a place to hold the bread. We lift up the cup, we give thanks to God for the gift of his Son, Jesus and invite God to share it with us, inviting in as well: Jesus, the Holy Spirit, the Holy Angels, Mother Mary, all his Saints, all those who love and serve him, all those God sees fit to share this communion with, our Guides and for those who have given us permission to take it on their behalf as well, and those who are under our care. We lift up all our brothers and sisters, especially those who do not have the strength to life themselves up and we ask that all the captives be freed from the manipulations of the unHoly.

We invite the Lord Jesus to take the Holy communion up to God as a gift on our behalf and again, we remember to "Do this in remembrance of Jesus."

268

We take the Holy communion remembering that even a piece, even the bread or the wine, once blessed is complete unto itself, for no bone was found broken on his Son. We place it in our mouths, drink the wine with humility and thanksgiving.

As part of communion, next we take the Holy Water and pour a little into the chalice or cup saying "Lord, I ask that anything that is not of your light and you love in this area of the world (city or country, old or current) be rinsed away as the Blood of Your Son is rinsed from this cup. We ask that this be done through the eyes of love, compassion and forgiveness, in Jesus' name. Amen." During this sacred time, we listen for the word of God to place in our heart the name of the city or country to be blessed and cleansed at that time.

The Holy Eucharist can also be used in land blessings as noted above. The Holy Eucharist is to be taken at least once a day. The Holy Eucharist is blessed and cannot be tarnished in any way. It is always a bright reflection of the fact that the Loving Act of Christ can also never be tarnished. It is always to be treated with the respect it deserves and use it to strengthen whenever needed.

<u>What Do We Do with the Spilled Wine in Communion?</u>

This is to be returned to Father by taking a tissue, napkin or paper towel, wiping it up and taking it outside to be rinsed out on the ground, or buried in the soil, returning the gift of the Blood to Father with a prayer of thanksgiving.

"Father, I return this blood to you. May not another drop of your Blood be shed, Father. All life comes from you and goes back to you. We recognize this most Holy gift and thank you for sharing it with us, and we offer it back in the fulfillment of Love. I ask that this ground here be made into sacred ground + and remain so until the end of days. I ask that your Holy Angels may have free will access to protect all my brothers and sisters here in this perimeter keeping them free from any manipulation or harm by the evil one + Thank you Heavenly Father, In Jesus' name, Amen." +

Any blood from the Holy Stigmata is to be treated the same way, to be returned to the ground. However, with the blood from those who have been blessed with the Holy Stigmata it is suggested that whatever the blood has spilled on such as clothes, sheets or towels, be rinsed outside that the water and blood may flow into the ground. Then after using the blessing listed above, the articles can be placed in the laundry and washed as usual.

It is important to remember that the Body and Blood of Christ are always to be treated with the utmost respect. The information that was shared with us was that no matter how the Body and Blood of Christ (the bread and wine once consecrated) are treated, it will never debase the Holiness of the sacrament. Nevertheless, all those who are given the ability to bless and consecrate bread and wine through God are to treat the Body and Blood of Christ with the utmost respect. It is an honor to be able to share in this work with God and only right that we demonstrate our love and admiration for the one who of his own free will, came down and became man, shared the love of God, was beaten, tortured and crucified, surrendering his life and dying for us (allowing God to feel the pain of death through the only one bright enough to share fully with God), and shattering the bonds of sin and death, resurrected and our redeemer. Jesus Christ was responsible for the salvation of all mankind, through the love of God and following through to God's Will for him. We honor this and literally *"do this in remembrance of me." (Matthew 26:26-28)*

This information is shared with you that you may recognize the source of your strength and follow through on God's Will for you just as Christ followed through on God's Will for him. While we are not as perfect as Christ was, we are given this information to draw strength from Christ who was perfect. Sharing or communing with God through Christ is a gift that will sustain you throughout this shifting into timelessness. Take communion whenever you feel it necessary, knowing that it is *always okay* to ask God for help. May it bring you as much peace and joy as it has for all those who have recognized the love of God and the Grace and salvation through his son, who is as life-sustaining as daily bread to us.

How Do We Transform Fear?

We are to transform fear. By being a place of love and light, we illuminate the darkness, dispersing the shadow that the light shines the way. There is no need for fear in this work for this is a work of love. Even when it seems difficult, God is the one who is doing it all with and through you and the Holy Angels. Trust in God and remember that *"Perfect love casts out fear. Fear has to do with punishment."* *(1John 4:18)*

Specifically, remembering what fears that the unHoly Angels like to target the most:

(1). *Fear* of complete destruction of the earth. We know this will not happen. The earth will fulfill what God intends, the earth will remain as a testament to the answered questions of the original issues. We know that the surface orientation of the earth will change but the earth itself will still be in existence.

(2). *Fear* of the complete and utter destruction of mankind. We know as well that many will survive the end time while still being in the body. Many will not die at that time. One of the main reasons for sharing this information is so that less of our brothers and sisters will suffer at this end of days and the shift into timelessness.

(3). *Fear* of alien takeover or destruction from the skies above. The unHoly Angels will seek to manipulate the fears of mankind and they will attempt to manifest images in the sky to cause fear and intimidation. Know that Father has us well protected and that all others can only watch but not interfere, these issues will be solved through the ones that have been manipulated, mankind and the Mighty Hand of God. We are reminded again, no matter what things may seem like, not to be afraid, we know the outcome of it all, God's Will being fulfilled, God's word coming to fruition.

(4). *Fear* of complete and total anarchy and lawlessness. Even when things seem like they are falling apart we are to remember that again, God is in control. God will not allow his children to be condemned for eternity. God

271

will save the day, just like he has already done, many times over.

(5). *Fear* of being wiped out by natural disasters. Again, we know that there will be changes upon the earth but we are to remember, we also have the power to transform the darkness into light by the Glory and Grace of God. Remembering that the unHoly Angels attempt to pervert what is natural, twist it and make it unnatural to harm the sons of man and God himself. Remember what you have been told, be not afraid.

(6). *Fear* of being wiped out by a health epidemic. The unHoly Angels have always preyed upon mankind's focus on the health of the body. We are to remember that we are greater than just this body, this body and this blood are both gifts from God. Our Father will give us the opportunity to heal, to bless the air and water that they not carry any disease or toxin. We have the tools needed to transform any substance, through The Divine Decrees, our Holy prayers and Holy intentions as well

(7). *Fear* of destruction through nuclear war. Our Lord has kept this from destroying the sons of man already for a long time. Do not be afraid. Father will keep us around and help us to transform and keep fear from taking over. Even more reason to choose love and not be reactionary but transformative! Trust here as well, as mentioned above, God will keep the earth here as a testament to the resolution of the original issues being solved.

The unHoly Angels look to manipulate the environment to make the earth unable to support life. People fear the effects of pollution, the greenhouse effect, global warming, polar ice caps melting, the increase of the ocean temperature and more, all leading to the earth not being able to sustain life. God will not let this happen. Our Father and his Holy Angels are hard at work and he calls us in to participate, to share in easing the suffering of our brothers.

The unHoly Angels prey upon man's fears with regard to abundance (attempting to create the illusion of lack) health (that man will be wiped out by disease, super-viruses, epidemics) and relationships (that man will not be able to trust anyone, governments, politics, religion, any relationships). Being the place of love in the world is standing up in the face of an adversity, any terror whether real or unreal, perceived or imagined and bringing love into it to transform and heal the situation.

Trust in God. You are doing Holy work, blessed by God to assist our brothers and sisters that there may be less suffering in this world. Be kind to yourself and all those around you. Use these as opportunities to heal, transform, forgive and be the place of love for God to use!

What Else is Needed to Assist with the World Shift?

Love is the focus, we look to God, seek his Will for us and follow through on what has been asked. And no matter how great or how small for each time we answer yes to Love and follow through, we add our evidence to the court case demonstrating his sovereignty, God's right to rule.

This is imperative to remember, this is in the original issues, will man try to rule on his own or will man recognize the sovereignty of Love and allow God to show the way. We show reverence to God by inviting God in. We share the day with God and make it clearly known that we cannot do it on our own. The Divine Decrees are an essential part of this. The Divine Decrees align our will with the Will of God.

What else is needed to assist the sons of man for the shift? Prayers, Decrees, books, info, sharing, helping them to connect, sharing with others, training, classes, strengthening connection with Father, spend time doing what to connect, best ways to connect. We can always pray for one another, pray for his Holy Kingdom to come now, pray for greater discernment on all things.

How Do We Keep the Work Expanding?

God will show the way. Do not be afraid. Many may come against but do not fear. This is why we are chosen, for our heart of righteousness, our compassion, our love and service to God and his strength. *"In God, whose word I praise, in God I trust; I will not be afraid. What can mortal man do to me?"(Psalm 56:4)*

Keeping people listening to God's Will for them, not giving their power away to others who may tell them what to do, but seeking their answers from God. All are asked to discern what is of love, what is of God and what is not. We are all given the ability to know love and many of us have worked very hard at love for a very long time. We are to pay attention to what God calls us to do in this love for him and for one another.

This is a personal communion with Love that each of us is called to follow. It is our responsibility to spend time listening to God, hearing his voice and recognizing that it is his. This is not about having someone else take your personal responsibility and connect for you, listen for you and tell you what to do. God himself is the one you listen to, just as we have done in bringing this information to you. He knows that his children will recognize his voice and know his love for them. Go direct and hold everything up to what you know to be true, discerning what is of love and what is not. Paying attention and remembering that you never have to earn the Love of God, it is already given to you and that you will never have to earn redemption for that to is already given through Jesus Christ for all the sons of man. No amount of personal growth or knowledge could have ever freed us, this was done for us by God. Not letting anyone deceive you into thinking you have to earn God's love, know that you have it, that you are God's child and he loves you now, perfectly!

Follow The Divine Decrees and the revelations given through the books and articles written and given through Holy Stigmata, holding these up to your spirit and letting it resonant within. There are many things that Love has taught us through signs and wonders.

Holy Stigmata was a gift, a sharing from God to enable us to bring forth these gifts from God, to help us all at this crucial time, but there are many, many more gifts! It was and is never about us, we are simply the ones that were blessed to bring it forth. It was, is and always will be about the glorification of God's name.

Paying attention to what was shared, what signs were presented that you have been foretold so that when they came true you may recognize that the one who gave them to you through his little ones may show you his truth. The Divine Decrees are powerful. Your prayers are your love song to God, The Divine Decrees are God's love song to you. He gives his children to opportunity to have The Divine Decrees and use them for their protection, health, abundance, happiness, understanding, well-being, knowledge, joy, relationships, interaction with community and the world around. They are not to be taken lightly, they are a powerful, transformative gift that God in his infinite mercy, love and compassion has given as a tool to be used by his children that we may be equipped to deal with what the unHoly Angels attempt to do to us. State them according to their time parameters. Remember, we are locking the door for we know not the time the thief will come, so we will be prepared and lock the door so no matter what time, the thief cannot enter into our house. Say them in accordance with what has been given.

Continual prayer helps with everything. Living in an undertone of prayer is that place of Divine connection between heaven and earth, where we look for and receive guidance for our entire journey. We are told: *Devote yourselves to prayer, being watchful and thankful. (Colossians 4:2)* Keep in prayer, keep making your love song for God. You will not run out of things to pray for. Simply look around, see what is going on in the world, in your life, in the lives of your family and friends, those you love and care about. Make prayer as precious as your breath.

What we have taught will continue on. Many will feel the call to carry the torch and share what has been shared. This is about the message God has for his children, that they may know that they are loved and cared for and how God gives them the tools they need to make it.

275

Those who teach the Divine Decree classes must stay in touch with us and with one another. Many will come against; many will attempt to squash the information to keep it from reaching the hands of the sons of man. But have no fear for this is the word of Love going out, being completed and returning to God, fulfilled.

We must be loving and strong in this time to share this message of love from God with our brothers to ease the suffering of the sons of man. Keep sharing the information, The Divine Decrees, the knowledge given through the sharing, the Holy Stigmata and always remember it is to be taught in love and with love, for God and for one another. Support one another, reach out and connect and share, pray for one another, love one another. Remember that you are the ones taking care of all those in need as if you were tending to God himself. So do this work with humility, patience, passionate desire and continual obedience to the Will of God.

Those that have been appointed as commissioned heads will have greater responsibility laid upon them, for as more is given, more is asked. You will be the place of love, reflecting God's love for his children. You will be vigilant in the work, recognizing the 1/3 that will be used as pawns by the unHoly Angels to come against you and keep you from progressing. Do not fear. God will show his hand mighty upon those that are true to his Holy name. As the commissioned heads you also have the responsibility of knowing what we have known, that it is not about us, we are the messengers. It is about the Glory of God. As such, we are no greater and no lesser than those around us, it is God who all the Glory, honor and praise belongs. Stay humble and true to your commission especially in the face of adversity and temptation.

What Do We Need to Pay Attention To with Others Involved?

The ability of all involved to be strong in their relationship with God. Letting everyone know whose side we are on, the side of love, and Love Wins! Christ has already redeemed us all! And, God gives us the opportunity to participate in the shifting out of time into timelessness.

God gives us the chance to be the place of love in the world, teaching our brothers and sisters, helping them to see this as well. Remember it is about building one another up and never about tearing down. We all have the ability to learn from our own actions, from cause and effect and God gives us even greater assistance through his Divine love and mercy, The Divine Decrees and the wonderful example of Jesus Christ of how to live in God's Will. Be the place of love and compassion, teaching all others around you about faith, love, hope, trust and discernment.

How Do We Strengthen and Unite With All His Light Workers?

First, we keep them in our prayers. It will be easy to recognize our fellow light workers for they serve him in love and with love. All those who share this love and remember that we do not have to earn God's love, it is a gift already given, how we are already redeemed through Christ. Even for those who are of different religions and faiths for Christ redeemed all of mankind through the ransom sacrifice.

We can support and encourage one another when we meet, remembering that we are united through Love, all having important purposes, no one greater or lesser than any one else, we are all in this together in union with each other for the glorification of God's Love. Remember that many of our brothers and sisters are covered in our prayers and The Divine Decrees. And many are covered through the specific Divine Decrees for unity of the Called and Commissioned as well.

With all that we do, we are to do it: *"In Remembrance of Me" (Luke 22:19)* Always in remembrance of Christ, doing what is asked of us and in balance and depending on Love the entire way! We indent all that we do with the tone that we do it in. We are to do all this work out of love and service to God, do this work, even the difficult work with kindness and love. Leave the mark of the Master upon the handiwork of the servant. Let love be the spirit we act in.

"Be joyful always, pray continuously and be thankful for all things" (1Thessalonians 5:16-18)

SCRIPTURES foretelling the two called to dispense The Divine Decrees.

The Gold Lampstand and the Two Olive Trees (Zechariah 4)

"Then the angel who talked with me returned and wakened me, as a man is wakened from his sleep. He asked me, "What do you see?"
I answered, "I see a solid gold lampstand with a bowl at the top and seven lights on it, with seven channels to the lights. Also there are two olive trees by it, one on the right of the bowl and the other on its left."
I asked the angel who talked with me, "What are these, my lord?"
He answered, "Do you not know what these are?"
"No, my lord," I replied.
So he said to me, "This is the word of the LORD to Zerubbabel: 'Not by might nor by power, but by my Spirit,' says the LORD Almighty.
"What are you, O mighty mountain? Before Zerubbabel you will become level ground. Then he will bring out the capstone to shouts of 'God bless it! God bless it!"
"Then the word of the LORD came to me: "The hands of Zerubbabel have laid the foundation of this temple; his hands will also complete it. Then you will know that the LORD Almighty has sent me to you.
"Who despises the day of small things? Men will rejoice when they see the plumb line in the hand of Zerubbabel.
"(These seven are the eyes of the LORD, which range throughout the earth.)"
Then I asked the angel, "What are these two olive trees on the right and the left of the lampstand?"
Again I asked him, "What are these two olive branches beside the two gold pipes that pour out golden oil?"
He replied, "Do you not know what these are?"
"No, my lord," I said.
So he said, "These are the two who are anointed to serve the Lord of all the earth."

The Two Witnesses (Revelation 11:1-14)

I was given a reed like a measuring rod and was told, "Go and measure the temple of God and the altar, and count the worshipers there. But exclude the outer court; do not measure it, because it has been given to the Gentiles. They will trample on the Holy city for 42 months. And I will give power to my two witnesses, and they will prophesy for 1,260 days, clothed in sackcloth." These are the two olive trees and the two lampstands that stand before the Lord of the earth. If anyone tries to harm them, fire comes from their mouths and devours their enemies. This is how anyone who wants to harm them must die. These men have power to shut up the sky so that it will not rain during the time they are prophesying; and they have power to turn the waters into blood and to strike the earth with every kind of plague as often as they want.

Now when they have finished their testimony, the beast that comes up from the Abyss will attack them, and overpower and kill them. Their bodies will lie in the street of the great city, which is figuratively called Sodom and Egypt, where also their Lord was crucified. For three and a half days men from every people, tribe, language and nation will gaze on their bodies and refuse them burial. The inhabitants of the earth will gloat over them and will celebrate by sending each other gifts, because these two prophets had tormented those who live on the earth.

But after the three and a half days a breath of life from God entered them, and they stood on their feet, and terror struck those who saw them. Then they heard a loud voice from heaven saying to them, "Come up here." And they went up to heaven in a cloud, while their enemies looked on. At that very hour there was a severe earthquake and a tenth of the city collapsed. Seven thousand people were killed in the earthquake, and the survivors were terrified and gave glory to the God of heaven.

<u>The Divine Decrees</u>

BOOK ONE – The Unification Act

(1). I Decree as a Spirit of God, born as a child of man, full alignment, communication and unity of this soul's Holy Prayers and Holy Intentions with God, the Word of God, the Holy Spirit, the Holy Ones Guides assigned, All Holy Angels assigned (and my husband/wife and those under my care). By free will I agree to receive and connect with Love to strengthen Love, choose the way of Love, encourage Love and expand Love wherever it may be found, whenever it may be found, in whatever amount it may be found, throughout all creation that has been formed, is being formed and will be formed.

(2). I Decree full authority and free will interaction to All Holy Angels assigned to utilize the indent of this soul through all interactions past, present and future to continue the experience and expansion of the Love of God.

(3). I Decree this as binding on earth as it is in heaven by the alignment of the will of God and man, bridging all past, present or future events until the One King of the Kingdom of God assumes full authority by the order of the Unification Act as ordained by the Blood of the Covenant as witnessed and given through the Holy Spirit by the Love of God, Amen.

(Visualization: Falling snow, blanketing everything. Color: White. Duration: 5 Days)

BOOK TWO – The Arrival Act

(4). I Decree as a Spirit of God, born as a child of man, full trust and opportunity to allow my soul or spirit to manifest and aid as needed in any past, present and future event of God's Love. By free will I accept full escort and call in All Holy Angels assigned to render harmless any unHoly indent while interacting in the body or in the spirit, granting safe passage to this soul and any Guides assigned as well. By free will I accept and ask for transformation of any gift or material made by man or substance of creation darkened by unHoly intentions or manipulations, and

(5). I Decree a cleansing of these through All Holy Angels assigned including a purification and bringing back the perfect creation within agreed parameters of interaction of the creations of the children of man to the fullness of potential made.

(6). I Decree full authority and free will interaction of All Holy Angels assigned to protect any and all methods of communication, interaction and information devices from manipulations and unHoly intentions, including any present methods and future methods and inventions.

(7). I Decree this as binding on earth as it is in heaven by the alignment of the will of God and man, bridging all past, present and future events until the King of All Dimensions in the Kingdom of God assumes full authority by order of the Arrival Act as ordained by the Blood of the Covenant as witnessed and given through the Holy Spirit by the Love of God, Amen.

(Visualization: The sun coming up over the horizon, going overhead and then the sun going down on the other side. Color: Yellow. Duration: 5 Days)

283

BOOK THREE – The Transformation Act

(8). I Decree as a Spirit of God, born as a child of man, full healing of this soul, spirit, body and mind by full alignment of the will of God and man by the receiving of wholeness and wellness in perfection, within the present parameters set by the original choices of man and agreed upon purpose and commission for this life. By free will I offer my faith and trust, in the power and Love of God as an indent for healing, for All Holy Angels assigned to offer aid of healing of the soul, spirit, body and mind to any and all of the children of man whenever they may call out to God for healing, knowing this will occur within the present parameters set by the original choices of man and agreed upon purpose and commission for these lives, and within the present parameters of the interaction of indents.

(9). I Decree full authority and free will interaction of All Holy Angels assigned to manifest additional opportunities and to aid these souls to recognize all choices of Love and healing and to choose without manipulations or unHoly intentions.

(10). I Decree this as binding on earth as it is in Heaven by the alignment of the will of God and man, bridging all past, present or future events until the King of Re-Creation of the Kingdom of God assumes full authority by order of the Transformation Act as ordained by the Blood of the Covenant as witnessed and given through the Holy Spirit by the Love of God, Amen.

(Visualization: Old becoming young, bodies deformed and bent standing straight and full, flowers going from bud to full bloom. Color: Orange. Duration: 5 Days)

BOOK FOUR - The Protection Act

(11). I Decree as a Spirit of God born as a child of man full protection of this soul, spirit, body and mind (and that of my husband/wife and those under my care) and all attending delegates by giving full authority and free will interaction to All Holy Angels assigned to render harmless any and all manipulations or unHoly intentions sent toward us.

(12). I Decree as welcome and valid all methods and signs approved by God and conducive to the further allowance of the veil, including full awareness of my spirit and any and all interactions of the human senses or God-given gifts to aid alignment with messages and power and action needed and made available through All Holy Angels assigned Guides assigned, and empowerment given to the faithful and aware children of man through all Divine Decrees and the Twelve Books of Acts of the Love of God.

(13). I Decree this soul's free will ability to call in All Holy Angels assigned and grant full authority and free will interaction to defend, battle, attack and render harmless as needed and to aid Guides assigned and all Holy Ones with containment of all manipulations and unHoly intentions sent.

(14). I Decree this soul's free will choice of asking for greater faith, trust and discernment of what my interaction is in every event and opportunity and utilizing this soul's abilities and God-given gifts when asked and in the parameters suggested and at the times recommended through all Divine Decrees and the Twelve Books of Acts of the Love of God....(cont.)

(15). I Decree this as binding on earth as it is in heaven by the alignment of the will of God and man, bridging all past, present or future events until the Warrior Son of the Kingdom of God and his Holy Army assumes full authority by order of the Protection Act as ordained by the Blood of the Covenant as witnessed and given through the Holy Spirit by the Love of God, Amen.

(Visualization: Warrior Angels encircling and the sound of marching and shouting in unison. Color: Red. Duration: 5 Days)

BOOK FIVE – The Forgiveness Act

(16). I Decree as a Spirit of God born as a child of man full forgiveness to all children of man who have harmed or intentioned to harm this soul (my husband/wife and those under my care). By free will I ask God for forgiveness and to erase and cleanse any indent of harm or intention to harm from this soul toward myself and all other children of man, attending delegates, the earth and all living creation in relationship to man, and any and all transgressions toward God, God's Word, The Holy Spirit, all Angels Guides, the Holy Ones and all Spirit Beings, and I send Holy Prayers and Holy Intentions to all.

(17). I Decree full authority and free will interaction to All Holy Angels assigned to aid awareness of any and all opportunities where Love can be expanded by forgiveness in past or present events. By free will I agree with the continuing redemption of unHoly Angels as offered by the Love of God and stand as a representative of redeemed mankind accepted into unification and light once more and in this capacity and by the example of the Love of God, I grant forgiveness to all unHoly ones who have requested and gained forgiveness from God for their manipulations toward this soul (my husband/wife and those in my care).

(18). I Decree this as binding on earth as it is in heaven by the alignment of the will of God and man, bridging all past, present or future events until the Mighty Counselor of the Kingdom of God assumes full authority by order of the Forgiveness Act as ordained by the Blood of the Covenant as witnessed and given through the Holy Spirit by the Love of God, Amen. *(Visualization: One on knees is tapped on the shoulder, asked to stand. Color: Brown. Duration:10 Days)*

BOOK SIX – The Abundance Act

(19). I Decree as a Spirit of God born as a child of man full ability to attain and maintain abundance in all things beneficial to this soul (my husband/wife and those under my care) and

(20). I Decree full authority and free will interaction to All Holy Angels assigned to render harmless any and all manipulations or unHoly intentions toward health, finances or relationships and for expanded awareness of any and all points of damage or potential damage where conscious or unconscious choices need to be transformed and healed. I acknowledge this soul's birthright as a Spirit of God and my redemption as a child of man to live each day in full abundance and expansion of Love with God, one another and myself to the full potential of understanding and experiencing of Love this soul has been, is presently and will be accomplishing, including giving and receiving, and acceptance, gratitude and application of gifts and abilities.

(21). I Decree this soul's free will to share abundance with all children of man in whatever way it is most needed and is most efficient and beneficial and

(22). I Decree All Holy Angels assigned to aid in this recognition and completion through free will interaction and full authority and to render harmless any and all manipulations or unHoly intentions sent to impede this….(cont.)

(23). I Decree this as binding on earth as it is in heaven by the alignment of the will of God and man, bridging all past, present or future events until the King of the Over-Flowing Cup of the Kingdom of God assumes full authority by order of the Abundance Act as ordained by the Blood of the Covenant as witnessed and given through the Holy Spirit by the Love of God, Amen.

(Visualization: Sounds of coins, the smell of fresh bread and a vision of golden fields of wheat that never end. Color: Green. Duration: 7 Days)

BOOK SEVEN – The Purification Act

(24). I Decree as a Spirit of God born as a child of man full cleansing of the air, water and land and all living creation in relationship to man and the earth through free will acceptance and interaction of All Holy Angels assigned to render harmless any and all manipulations or unHoly intentions including rendering harmless any and all harmful choices made by the conscious or unconscious mind of the children of man.

(25). I Decree full authority and free will interaction of All Holy Angels assigned to purify and sanctify any and all movements of elements beyond normal measures and to return all unHoly manipulations to the original parameters as first ordained by The Word of God, including peaceful and respectful interaction of man within the environment and man's transformation and balance of good and natural for all living creation in relationship to man and the earth in God's perfect plan of perpetual abundance as first ordained and commissioned.

(26). I Decree the full authority of All Holy Angels assigned to aid remembrance and giving of additional opportunities to all children of man to elicit gentleness, awareness and peaceable actions toward the air, water and land and all living creation in relationship to man and the earth…..(cont.)

(27). I Decree this as binding on earth as it is in Heaven by the alignment of the will of God and man, bridging all past, present or future events until the fullness of the shift of transformation arrives and The Master Caretaker of the Kingdom of God assumes full authority by the order of the Purification Act as ordained by the Blood of the Covenant as witnessed and given through the Holy Spirit by the Love of God, Amen.

(Visualization: A cloud forming a raindrop, falling onto Earth which then turns from brown to green and full. Color: Blue. Duration: 10 Days)

BOOK EIGHT – The Awareness Act

(28). I Decree as a Spirit of God born as a child of man full ability of discernment between Holy and unHoly. By free will,

(29). I Decree Guides assigned and All Holy Angels assigned full access, ability and free will interaction to consistently communicate with this soul in a manner conducive to the allowance of the veil and the full potential of connection allowed at the present time of understanding. By free will this soul asks for additional opportunities of awareness of conscious or unconscious choices of cause and effect even before any decision or action is made, and clear discernment and ability to choose without manipulations or unHoly intentions sent toward this soul.

(30). I Decree this soul's free will ability to immediately recognize and call in All Holy Angels assigned in all potential events of protection or harm to this soul (or to my husband/wife and those under my care) and for continuing expansion of awareness and acting in accordance with Holy signs and wonders and God-given methods of interaction and aiding personal connection, amplification, frequency and brightening of prayer.....(cont.)

(31). I Decree this soul's free will to remember and act upon God's Will and agreed-upon purpose and commission for this life and to easily recognize all God-given opportunities and realizations, and to resist opportunities for unHoly actions and turn away from unHoly manifestations and to act without doubt, hesitation or fear upon every God-given opportunity and transform dark to light, and fear to Love and I ask Guides assigned and All Holy Angels assigned in assisting this soul with this, and assisting all children of man to full faith and trust in God and his Word.

(32). I Decree this as binding on earth as it is in heaven by the alignment of the will of God and man, bridging all past, present or future events until the veil is fully lifted and the Holy One of the Kingdom of God assumes full authority by order of the Awareness Act as ordained by the Blood of the Covenant as witnessed and given through the Holy Spirit by the Love of God, Amen.

(Visualization: A supernova expansion, starburst in the sky, a light turned on in the darkness Color: Purple. Duration: 7 Days)

BOOK NINE – The Representation Act

(33). I Decree as a Spirit of God born as a child of man this soul's free will Holy Prayers and Holy Intentions that all those in designations of authority and divisions of government act for the betterment of the children of man.

(34). I Decree full authority and free will interaction of All Holy Angels assigned to render harmless any and all manipulations or unHoly intentions sent toward these representatives, and I further ask for additional opportunities of awareness of conscious or unconscious choices of cause and effect for each decision and action where it impacts the children of man and all living creation in relationship to man, by free will this soul asks for the consistent free will interaction of All Holy Angels assigned to expand the justice, support and protection for those under the greatest attack and to give additional opportunities to each representative to elicit peace and harmony between all people and nations, to assist with abundance for any and all in need, and to enact any and all laws and policies that will only benefit and serve the people in the highest good as a reflection of the recognition of the sovereignty of the God of Love and his justice, mercy, support and protection.....(cont.)

(35). I Decree full authority and free will interaction of All Holy Angels assigned to aid the protection of all children and any and all vulnerable children of man who are in need in body, mind, soul and spirit and rendering harmless any and all manipulations or unHoly intentions sent toward these vulnerable ones, and giving them additional opportunities to communicate with God, the Holy Ones, their Guides assigned and one another without restraint or fear.

(36). I Decree this as binding on earth as it is in heaven by the alignment of the will of God and man, bridging all past, present or future events until the King of Kings and True Ruler of the Kingdom of God assumes full authority by order of the Representation Act as ordained by the Blood of the Covenant as witnessed and given through the Holy Spirit by the Love of God, Amen.

(Visualization: A pebble being cast into a pond, the ripples going out to distant shores. Color: Black. Duration: 10 Days)

BOOK TEN – The Salvation Act

(37). I Decree as a Spirit of God born as a child of man full surrender of my spirit and all attending delegates to the sanctity of baptism of Blood and Water, and I acknowledge that which was created pure became unclean unto itself, and was made clean and Holy once more by the Redemption of Grace, and through this Grace this soul stands in the light once more, and darkness has no authority.

(38). I Decree by free will my bending of knee in humility and spirit aligned with the Spirit and will of God, now and through timelessness.

(39). I Decree by free will my full awareness of the Original Issues and I offer this soul's testimony to the rightness and truth of God's right to rule over his creation and that it has not been possible for the sons of man to successfully choose for themselves what is right or wrong and that the children of man call for the interaction of God and continue to seek for God and desire to learn and accomplish God's Will even when manipulations occur to their body's destruction or when their soul is not satisfied by gifts….(cont.)

(40). I Decree by free will the complete fullness of Love even in suffering by the Son of God's Love, as testified to and witnessed in the life of his Life, Death and Life Again while maintaining fullness of purity and rebuking darkness, thereby breaking the bondage upon pure creation forevermore and freeing this soul and all children of man to continue the experience and expansion of Love. I receive by free will my birthright as a Child of God created by Love, in Love and for Love.

(41). I Decree this as binding on earth as it is in heaven by the alignment of the will of God and man, bridging all past, present and future events until the Savior of the World and King of the Kingdom of God assumes full authority by order of the Salvation Act as ordained by the Blood of the Covenant as witnessed and given through the Holy Spirit by the Love of God, Amen.

(Visualization: Golden light falling like raindrops from Heaven, covering all, body levitating on gold light, lifting to God. Color: Gold. Duration: 7Days)

BOOK ELEVEN - The Hierarchy Act

(42). I Decree as a Spirit of God born as a child of man this soul's free will Holy Prayers and Holy Intentions that all those in designations of sacred office and Holy Orders by vows given before God remain faithful and true in submission and humility for the consistent disbursement of acts of ministry to children of man as though ministering to God.

(43). I Decree full authority and free will interaction of All Holy Angels assigned to render harmless any and all manipulations or unHoly intentions sent toward these servants, and I further ask for additional opportunities of awareness of conscious or unconscious choices of cause and effect for each decision and action where it impacts the spirit and soul of the children of man and their delegates and all living creation in relationship to man. By free will this soul asks for the consistent free will interaction of All Holy Angels assigned to expand the houses of prayer and fellowship to all children of man throughout all the nations, granting Divine guidance, protection and discernment in teaching and reaching the hearts of man through Love and unification of those Holy in reflection of the Love of God and the magnification and sanctification of the fullness of the Name of God.

(44). I Decree this soul's free will Holy Prayers and Holy Intentions for all religions and faiths to serve as ambassadors of peace and unity under One God of Love, and that all these may shelter, feed, nurture, encourage, counsel, protect, defend, guide and give service by God's Words and Authority and not their own. (cont.)

(45). I Decree this as binding on earth as it is in heaven by the alignment of the will of God and man, bridging all past, present or future events until the Anointed High Priest of the Kingdom of God assumes full authority by order of the Hierarchy Act as ordained by the Blood of the Covenant as witnessed and given through the Holy Spirit by the Love of God, Amen.

(Visualization: Succession of shepherd's staff being given from one to the other from God, through mankind and mankind giving it back to God, row of hundreds of people. Color: Silver. Duration: 10 Days)

BOOK TWELVE – The Rainbow Act

(46). I Decree as a Spirit of God born as a child of man full agreement and free will alignment to the completion and fulfillment of the Will of God as originally ordained, including the perfection of the children of man and all living creation in relationship to man and the earth, including the air, water and land.

(47). I Decree this soul's full agreement and free will alignment of full unity and communication through sacred interactions and sharing of experiences of Love's expansion and validation of answered questions in the Original Issues of the Sovereignty of God's Love over this soul and all creation as was commissioned and comes to be in perfect fruition.

(48). I Decree this soul's full agreement and free will alignment of the end and fulfillment of time and the never-ending expansion of timelessness and the full availability of mobility, unity, communication and interaction between all Spirit Beings and creations of the Love of God.

(49). I Decree this soul's full agreement and free will alignment to utilize all Divine Decrees and the Twelve Books of Acts of the Love of God to ease the manipulations and unHoly intentions toward the children of man during the end of time and the shift into timelessness, and to call in All Holy Angels assigned and give full authority and free will interaction to render harmless these manipulations and unHoly intentions toward this soul ….(cont.)

(and that of my husband/wife and those under my care) and to transform any unnatural manifestations and to purify and sanctify any and all movements of elements beyond normal measures and decommission, bind and encapsulate all unHoly until the fulfillment of the Word of God is satisfied through the Warrior Son and his Holy Army.

(50). I Decree this as Binding on Earth as it is in Heaven by the alignment of the Will of God and man, bridging all past, present or future events, and the Prince of Peace of the Kingdom of God and his Holy Army will assume full authority and triumph victorious and return timelessness and rightful sovereignty of the Kingdom of God by the order of the Rainbow Act as ordained by the Blood of the Covenant as witnessed and given through the Holy Spirit by the Love of God, Amen.

(Visualization: Arrows like comets racing across the sky, all heading to a purified and sparkling Earth. The sound of myriads of Angels singing. Colors: All the colors of the previous 11 Acts: white, yellow, orange, red, brown, green, blue, purple, black, gold, silver in a beautiful rainbow! Duration: 12 Days)